Praise for *Messy*

"Engrossing . . . The most powerful part of the book isn't in the examples of corporate or creative success, but in the realization that mess—the autonomy that comes from discarding inflexible rules and neat labels—is important even when we don't actually want it." —*The New York Times Book Review*

"Utterly fascinating. Tim Harford shows that if you want to be creative and resilient, you need a little more disorder in your world. It's a masterful case for the life-changing magic of cluttering up."
—Adam Grant, *New York Times*–bestselling author of *Originals* and *Give and Take*

"*Messy* masterfully weaves together anecdote and academic work." —*The Economist*

"*Messy* is neither a broadside at Marie Kondo and her cult of minimalism nor a case for the hidden virtues of hoarding. Harford, an acclaimed economics journalist, isn't so much extolling squalor as questioning the notion that order is inherently preferable for creative endeavors." —*Time*

"Tim's best and deepest book."
—Tyler Cowen, *New York Times*–bestselling author of *Average Is Over*

"It's a very, very good book, full of wise counter-intuitions and clever insights."
—Brian Eno

"A book that presents itself as an impossibly simple account of the virtues of a messy workspace, then builds to something extraordinary." —The Age

"This absorbing book offers a different approach from instructional decluttering manuals by celebrating the successes derived from the unplanned, unscripted, and unknown." —*Library Journal*

"Weaving together lessons from history, art, technology, and social and scientific research, Harford's theories have many potential benefits for individuals and businesses seeking to remain on the creative cutting edge, as well as profound implications for society." —*Publishers Weekly*

“Harford presents the strategies of disorganization as unique and enlightening and convincingly offers reinforced encouragement to those who may find themselves ‘tempted by tidiness’ to instead ‘embrace some mess instead.’ ” —*Kirkus Reviews*

“Ranging expertly across business, politics, and the arts, Tim Harford makes a compelling case for the creative benefits of disorganization, improvisation, and confusion. His liberating message: you’ll be more successful if you stop struggling so hard to plan or control your success. *Messy* is a deeply researched, endlessly eye-opening adventure.”

—Oliver Burkeman, author of *The Antidote: Happiness for People Who Can’t Stand Positive Thinking*

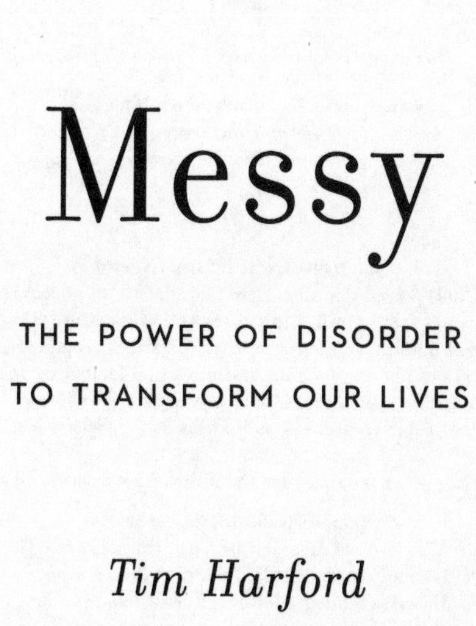

Messy

THE POWER OF DISORDER TO TRANSFORM OUR LIVES

Tim Harford

RIVERHEAD BOOKS
NEW YORK

Riverhead Books
An imprint of Penguin Random House LLC
375 Hudson Street
New York, New York 10014

The Library of Congress has catalogued the Riverhead hardcover edition as follows:

Names: Harford, Tim, author.
Title: Messy : the power of disorder to transform our lives / Tim Harford.
Description: New York : Riverhead Books, 2016. |
Includes bibliographical references and index.
Identifiers: LCCN 2016026363 | ISBN 9781594634796 (hardcover)
Subjects: LCSH: Creative ability. | Resilience (Personality trait) |
Orderliness—Psychological aspects.
Classification: LCC BF408 .H297 2016 | DDC 153.3/5-dc23
LC record available at https://lccn.loc.gov/2016026363
p. cm.

First Riverhead hardcover edition: October 2016
First Riverhead trade paperback edition: October 2017
Riverhead trade paperback ISBN: 9781594634802

Printed in the United States of America
3 5 7 9 10 8 6 4 2

Book design by Amanda Dewey

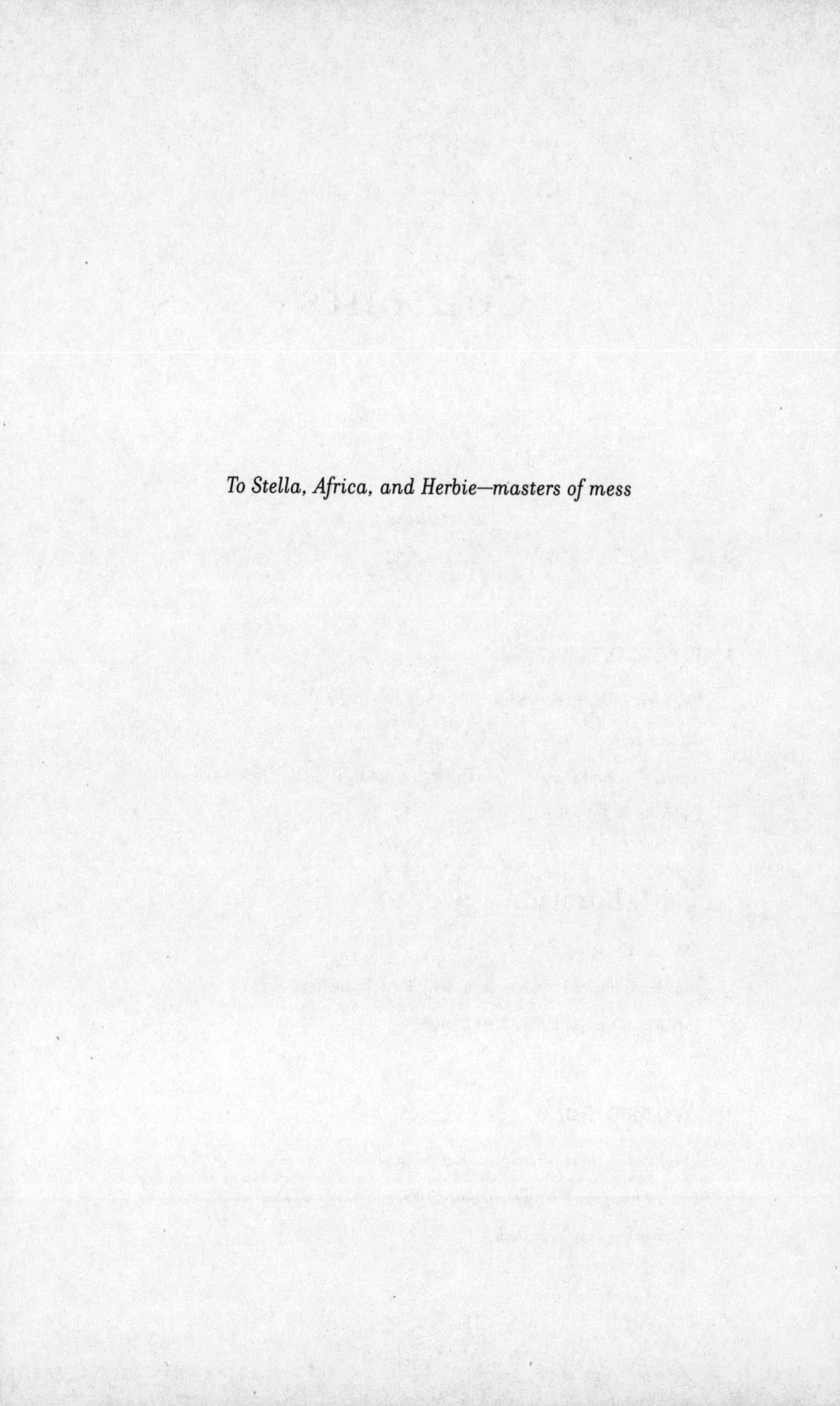

To Stella, Africa, and Herbie—masters of mess

Contents

Introduction

"It was unplayable."

On the 27th of January, 1975, a seventeen-year-old German girl named Vera Brandes stepped out onto the vast stage of the Cologne opera house. The auditorium was empty, and lit only by the dim green glow of the emergency exit sign, but this was the most exciting day of Vera's life. She was the youngest concert promoter in Germany, and she had persuaded the Opera House to host a late-night concert of improvised jazz by the American pianist Keith Jarrett. The concert was a sellout, and in just a few hours, Jarrett would stride out in front of 1,400 people, sit down at the Bösendorfer piano, and without sheet music or rehearsal would begin to play.[1]

But that afternoon, Vera Brandes was introducing Keith Jarrett and his producer Manfred Eicher to the piano—and it wasn't going well.

"Keith played a few notes," recalls Brandes. "Then Eicher played a few notes. They didn't say anything. They circled the instrument several times and then tried a few keys. Then after a long silence, Manfred came to me and said, 'If you don't get another piano, Keith can't play tonight.'"[2]

Vera Brandes was stunned. She knew that Jarrett had requested a specific instrument and the Opera House had agreed to provide it. What she hadn't realized was that, caring little for late-night jazz, they'd failed and didn't even know it. The administrative staff had gone home, the piano movers hadn't been able to find the Bösendorfer piano that had been requested, and so they had instead installed, as Brandes recalls, "this tiny little Bösendorfer, that was completely out of tune, the black notes in the middle didn't work, the pedals stuck. It was unplayable."[3]

Brandes tried everything to find a replacement. She even rounded up friends to push a grand piano through the streets of Cologne, but it was raining hard, and the local piano tuner warned her that the substitute piano would never survive the trip. Instead, he worked to fix up the little instrument that was onstage already. Yet he could do nothing about the muffled bass notes, the plinky high notes, and the simple fact that the piano—"a small piano, like half a piano"—just didn't make a loud enough sound to reach the balconies of the vast auditorium.

Understandably, Jarrett didn't want to perform. He left and went to wait in his car, leaving Brandes to anticipate the arrival of 1,400 soon-to-be furious concertgoers. The best day of her life had suddenly become the worst; her enthusiasm for jazz and her precocious entrepreneurial spirit brought the prospect of utter humiliation. Desperate, she caught up with Jarrett and through the window of his car, she begged him to play. The young pianist looked out at the bedraggled German teenager standing in the rain and took pity on her. "Never forget," Jarrett said. "Only for you."

A few hours later, as midnight approached, Jarrett walked out to the unplayable piano in front of a packed concert hall, and began.

"The minute he played the first note, everybody knew this was magic," recalls Brandes.

That night's performance began with a simple chiming series of notes, then quickly gained complexity as it moved by turns between dynamism and a languid, soothing tone. It was beautiful and strange, and it is enormously popular: the *Köln Concert* album has sold 3.5 million copies. No other solo jazz album or solo piano album has matched that.

When we see skilled performers succeeding in difficult circumstances, we habitually describe them as having triumphed over adversity, or despite the odds. But that's not always the right perspective. Jarrett didn't produce a good concert in trying times. He produced the performance of a lifetime, but the shortcomings of the piano actually helped him.

The substandard instrument forced Jarrett away from the tinny high notes and into the middle register. His left hand produced rumbling, repetitive bass riffs as a way of covering up the piano's lack of resonance. Both of these elements gave the performance an almost trancelike quality. That might have faded into wallpaper music, but Jarrett couldn't drop anchor in that comfortable musical harbor, because the piano simply wasn't loud enough.[4]

"What's important to understand is the proportion between the instrument and the magnitude of the hall," recalls Vera Brandes. "Jarrett really had to play that piano very hard to get enough volume to get to the balconies. He was really—*pchow*—pushing the notes down."

Standing up, sitting down, moaning, writhing, Jarrett didn't hold back in any way as he pummeled the unplayable piano to produce something unique. It wasn't the music that he ever imagined playing. But handed a mess, Keith Jarrett embraced it, and soared.

Keith Jarrett's instinct was not to play, and it's an instinct that most of us would share. We don't want to work with bad tools, especially when the stakes are so high. But in hindsight, Jarrett's instinct was wrong. What if our own similar instincts are also wrong, and in a much wider range of situations?

The argument of this book is that we often succumb to the temptation of a tidy-minded approach when we would be better served by embracing a degree of mess. Keith Jarrett's desire for a perfect piano was one example of this tidiness temptation. Others include the public speaker who cleaves to a script; the military commander who carefully strategizes; the writer who blocks out distractions; the politician who sets quantifiable targets for public services; the boss who insists on tidy desks for all; the team leader who makes sure everyone gets along. We succumb to the tidiness temptation in our daily lives when we spend time archiving our e-mails, filling in questionnaires on dating websites that promise to find our perfect match, or taking our kids to the local playground instead of letting them run loose in the neighborhood wasteland.*

Sometimes, of course, our desire for tidiness—our seemingly innate urge to create a world that is ordered, systematized, quantified, neatly structured into clear categories, planned, predictable—can be helpful. It wouldn't be such a deeply rooted instinct if it weren't helpful.

But often we are so seduced by the blandishments of tidiness that we fail to appreciate the virtues of the messy—the untidy, unquantified, uncoordinated, improvised, imperfect, incoherent, crude, cluttered, random, ambiguous, vague, difficult, diverse, or even dirty. The scripted speech misreads the energy of the room; the careful commander is disoriented by a more impetuous opponent; the writer is

---

*And of course there is also the popularity of Marie Kondo's bestselling book *The Life-Changing Magic of Tidying Up*. Ironically, Kondo herself warns against the tidiness temptation: she says that carefully organizing one's possessions in clever storage solutions is a "booby trap." She's right. Trying to impose order by rearranging a house stuffed full of possessions feels like it should help, but it doesn't. A more accurate title would be *The Life-Changing Magic of Throwing Out All Your Stuff*, a policy on which this book takes no view either way. But "tidying" in the sense of "categorizing and storing" is overrated. Chapter 9 of this book shows, for example, that people who carefully file their documents are more likely to be overwhelmed by them.

serendipitously inspired by a random distraction; the quantified targets create perverse incentives; the workers in the tidy office feel helpless and demotivated; a disruptive outsider aggravates the team but brings a fresh new insight. The worker with the messy inbox ultimately gets more done; we find a soul mate when we ignore the website questionnaires; the kids running loose in the wasteland not only have more fun and learn more skills, but—counterintuitively—have fewer accidents.

And the pianist who says, "I'm sorry, Vera, that piano is simply unplayable," and drives off into the rainy Cologne night, leaving a seventeen-year-old girl sobbing on the curbside, never imagines that he has passed up the opportunity to make what would have been his most-loved piece of work.

I hope this book will serve as the Vera Brandes in your life—the nudge, when you are tempted by tidiness, to embrace some mess instead. Each chapter explores a different aspect of messiness, showing how it can spur creativity, nurture resilience, and generally bring out the best in us. That is true whether we are performing with a piano in front of a concert hall audience or a slide deck in front of a boardroom; whether we are running a corporation or manning a call center; whether we are commanding an army, dating, or trying to be a good parent. The success we admire is often built on messy foundations—even if those foundations are often hidden away.

I will stand up for messiness not because I think messiness is the answer to all life's problems, but because I think messiness has too few defenders. I want to convince you that there can sometimes be a certain magic in mess.

1

Creativity

"You're asking the blood in your brain to flow in another direction."

Bowie, Eno, and Darwin: How Frustration and Distraction Help Us Solve Problems in Art, Science, and Life

Keith Jarrett's predicament was a happy accident. But there are those who take it for granted that such accidents can and should be planned; they feel that messy situations will tend to provide fertile creative soil.

In 1976, David Bowie fled to West Berlin. The unearthly, ambisexual rock star had repeatedly shredded the rule book for rock and roll, creating one persona after another—from Ziggy Stardust to the Thin White Duke—until he found himself stuck. He was beset by legal troubles, his marriage alternated between indifference and contempt, and he was taking too many drugs—which he planned to kick, in the words of his friend and housemate Iggy Pop, "in the heroin capital of the world."

"It was a dangerous period for me," Bowie reflected over twenty years later. "I was at the end of my tether physically and emotionally and had serious doubts about my sanity."[1]

Bowie put down roots near the Berlin Wall. Hansa Studios, where he and Iggy Pop recorded a series of groundbreaking albums, were overlooked by East German machine gun nests. Bowie's producer, Tony Visconti, remarked that everything about the place screamed "you shouldn't be making a record here."[2] But amid Berlin's great museums, legendary bondage clubs, and tormented geopolitics, Bowie found what he needed: new ideas, new constraints, and new challenges. And then, of course, there was Brian Eno.

Eno had already found fame as Roxy Music's crazy keyboard player, and as the creator of a new sonic aesthetic called ambient music. Now Bowie had brought him in to play an undefined collaborative role alongside Tony Visconti. Visconti himself was recruited by Bowie with this sales pitch: "We don't have any actual songs yet . . . this is strictly experimental and nothing might come of it in the end."[3]

As Visconti and Bowie struggled to find a new direction—not so much composing songs as carving them out of blocks of sound—Eno took to showing up at the studio with a selection of cards he called Oblique Strategies. Each had a different instruction, often a gnomic one. Whenever the studio sessions were running aground, Eno would draw a card at random and relay its strange orders.

Be the first not to do what has never not been done before

Emphasize the flaws

Only a part, not the whole

Twist the spine

Look at the order in which you do things

Change instrument roles

For example, during the recording of the *Lodger* album, Carlos Alomar, one of the world's greatest guitarists, was told to play the drums instead. This was just one of the challenges that Eno's Oblique Strategies cards imposed, apparently unnecessarily. The cards drove the musicians crazy. (This annoyance cannot have come as a surprise to Eno. During work on an earlier Eno album, *Another Green World*, the cards reduced Phil Collins, the superstar drummer from Genesis, to hurling beer cans across the studio in frustration.[4]) Faced with one piece of card-inspired foolishness, Carlos Alomar told Eno that "this experiment is stupid"; the violinist Simon House commented that the sessions often "sounded terrible. Carlos did have a problem, simply because he's very gifted and professional . . . he can't bring himself to play stuff that sounds like crap."[5]

Yet the strange chaotic working process produced two of the decade's most critically acclaimed albums, *Low* and *"Heroes,"* along with Iggy Pop's most respected work, *The Idiot* and *Lust for Life*. *Low* was arguably the bravest reinvention in pop history—imagine Taylor Swift releasing an album full of long, pensive instrumentals and you get a sense of the shock. It's hard to argue with such results, and Brian Eno's Oblique Strategies now have a cult following in creative circles.

The Berlin trilogy of albums ends with Bowie's *Lodger*, a record with a revealing working title. It was originally called *Planned Accidents*.

Given both Jarrett's and Bowie's experiences, it seems that arbitrary shocks to a project can have a wonderful, almost magical effect. But why is that? One might expect that the answer lies in our psychological response to these curveballs, but that is only partly true. The advantage of random disturbances can also be seen in a far more technical realm—mathematics—full of practical applications.

Take the question of how to lay out a circuit on a silicon chip. Starting with a description of what the circuit should do tells us which parts of which components should be wired to other components, but there are trillions upon trillions of conceivable ways to lay out the wiring and the digital logic gates that make up the circuit—and some are much more efficient than others, making a big difference to the performance of the chip.[6] This is an example of what mathematicians call an NP-hard problem. NP-hard problems are a bit like enormous combination locks: if you're given a solution it is easy to check if it works, but it would take an impossibly long time to find the solution yourself by systematically trying every combination.

Fortunately, there is a sense in which the silicon chip problem differs from a combination lock. With a lock, only one solution will work. But with a chip, manufacturers don't need to find the ultimate circuit layout; they just need to find one that's good enough. To do that, they use an algorithm, which is a recipe for a computer to work through different possibilities. A good algorithm will get you a decent solution without taking forever.

But what makes for a good algorithm? One recipe that won't get very far is a systematic check of every possible layout: that's hopeless, because it might take a lifetime to stumble across a good answer. Another is to start with a random layout and look for incremental improvements: a small change that makes the layout work better, moving just a single component and redrawing the wiring to fit. Find another small improvement; then another; then another. Unfortunately, this method is likely to send you down a dead end. There'll be a point where no single change can make the circuit more efficient, even though making several changes at once—perhaps moving several components together into a cluster—would produce a big improvement.

The better method is to emulate Brian Eno and introduce a judicious dose of randomness. For example, an algorithm called "simulated annealing" starts with an almost random search, willing to try any change, good or bad. Then it slowly becomes fussier and fussier about what changes it will accept, until eventually it has turned into a rigid search for small step-by-step improvements. There's no guarantee of finding the very best circuit layout, but this kind of approach will usually find a good one. The combination of gradual improvements and random shocks turns out to be a very effective way to approach a host of difficult problems. One example: evaluate a complex new molecule for possible medical use by comparing its structure with that of many other complex molecules with known medical properties. Other examples involve scheduling (find a timetable for exams in which no student faces a clash between the subjects she is taking) or logistics (planning the optimal route for delivering packages).

Here's an analogy: imagine participating in a strange competition to find the highest point on the planet, without being allowed to look at a map. You can name any set of coordinates you like, and you'll be told its altitude: say, "50.945980, 6.973465," and you're told: "That's 65 meters above sea level." Then you can name another point, and another, as often as you like until you run out of time.

What strategy will you use? As with all the other problems, you could try a methodical search: start with "0.000001, 0.000001" and work your way up. You're unlikely to have found a competition-winning high altitude by the time the clock runs out.

Or you could try a strategy of purely random leaps: pick one set of random coordinates after another, and when time runs out, look back through them and pick the highest point. You might get lucky and just happen to suggest some coordinates near the top of Everest, but pure randomness is probably not going to win you the contest.

An alternative extreme strategy is pure hill-climbing, analogous to the step-by-step search for improvements in the silicon chip design. Start at a random point and then look at all the nearby coordinates—say, a meter away in each direction. Pick the highest of those, and repeat the process over and over. The hill-climbing algorithm is guaranteed to bring you to a local summit—a point from which every direction is down. This strategy will serve you well if your first random guess was on the foothills of a cloud-capped pinnacle, but it may have been just a sand dune or a pitcher's mound. Hill-climbing strategies get stuck if they meet small hills.

The most likely winning approaches will be a blend of randomness with hill-climbing. You might start by trying purely random coordinates for a while. Then, with time ticking on, you pick the highest you've hit so far and try some more random coordinates within a few kilometers of that point—hopefully, by now, you're fishing in a mountain range. Finally, you pick the highest point so far and switch to a pure hill-climbing algorithm until time runs out.

Improvising at the piano seems a world away from laying out an efficient array of electronic components on a silicon wafer, but the analogy of random leaps and hill-climbing helps to make sense of what happened in Cologne. Keith Jarrett was already a highly accomplished pianist: we might imagine his performances as habitually scaling peaks in the Alps. When faced with the unplayable piano, with its harsh treble and anemic bass, it was as if a random disruption had plucked him from an Alpine peak and deposited him in an unfamiliar valley. No wonder he was annoyed. But when he started to climb, it turned out that valley was in the Himalayas, and his skill enabled him to ascend to a higher and more wonderful destination than he had ever reached before.

It's human nature to want to improve, and this means that we tend to be instinctive hill-climbers. Whether we're trying to master a hobby, learn a language, write an essay, or build a business, it's natural to want every change to be a change for the better. But like the problem-solving algorithms, it's easy to get stuck if we insist that we will never go downhill.

There are some situations in which a relentless hill-climbing search for marginal improvements seems to work well even without the occasional random leap. For example, the fortunes of British cycling were transformed by adopting a philosophy of "marginal gains." Thanks to this approach, British cyclists won seven out of the ten gold medals available on the track at the 2012 Olympics—as well as winning the Tour de France in 2012, 2013, and 2015 after almost a century of failure. But this turns out to be an exception that proves the rule, because the cycling authorities had stacked the deck in favor of tidy step-by-step approaches. In the 1990s, Graeme Obree, a maverick cyclist nicknamed "The Flying Scotsman," made some random leaps—he experimented with radical changes, building his own bike from odd components, including parts of a washing machine, and adopting unusual riding positions, one of which involved tucking his hands into his breastbone with no handlebars to speak of, and another with hands straight out like Superman.

Obree's experimentations enabled him to break the world hour record twice, until the world cycling body, the Union Cycliste Internationale, simply banned his riding position. He switched to another unconventional position and won the world championship; the UCI banned that position, too. Given the UCI's attitude, we should not be surprised that the best cyclists and cycling teams now focus largely on marginal gains. But in most endeavors, there is no UCI to artificially constrain our crazy ideas.

Most of us are not virtuoso jazz pianists, silicon chip designers, or elite cyclists. But many of us are commuters, and even the repetitiveness of the daily commute illustrates the power of randomness to unstick us when we don't even know we're stuck.

In 2014, some of the workers on London's Underground system went on strike for two days. The strike closed 171 of the system's 270 stations, leaving commuters scrambling to find alternative routes using buses, aboveground trains, or the stations that remained open. Many commuters in London use electronic fare cards that are valid on all forms of public transport, and after the strike, three economists examined data generated by those cards. The researchers were able to see that most people used a different route to get to work on the strike days, no doubt with some annoyance. But what was surprising is that when the strike was over, not everybody returned to their habitual commuting route. One in twenty of the commuters who had switched then stayed with the route that they had used during the strike; presumably, they had discovered that it was faster or cheaper or preferable in some other way to their old routine. We tend to think that commuters have their route to work honed to perfection; evidently not. A substantial minority promptly found an improvement to the journey they had been making for years. All they needed was an unexpected shock to force them to seek out something better.[7]

Messy disruptions will be most powerful when combined with creative skill. The disruption puts an artist, scientist, or engineer in unpromising territory—a deep valley rather than a familiar hilltop. But then expertise kicks in and finds ways to move upward again: the climb finishes at a new peak, perhaps lower than the old one, but perhaps unexpectedly higher.

As long as you're exploring the same old approaches, Brian Eno explains, "you get more and more competent at dealing with that place, and your clichés become increasingly clichéd."[8]

But when we are forced to start from somewhere new, the clichés can be replaced with moments of magic.

Brian Eno is annoyed. "I wish these people would go away." He's sitting in the sunshine in a mews in Notting Hill, West London, and a group of people have emerged from a nearby house. "I don't know why they've chosen to have this fucking conversation outside right now."[9]

Eno is being interviewed by my colleague, Ludovic Hunter-Tilney. The interview moves indoors, but even there things aren't quiet enough. Eventually, he moves to the holy of holies—his recording studio. Only there, free from all auditory distractions, can Eno concentrate on talking about music.

Nothing gets past Brian Eno's ears, it seems.

I meet Eno one February afternoon in the same Notting Hill studio. It's a warehouse space with a wrought-iron spiral staircase in the center and a kitchenette in one nook. Architecturally the place is defined more by what it is not than what it is: it feels like someone put a flimsy roof over a space that was hemmed in on all sides by expensive town houses. The only daylight comes through the skylights.

While the spaciousness of the place stops it from feeling claustrophobic, it is engagingly messy. We are surrounded by a piano and some guitars, speakers and laptops, towering bookshelves packed with curiosities, bits and pieces of half-built instruments, plastic crates full of cables and wires and art supplies, and in a desk in a corner, a perfume collection.

Eno himself is a man who once dressed like a wizard, long locks dyed silver as he played the synthesizer with a giant plastic knife and fork. Now in his mid-sixties, the glam look is long gone. He is dressed expensively but casually. Where his head isn't bald, it is shaved. He has the veteran cool of a star architect.

He hasn't stopped making music. A new ambient work is being randomly generated by an Eno-tweaked algorithm even as we greet each other. As our interview begins he switches it off—otherwise we'd never be able to talk. "It's a problem for me in social situations . . . I can't be in a restaurant when there's music playing," he says. "I just can't get my ears off it."[10]

Brian Eno is easily distracted.

We're often told that good work comes from the ability to focus, to shut out distractions. To choose from a plethora of self-help tips along these lines, a Mayo Clinic psychologist, Dr. Amit Sood, advises us to focus more effectively by turning off the TV, logging out of e-mail, and taking up "attention training" to "train your brain." An article on the Psych Central website offers similar tips, counseling us to "limit distractions"—alas, on a webpage that is surrounded by sponsored links about wrinkle cream, sex addiction, and ways to save money on insurance. Some people turn to methylphenidate (better known as Ritalin) to help them concentrate. The science writer Caroline Williams even visited the Boston Attention and Learning Lab—an affiliate of Harvard and Boston Universities—to have her left prefrontal lobe zapped with magnetic pulses, all in an attempt to resolve what one of the lab's neuroscientists called her "issues with attention and distractibility."[11]

Yet here is a creative icon, one of the most influential people in modern music, who seems unable to hold a conversation outside a soundproof box. Look around a record shop and Eno is everywhere: as a glam rocker with Roxy Music; composing ambient work such as *Music for Airports*; creating *My Life in the Bush of Ghosts*, a collaboration with David Byrne in which two white geeks anticipated hip-hop; and making *Another Green World*, the record that Prince once named as his biggest inspiration. (It's the one featuring Phil Collins and the beer cans.) But the albums with Eno's name on the front are just the start. Look in the small print and he is everywhere, a zephyr of cerebral chaos blowing back and forth across the frontal lobes of pop. Famous for his contributions to David Bowie's albums, Eno has also worked with Talking Heads, U2, Paul Simon, and Coldplay. Along the way he collaborated with punks, performance artists, experimental composers, and even the film director David Lynch.* When the music magazine *Pitchfork* listed its top 100 albums of the 1970s, Brian Eno had a hand in more than a quarter of them.

Distractibility can indeed seem like an "issue," or even a curse. But that's if we're looking only at the hill-climbing part of the creative process. Distractible brains can also be seen as brains that have an innate tendency to make those useful random leaps. Perhaps, like Keith Jarrett's unplayable piano, distractibility is a disadvantage that isn't a disadvantage at all. Certainly to psychologists who study creativity, the fact that Brian Eno is easily distracted comes as little surprise.[12]

A few years ago a team of researchers including Shelley Carson of Harvard tested a group of Harvard students to measure the strength of their ability to filter out unwanted stimulus.[13] (For example, if you're having a conversation in a busy restaurant, and you can easily filter out the other conversations going on around you and focus only on the conversation at hand, you have strong attentional filters.) Some of the students they studied had very weak filters—their thoughts were constantly being interrupted by the sounds and sights of the world around them.

You might think that this was a disadvantage. Yet these students were actually more creative on all sorts of measures. The most striking result came when the researchers looked at precociously creative students—those who had already released their first album, published their first novel, produced a stage show of sufficient prominence to be reviewed by the national press, been awarded a patent, or some similar achievement. There were twenty-five of these super-creatives in the study; twenty-two of them had weak or porous attention filters. Like Brian Eno, they simply couldn't filter out irrelevant details. But then, who is to say what is irrelevant?

---

*Aside from superstars such as Bowie and U2, the list of Eno collaborators includes DNA, Laurie Anderson, Gavin Bryars, Michael Nyman, Twyla Tharp, and Devo—artists with little in common except the admiration of the critics.

Holly White of the University of Michigan and Priti Shah of the University of Memphis found something similar in a study of their own.[14] They looked at adults with attention deficit/hyperactivity disorder at a severe enough level to have sought professional help. As with Shelley Carson's research, the ADHD sufferers were more creative in the laboratory than non-sufferers, and were more likely to have major creative accomplishments outside the lab. The people who were most easily distracted were also the ones whose first album had been released, whose poetry had been published in *The New Yorker*, or whose play was showing off-Broadway.

Clearly, these people were not so completely incapable of focus that they couldn't finish the album, the poem, or the script. There needs to be at least some hill-climbing between the random leaps. But looking at these achievements, the word "hyperactivity" takes on more positive connotations. One is reminded of the sardonic headline in *The Onion*: "RITALIN CURES NEXT PICASSO."

Psychologists have conducted several laboratory studies of ordinary people struggling with messy disruptions, distractions, or constraints in situations that ask them to be creative.

In one, Charlan Nemeth and Julianne Kwan showed pairs of people bluish/greenish slides, asking them to shout out whether they were blue or green. The experimenters had a trick to play, however: one member of each pair was actually a confederate of the researchers, who would sometimes call out baffling responses—"green" when the slide was clearly blue. Having been thoroughly baffled, the experimental subjects were then asked to free-associate words connected with "green" and "blue"—*sky, sea, eyes*. Those who had been subjected to a confusing mess of signals produced more original word associations: *jazz*, *flame*, *pornography*, *sad*, *Picasso*. There was something about the sheer disruptiveness of the setup that unlocked creative responses.[15]

In another study, led by psychologist Ellen Langer, researchers assigned creative tasks to their subjects, then started messing with them. For example, as a subject was halfway through drawing a cat, the psychologists would say, "Oh, the animal has to be one that lives underwater." Other people were given an exercise about breakfast, and then told, verbally, to write an essay about "morning." Halfway through the exercise, they were asked to fill in a quick questionnaire asking how it felt to be writing an essay about "mourning." As long as people had been appropriately briefed ("mistakes are human, try incorporating them into your work") they did better work and reported that they had more fun.[16]

A third experiment was conducted by a team including Paul Howard-Jones, a neuroscientist at the University of Bristol. Researchers showed their experimental subjects a set of three words, and then asked them to tell a brief story involving the three words. Sometimes the words had obvious connections, such as "teeth, brush, dentist" or "car, driver, road." Sometimes the words were unconnected, such as "cow, zip, star" or "melon, book, thunder." The more random, obscure, challenging combinations spurred the subjects into spinning far more creative tales.[17]

These are, admittedly, artificial one-off situations with nothing at stake for the experimental subjects. When someone relies on creativity for a living, mucking them around becomes much more fraught: think of poor Carlos Alomar, too talented and too professional to be comfortable playing "crap"; or Phil Collins, so frustrated with Eno's unpredictable requests that he started throwing beer cans around the studio. It's one thing to throw random noise into a computer algorithm, mechanistically forcing it to seek fresh horizons in its search for the perfect circuit layout. But algorithms don't have feelings. Is the mess of Oblique Strategies really a productive way to deal with human beings?

Brian Eno rubs his pate thoughtfully as we sit at a small circular table in the middle of his studio. The ambient music has been switched off, but he's placed me so that over his shoulder I can view one of his ventures into ambient visual art. Mounted on the wall beside the piano is a brushed-aluminum diamond-shaped frame housing four exactingly fitted plasma screens on which an ever-shifting Eno artwork is displayed in fourfold symmetry. The change is slow, beautiful, and soothing—unlike the Oblique Strategies cards, which can wrench and jar.

I mention Adrian Belew, another fine guitarist, who was drafted into the David Bowie recording session where Carlos Alomar was ordered to play the drums. He didn't really know what was happening, and had barely plugged in his Stratocaster when Eno, Visconti, and Bowie told him to start playing in response to a previously unheard track. Before he could ask why Carlos was on the drums, Belew was told that Alomar "would go one, two, three, then you come in."

"What key is it?" asked Belew.

"Don't worry about the key. Just play!"

"It was like a freight train coming through my mind," said Belew later. "I just had to cling on."[18]

"Poor Adrian," muses Eno. "He's such a great player that he can handle this kind of thing."[19] Still, he adds, "I think I would have a bit of difficulty doing that experiment now. I didn't really know enough about being a playing musician at that time . . . I didn't know how disruptive that was to players." Eno admits that his experiments with Belew, Alomar, and the other musicians in Berlin weren't much fun for them. Used to finding a comfortable groove, their routines were "entirely subverted" as Eno pushed them through arbitrarily chosen chord sequences by pointing at different notes on a blackboard in the studio.

The eventual result of the freight train coming through Belew's mind, sliced and spliced by Eno and producer Visconti, became a guitar solo that is the spine of Bowie's single "Boys Keep Swinging." The solo is now regarded as a classic. And from a creative point of view, the end may justify the means: when we listen to a Bowie album, we don't see the mess and frustration of the recording session; we can just enjoy the beauty that it produced.

On the table between me and Eno is a deck of the cards in a snug black box. Seeking an example, Eno jiggles the box open and pulls out a card. It says:

WATER

What impact might that card have on a group of musicians in a studio? Eno starts throwing out suggestions. Perhaps it would be a prompt to take a break and have a drink. One member of the band might argue that the music is too stiff and needs to be more fluid. Another might simply complain that the music already is soggy and wet. The point is that the card forces the group to take a new vantage point and to look carefully at what can be seen from that point.

What is more, he says, people respond to unexpected stimuli and constraints all the time. We just don't call it randomness. A good conversation is a constant stream of unexpected responses. A new collaboration forces fresh perspectives and demands attention. "That's why working with somebody new can be very exciting," Eno says.

Or consider a rhyme in a poem or a song. "When you start out with a line . . . 'Her hair was beautiful and red,' then immediately your mind is saying 'Dead . . . fled . . . instead . . . bled . . . lalala.' Immediately you've pushed yourself into a place where you have to make a choice between a set of random possibilities, because there's no connection between the word 'red' and the word 'instead' except they happen to sound the same. Suddenly you have a bunch of random possibilities thrown at you and of course as soon as you do that it pushes you into places that you really had not thought of going before."

And then Eno says something that sheds a new light on the way I see the Oblique Strategies cards and the unplayable piano.

"The enemy of creative work is boredom, actually," he says. "And the friend is alertness. Now I think what makes you alert is to be faced with a situation that is beyond your control so you have to be watching it very carefully to see how it unfolds, to be able to stay on top of it. That kind of alertness is exciting."[20]

That alertness is Keith Jarrett onstage in Cologne. It's Adrian Belew desperately trying to make sense of "Boys Keep Swinging." And it is the effect that the cards can have on a creative project. The cards force us into a random leap to an unfamiliar location, and we need to be alert to figure out where we are and where to go from here. Says Eno, "The thrill of them is that they put us in a messier situation."

This sudden sharpening of our attention doesn't just apply to pioneering artworks. It can be seen in an ordinary high school classroom. In a recent study, psychologists Connor Diemand-Yauman, Daniel M. Oppenheimer, and Erikka Vaughan teamed up with teachers, getting them to reformat the teaching handouts they used. Half their classes, chosen at random, got the original materials. The other half got the same documents, reformatted into one of three challenging fonts: the dense **Haettenschweiler**, the florid *Monotype Corsiva*, or the zesty *Comic Sans Italicized*. These are, on the face of it, absurd and distracting fonts. But the fonts didn't derail the students. They prompted them to pay attention, to slow down, and to think about what they were reading. Students who had been taught using the ugly fonts ended up scoring higher on their end-of-semester exams.[21]

Most of us don't have an academic researcher or a Brian Eno in our lives, forcing us to seek out these attention-grabbing challenges. We don't force ourselves to reformat our work into challenging fonts, perform on faulty instruments, or arbitrarily seek alternative commuting routes. However, there is another strategy for making random leaps which is altogether more achievable.

The journalist David Sheppard's biography of Brian Eno noted that his "frenetic multi-episodic life can sometimes present a thick miasma of cross-pollinated activity."[22] Erez Lieberman Aiden seems much the same. Aiden is not a chart-topping musician, although his CV suggests that little is beyond his grasp. He has been a physicist, an engineer, a mathematician, a molecular biologist, a historian, and a linguist, and he's won some big scientific prizes for his work.[23] All before he turned forty.

The science writer Ed Yong describes Aiden's working method as "nomadic. He moves about, searching for ideas that will pique his curiosity, extend his horizons, and hopefully make a big impact. 'I don't view myself as a practitioner of a particular skill or method,' he tells me. 'I'm constantly looking at what's the most interesting problem that I could possibly work on. I really try to figure out what sort of scientist I need to be in order to solve the problem I'm interested in solving.'"[24]

The nomadic approach isn't just about feeding Aiden's natural curiosity, although he has plenty of that. It pays off whenever he hits a dead end. For example, in his mid-twenties, Aiden tried to sequence the human immune system. Human antibodies are built from a Lego kit of different genes, snapping together quickly to meet the challenges of constant invasions from viruses, bacteria, and other nasties. Aiden wanted to catalogue all the Lego bricks in the set—all the different genes that could be deployed to fight germs.

After months of hard work, the project crashed. The gene sequencing techniques just weren't up to distinguishing among countless subtly different genes. But then Aiden went to an immunology conference, wandered into the wrong talk, and ended up solving a ferociously difficult problem—the three-dimensional structure of the human genome—by combining everything he had learned in failing to sequence antibodies with an obscure idea he'd stumbled upon from mathematical physics.

This wasn't a fluke. It was a strategy. Aiden seeks the hardest, most interesting problems he can find, and bounces between them. A failure in one area gives fresh insights and new tools that may work elsewhere. For example, Aiden helped Google launch "n-grams," graphs showing the popularity of words across history thanks to a quantitative analysis of five million digitized books. He's now moving on to a similar analysis of music. This poses some formidable technical challenges, but fortunately Aiden already solved a key one while he was failing to sequence the human immune system.[25]

Erez Aiden is clearly an unusual man. But how unusual?

In 1958, a young psychologist by the name of Bernice Eiduson began a long-term study of the working methods of forty mid-career scientists. For twenty years, Professor Eiduson periodically interviewed the scientists and gave them a variety of psychological tests, as well as gathering data on their publications. Some of the scientists went on to great success: there were four Nobel Prize winners in the group, and two others widely regarded as Nobel-worthy. Several other scientists joined the National Academy of Sciences. Others had disappointing careers.

In 1993, several years after Bernice Eiduson's death, her colleagues published an analysis of this study, trying to spot patterns. A question of particular interest was: What determines whether a scientist keeps publishing important work throughout his or her life? A few highly productive scientists produced breakthrough paper after breakthrough paper. How?[26]

A striking pattern emerged. The top scientists switched topics frequently. Over the course of their first hundred published papers, the long-lived high-impact researchers switched topics an average of forty-three times. The leaps were less dramatic than the ones Erez Aiden likes to take, but the pattern is the same; the top scientists keep changing the subject if they wish to stay productive. Erez Aiden is less of an outlier than one might think. As Brian Eno says, the friend of creative work is alertness, and nothing focuses your attention like stepping onto unfamiliar ground.

Eiduson's research project isn't the only one to reach this conclusion. Her colleagues looked at historical examples of long-term scientific achievers, such as Alexander Fleming and Louis Pasteur, and compared them to "one-hit wonders" such as James Watson, co-discoverer of DNA, and Jonas Salk, who developed the polio vaccine. They found the same pattern: Fleming and Pasteur switched research topics frequently; Watson and Salk did not.

This sort of project switching seems to work in the arts as well as the sciences. David Bowie himself is a great example. In the few years before he went to Berlin, Bowie had been collaborating with John Lennon, had lived in Geneva, Los Angeles, and Philadelphia, and had acted in a feature film, *The Man Who Fell to Earth*, as well as working abortively on its soundtrack. He had been drafting an autobiography. In Berlin, he produced and cowrote Iggy Pop's albums in between working on his own.

Another example is Michael Crichton, who in the 1970s and 1980s had written several novels, directed the mid-budget sci-fi thriller *Westworld*, and written nonfiction books about art, medicine, and even computer programming. This remarkable range of interests served him well: by 1994 Crichton had the astonishing distinction of having created the world's most commercially successful novel (*Disclosure*), TV show (*ER*), and film (*Jurassic Park*).[27]

A study of this sort of project-juggling behavior has been conducted by a team including creativity researchers Keith Sawyer and Mihaly Csikszentmihalyi, who popularized the idea of *flow*. The researchers investigated the creative habits of almost a hundred exceptionally creative people, including performers such as Ravi Shankar; Paul MacCready, who built the first human-powered airplane; Nobel laureates in literature such as Nadine Gordimer; twelve-time Emmy Award–winning TV producer Joan Konner; great nonfiction writers such as Stephen Jay Gould; and a pair of double Nobel laureates, Linus Pauling and John Bardeen. Every single one of this galaxy of creative stars had multiple projects on the go at the same time.[28]

In the business world, too, different fields can cross-fertilize. Dick Drew was a sandpaper salesman at the Minnesota Mining and Manufacturing Company. In the 1920s he noticed the challenges of painting automobiles, and with a leap of intuition he realized that sandpaper could help. All he needed to do was produce a roll of sandpaper without the sand: the result was masking tape. Later, Drew saw DuPont's new wrapping paper, "cellophane." Again, he saw an opportunity. Cellophane didn't have to be a wrapping paper at all: it could be one more product to be coated with glue and stored on a roll. Thus was Scotch tape invented.[29]

These days Minnesota Mining and Manufacturing is called 3M, one of the most consistently innovative companies in the world. Given its origins, should we be surprised to discover that 3M has a "flexible attention" policy? In most companies, flexible attention means goofing off on the company dime. In 3M it means playing a game, taking a nap, or going for a walk across an extensive campus to admire the deer. 3M knows that creative ideas don't always surrender to a frontal assault. Sometimes they sneak up on us while we are paying attention to something else.[30]

3M also rotates its engineers from one department to another every few years. This policy is one that many companies—not to mention some employees—resist. Why make someone with years of expertise in soundproofing or flat-screen displays work on a vaccine or an air conditioner? For the company it seems wasteful and for the employee it can be stressful. But for a company that makes masking materials out of sandpaper and sticky tape out of wrapping paper, the real waste would be to let ideas sit in their tidy silos, never to be released.

Two leading creativity researchers, Howard Gruber and Sara Davis, have argued that the tendency to work on multiple projects is so common among the most creative people that it should be regarded as standard practice.[31] Gruber had a particular interest in Charles Darwin, who throughout his life alternated between research in geology, zoology, psychology, and botany, always with some projects in the foreground and others in the background, competing for his attention. He undertook his celebrated voyage with the *Beagle* with "an ample and unprofessional vagueness in his goals."

And then there are the earthworms. Darwin could not get enough of earthworms. This great scientist, who traveled the world, studied the finches of the Galápagos, developed a compelling account of the formation of coral reefs, and—of course—crafted the brilliant, controversial, meticulously argued theory of evolution, studied earthworms from every possible angle for more than forty years. The earthworms were a touchstone, a foundation, almost a security blanket. Whenever Darwin was anxious, puzzled, or at a loss, he could always turn to the study of the humble earthworm.[32]

Gruber and Davis call this pattern of different projects at different stages of fruition a "network of enterprises." Such a network of parallel projects has four clear benefits, one of them practical and the others more psychological.

The practical benefit is that the multiple projects cross-fertilize.

The knowledge gained in one enterprise provides the key to unlock another. This is Erez Aiden's advantage. He moves back and forth across his network of enterprises, solving an impasse on one project with ideas from another, or unexpectedly fusing two disparate lines of work. Dick Drew did much the same at 3M. Or as David Bowie once put it, "The idea of mixtures has always been something that I've found absolutely fascinating, using the wrong pieces of information and putting them together and finding a third piece of information."[33]

The psychological advantages may be just as important. First is the point emphasized by Brian Eno, that a fresh context is exciting; having several projects may seem distracting, but instead the variety grabs our attention—we're like tourists gawping at details that a local would find mundane.

The second advantage is that while we're paying close attention to one project, we may be unconsciously processing another—as with the cliché of inspiration striking in the shower. Some scientists believe that this unconscious processing is an important key to solving creative problems.[34] John Kounios, a psychologist at Drexel University, argues that daydreaming strips items of their context.[35] That's a powerful way to unlock fresh thoughts. And there can be few better ways to let the unconscious mind chew over a problem than to turn to a totally different project in the network of enterprises.

A third psychological benefit is that each project in the network of enterprises provides an escape from the others. In truly original work, there will always be impasses and blind alleys. Having another project to turn to can prevent a setback from turning into a crushing experience. The philosopher Søren Kierkegaard called this "crop rotation." One cannot use the same field to grow the same crop indefinitely; eventually the soil must be refreshed, by planting something new, or simply taking a break.[36]

Gruber and Davis observe that a dead end in one project can actually feel liberating. If one business model founders, an entrepreneur can pivot to something fresh. The writer can pull out some old jottings, the scientist can turn to an anomaly she had long wanted to investigate. What would have been a depressing waste of time for a single-minded person can become a creative lease of life for someone with several projects on the go.

That's the theory, but in practice it can be a source of anxiety. Having many projects on the go is a stressful experience that can quickly degenerate into wheel-spinning. (Rather than turning to the study of earthworms for a break, we turn to Facebook instead.) How do we prevent it from becoming psychologically overwhelming?

Here's one practical solution, from the great American choreographer Twyla Tharp. Over the past fifty years she has won countless awards while blurring genres and dancing to the music of everyone from Mozart to Billy Joel, and somehow has found the time to write three books. "You've got to be all things," she says. "Why exclude? You have to be everything."[37] Tharp uses the no-nonsense approach of assigning a box to every project. Into the box she tosses notes, videos, theater programs, books, magazine cuttings, physical objects, and anything else that has been a source of inspiration. If she runs out of space, she gets a second box. And if she gets stuck, the answer is simple: begin an archaeological dig into one of her boxes. She writes:

> The box makes me feel connected to a project. It is my soil. I feel this even when I've back-burnered a project: I may have put the box away on a shelf, but I know it's there. The project name on the box in bold black lettering is a constant reminder that I had an idea once and may come back to it very soon.
>
> Most important, though, the box means I never have to worry about forgetting. One of the biggest fears for a creative person is

> that some brilliant idea will get lost because you didn't write it down and put it in a safe place. I don't worry about that because I know where to find it. It's all in the box.[38]

I have a related solution myself, a steel sheet on the wall of my office full of magnets and three-by-five-inch cards. Each card has a single project on it—something chunky that will take me at least a day to complete. As I write this, there are more than fifteen projects up there, including my next weekly column, an imminent house move, a standup comedy routine I've promised to try to write, two separate ideas for a series of podcasts, a television proposal, a long magazine article, and this chapter. That would potentially be overwhelming, but the solution is simple: I've chosen three projects and placed them at the top. They're active projects and I allow myself to work on any of the three. All the others are on the back burner. I don't fret that I will forget them, because they're captured on the board. But neither do I feel compelled to start working on any of them. They won't distract me, but if the right idea comes along they may well snag some creative thread in my subconscious.

Whether it's a stack of boxes or a notice board full of cards, you can manage many projects like this. Rather than churning away at the front of your thoughts, ideas can be stored safely at the back of your mind, ready to pop up when unexpected inspiration strikes.

Eno's Oblique Strategies began as a tidy prototype: a checklist. Working on the first Roxy Music album in 1972, Eno and the rest of the band found themselves in a proper recording studio for the first time. That was intimidating.

"It was a lot of money," he says. "We were just working away and working away. And sometimes I would go home at night and remember, think back over the day's work, and think, God, if we'd only remembered such-and-such a thing, some idea, that would have been better."

Eno started making a list of ideas to remember in the high-pressure environment of the studio. The first was "Honor thy error as a hidden intention," a reminder that sometimes what is achieved by accident may be much more worthy of attention than the original plan. The list of reminders grew, "sitting out on the control room desk."

But Eno soon found that the list didn't work. It was too orderly. It was too easy to ignore the disruptive instructions. Your eye would run down the list and settle on exactly the item that would cause the least stress, something that felt safe. And so the idea emerged of turning the checklist into a deck of cards that would be shuffled and dealt at random. Eno's friend, the artist Peter Schmidt, had a flip-book filled with similar provocations. The two men teamed up to produce the Oblique Strategies deck—a guaranteed method of pushing artists out of their comfort zones.

The poet Simon Armitage, fascinated by the cards, says their effect is "as if you're asking the blood in your brain to flow in another direction."[39]

That does not sound like a pleasant experience. Carlos Alomar, the guitar maestro who once told Eno his experiment was stupid, still remembers what it was like having to take orders from the cards.

"I picked the card and the card simply said, 'Think like a gardener,'" he recalls. "The immediate impact of the thought of course throws you off. I think that's the purpose. It's like when you're feeling a pain in your foot and someone slaps you in the face, you're not feeling the pain in your foot anymore. I started thinking, how would I make things grow. So it allowed me to look at the sessions a little bit differently. I kind of let my guitar parts develop into being what they were. You know. Plant something, nurture it, water it, let it grow."[40]

Most of us don't like being slapped in the face. But it's possible to take that slap and turn it into something remarkable. Useful diversions can come from anywhere: an error from some piano movers and a guilt trip from a German teenager; the randomness of an algorithmic search; a strange order from a deck of mysterious cards; the background noise that you can't quite shut out; the side project that suddenly suggests a new solution. Or the annoying need to collaborate with other people, which is the subject of the next chapter.

Over the years, Carlos Alomar came to realize that the cards he once dismissed as "stupid" have unexpected benefits. "I mean some of it worked, some of it didn't," he said a quarter of a century later. "But quite honestly it did take me out of my comfort zone and it did make me leave my frustration at what I was doing and totally look at it from another different point of view and although I didn't like the point of view, when I came back, I was fresh."[41]

Alomar now teaches music at the Stevens Institute of Technology in New Jersey, and he regularly resorts to the Oblique Strategies. His students will sometimes experience creative block, and "I need for them to see what I saw, and feel what I felt, and the dilemma that I had when I had to come up with something out of nothing."[42]

He adds, "They're very curious cards."

When I tell Brian Eno this, he laughs.

2

Collaboration

"My brain is open!"

Paul Erdős and the Robbers Cave:
Why Tidy Teams Have More Fun
but Messy Teamwork Gets More Done

In 1999, as the Summer Olympics in Sydney approached, Ben Hunt-Davis was tantalizingly short of being one of the best rowers in the world. The British rowing team was built around one of the greatest Olympians of any era, Steve Redgrave, a man who was targeting the scarcely believable feat of winning a gold medal in a fifth consecutive Olympic games. Most teams placed their best rowers in the "8+," an event made famous by the annual Oxford and Cambridge Boat Race, with a boat that slices through the water fast enough to pull a water skier. But with the British team focused on Steve Redgrave's crew of four, the British 8+ was for the "nearly men," athletes who weren't fast enough and strong enough to row with him. Ben Hunt-Davis was one of a crew of unfancied underdogs even their opponents ignored. "Roland Baar, the stroke for the Germans, wouldn't have known who I was," says Hunt-Davis.[1]

Faced with an impossible task, Hunt-Davis and the rest of the 8+ crew embarked on a team-building project that took the monomaniacal tendencies of Olympic rowers to new extremes. They shut themselves off from the outside world—by which they meant not just evenings down at the pub, but the rest of the British Olympic team. Most of the British crews had a natural rivalry, noting their status on an informal leaderboard. The 8+ crew shrugged at such point scoring; they had no interest in where they stood relative to Redgrave or the women's 8+ or anyone else. Their crew rules forbade "performance talk" with outsiders; they dismissed the distracting chatter as "talking bollocks to Basil."[2] They even skipped the opportunity to stride out in national colors at the Olympic Opening Ceremony surrounded by superb athletes, cheering crowds, and the TV cameras of the world. They stayed back in the village, focused not on the spectacle or even the British team, but on one another.

Nobody was surprised when Steve Redgrave, the most famous oarsman on the planet, won his fifth gold medal. The next day, Hunt-Davis and his crewmates added a gold medal that had been entirely unexpected: the first British victory in the 8+ since 1912. They had done so by deliberately disconnecting from the rest of the world in an effort to connect with what mattered—one another.

It's a remarkable story of collaboration, of team-building through isolation. Such strategic isolationism has a long history, most famously in 1519 when the conquistador Hernán Cortés destroyed his own ships on the coast of an unknown land, forcing his men to face the mighty and warlike Aztec Empire rather than return to their homes in Cuba.[3] Japanese gangsters sever their little fingers, marking them out as different and making them less able to prosper by themselves. Loyalty to the gang becomes relatively more attractive.

Such strategic isolation can be brutally effective. If you want your teammates to be committed to one another, one way to achieve that is to give them no alternative. The British 8+ crew recognized this and demanded total commitment, because the crew was only as strong as its weakest member. Outsiders weren't merely a distraction; they were a threat to crew unity because they might tempt a crew member into slacking off. Olympic rowing is backbreaking work even by the standards of other professional sports, and the cost-benefit calculus is asymmetric: the crew member who skimps on the training enjoys all the benefits of doing so, while the rest of the crew must share much of the cost. No wonder Hunt-Davis and his crewmates made a pact to turn their gaze away from the world and toward one another. Collaboration is commitment.

But there is an alternative view of teamwork that could not be more different, and there is one man who personified the approach so completely that his name is now used to describe networks of collaboration. That name is Paul Erdős.

Erdős was a brilliant mathematician. He was once sipping coffee in the mathematics common room at Texas A&M University when he noticed some intriguing scribbles on the board. "What's that? Is it a problem?" he asked. It was indeed a problem, and two local mathematicians were delighted with the fact that they had just solved it, requiring a thirty-page chain of intricate reasoning. Erdős didn't recognize the symbols, because this was a totally unfamiliar branch of mathematics, so he asked for an explanation. He then sprang to the blackboard and immediately wrote down an elegant masterpiece of a solution. It was just two lines long.[4]

That is a kind of magic, but there have been many gifted individuals in twentieth-century mathematics. Erdős had a more important spell to weave: the Hungarian wizard was quite simply the most prolific collaborator in the history of science. The web of cooperation around the world and across the twentieth century spreads so far it is measured in an honorific unit: the "Erdős number." People who wrote articles jointly with Erdős himself are said by mathematicians to have an Erdős number of one. Over five hundred people enjoy this distinction. If you wrote a paper with one of them, your Erdős number is two. Over forty thousand people have Erdős numbers of three or less, all spinning in intellectual orbit around this astonishing man.

Erdős's achievement as the linchpin of so many mathematical partnerships is unsurpassed and perhaps unsurpassable. Think for a moment about his five hundred collaborating authors: each one represents Erdős's launching into a serious piece of intellectual teamwork—a peer-reviewed scientific paper—with a stranger. He did this, on average, every six weeks for sixty years. In his peak collaborative year, 1987—when he was seventy-four—he formed thirty-five new creative partnerships, one every ten days.[5]

These collaborations bear little resemblance to the self-sacrificing commitment of the tight-knit rowing crew. They do not have to be unbreakable bonds of comradeship. In fact, they rarely are—with five hundred people involved, how could they be?

In 1973, Mark Granovetter, an American sociologist, introduced the paradoxical idea of "the strength of weak ties." Granovetter looked at a simple sociological question: How do people with good jobs find those jobs? To answer it, he did something new: he looked at the structure of their social networks. After all, as the cliché goes: it's not what you know, but who. Granovetter observed that the most irreplaceable social connections were the distant ones. Jobs were often discovered through personal contacts, but not because they were handed out by close friends. Instead, the jobs were rooted out by following up leads from distant contacts—old acquaintances from college, perhaps, or colleagues from a previous job. More recent data-driven research—for example, using millions of mobile-phone call records—backs up Granovetter's claim that the vital ties are the weak ones.[6]

This seemingly paradoxical finding is obvious in retrospect. In a clique, everyone knows everyone and all your friends can tell you the same gossip. The more peripheral the contact, the more likely she is to tell you something you didn't know.[7]

Paul Erdős was the quintessential weak tie. He made the connections that nobody else could. He never stayed long in any particular university department or in any particular home. He was peripatetic, staying as a houseguest with one mathematician after another—his motto was "Another roof, another proof." His travel schedule was relentless. Erdős's biographer Bruce Schechter describes an itinerary:

> From Budapest to Moscow, then to Leningrad, back to Moscow and on to Beijing by way of Irkutsk and Ulan Bator. After three weeks in Beijing catching up with old friends . . . Erdős caught a flight to Shanghai, then boarded a train to Hangchow. Another flight took him to Canton, from whence another train, this time to Hong Kong; then he flew to Singapore and finally on to Australia.[8]

That was 1960, "and that wasn't even a particularly busy year." Before the Internet, Erdős was a one-man hub through which the world's mathematical insights flowed. During the iciest moments of the Cold War it was Erdős who linked mathematicians in the Soviet bloc to those in the West. And Erdős would step off each plane to be greeted by a welcoming committee of mathematicians, to whom he would announce, "My brain is open!"

Open it was. Erdős loved different branches of mathematics, and was often able to help a colleague focused on one type of problem by talking about a related advance from an entirely different field. This was partly a unique cognitive gift: Erdős could move around a hotel room full of mathematicians like a grand master playing simultaneous chess games, discussing progress, offering breakthrough suggestions, then moving on. But it was a preference as well as a skill: Erdős loved to connect with other people through mathematics.

Erdős was not your average sofa-surfer. Although he joked that a mathematician was "a machine for turning coffee into theorems," he relied on amphetamines for his prodigious output. This homeless, drug-dependent genius was an exhausting houseguest. If he wanted something to eat at four o'clock in the morning—and he often did, since he never cooked a meal for himself in his life—then he would get out a couple of saucepans and bash them until the owner of the house woke up to provide some service. He owned very few clothes, although his vest and underpants were made of silk—these needed to be hand-washed frequently, and not by Erdős. He couldn't drive, so his hosts were forced to drive him. He couldn't even pack his own suitcase. People found him impossibly demanding; it was like caring for an infant.[9]

And yet, everyone loved working with him. Years after his death, papers continued to be published listing Paul Erdős as a coauthor, as the seeds he planted continued to bear fruit.

Sociologists have a term for these different kinds of collaboration. When Hunt-Davis and his crewmates focused purely on one another and the task ahead of them, cutting themselves off from the temptations of the outside world, they were building up their "bonding social capital." Paul Erdős restlessly traversed that outside world with a plastic bag full of the latest mathematical offprints, bringing news from Beijing to Princeton to Manchester to Budapest—and from set theory to number theory to probability theory and back—and created "bridging social capital." We can think of bonding as the tidy-minded approach to collaboration. Minimize disruptions, distractions, obstacles; identify what you have to do; focus your energies on doing it as effectively as possible. It's analogous to the hill-climbing strategy, while the itinerant genius Erdős personifies the random leap.

In some circumstances, it may be appropriate to focus only on bonding: when it is absolutely clear how the goal needs to be achieved, and hard work is needed to put theory into practice. As we saw in the last chapter, elite sports is one field where there is relatively little scope for radical new approaches. If Hunt-Davis and his crew had sealed themselves off from the outside world for years on end, they might well have missed out on some useful advance in understanding nutrition, or an improved design of rowing machine. But for a few weeks or months of intense preparation, lack of contact with the outside world wasn't likely to deprive them of game-changing new ideas.

In many other circumstances, however, bridging takes on more importance. While Hunt-Davis showed that hard work could propel eight second-tier rowers to the pinnacle of their sport, second-tier mathematicians are unlikely to crack the hardest theorems by locking themselves away. What they need is a flash of inspiration, of the kind Erdős could swiftly conjure over coffee in a faculty lounge.

Most tasks require a combination of bonding and bridging: flashes of inspiration to identify the right approach, and long effort characterized by selfless teamwork to put it into practice. That means a compromise between bonding and bridging—a willingness to allow a degree of messiness into a tidy team. This chapter is all about why getting the best of both approaches can prove very challenging indeed.

If we're looking for a petri dish to examine the nature of teamwork in the twenty-first century, a computer game isn't a bad candidate. Game design requires a marriage of skills—visual, audio, and narrative artists work with skilled software engineers alongside commercial functions such as finance and marketing. The technical possibilities are always changing, and for many games it is important to take full advantage of the very latest technology. Like a Hollywood movie, a game is an extended yet temporary project with plenty of freelancers and ad hoc teams.

In modern working life, most projects are more like designing a computer game than solving a mathematical theorem or winning Olympic gold.

So when three sociologists wanted a case study of how teams produce products that are both original and commercially successful, they turned to the computer games industry. The three researchers, Mathijs de Vaan, David Stark, and Balázs Vedres, were also attracted by the rich data that was available about the game industry. They were able to assemble a vast database of the artists, programmers, and other individuals who had worked on computer games between 1979—the birth of the commercial game industry—and 2009. The data described 12,422 games, and the 139,727 different people who had worked on them.[10]

One crucial advantage of this approach was that they were able to develop a much more dynamic view of collaborative networks. Typically, when social scientists analyze networks they look at a snapshot of relationships at a given moment. Analyzing the gaming data set, however, revealed teams of designers and engineers forming and splitting to work on one game after another.

The researchers also had access to financial information and critical reviews, and they were able to develop a detailed picture of each game, identifying more than one hundred different stylistic elements—for example, whether the game was first person or third person, 2-D or 3-D, a shooter or a flight simulator. In short, they were able to understand both the best games—the "game changers" that were stylistically original, while also being critical and commercial hits—and the structure of the teams that created those games.

Think about what that structure might be. In some ways, making a great computer game is like training for a top rowing race. It requires bonding: focus, and trust, and commitment. Team members need to understand each other quickly and well. There is no room for free riders, or for disloyalty. But viewed another way, a great computer game is like a great mathematics paper. It requires bridging: the clever combination of disparate ideas. So what does a network analysis of great computer games reveal? Are they put together by tight-knit teams? Or created by a far-flung and diverse network?

The answer: neither, and both. What de Vaan, Stark, and Vedres found was that the outstanding games were forged by *networks of teams*. The social networks behind these games contained several different clusters, groups of people who had worked together many times before and so had the trust and commitment and mutual understanding necessary to pull long hours in pursuit of a shared goal. But the networks were also diverse, in the sense that each of these teams was different from the others, having worked on very different projects in the past.

This is not conventional social bridging, where a tidily packaged idea is carried from one cluster of people to a distinct cluster of people, where the idea can be used profitably in a fresh context. Instead, the researchers were uncovering creative tension, where two or three tightly bonded teams with very different creative histories had to find a way to work together over an extended period to produce something quite new. That sounds exciting, and it's not a shock to hear that the cognitive diversity of the teams was an asset, nor that close-knit teams could achieve remarkable things.

But the greater effectiveness of networks of diverse teams, knitted together at what Vedres calls "structural folds," comes at a cost.

"Structural folds shorten the lifespan of teams," he says. "They fall apart much quicker. The instability comes from different sources. Maybe there are concerns about loyalty, or perhaps just scheduling conflicts. But such groups fall apart much faster than a random baseline."[11]

Attempting to put two tight-knit teams together in a single organization can present the organization's leaders with a severe headache—as a remarkable adventure from the 1950s demonstrates.

On June 19, 1954, eleven boys were collected by bus from Oklahoma City and journeyed to a Boy Scout campsite at Robbers Cave State Park, a quiet, densely wooded area forty miles away from the nearest town. (It had once been a hideout for Jesse James.) The boys had never met but they had plenty in common—white, eleven years old, all from Protestant families of modest means—and before the bus had even collected them all, friendships were beginning to form. Loosely supervised by adult camp counselors, the boys chose their bunks, and around the campfire after supper they looked forward to three weeks of adventure—camping, swimming, boating, baseball, and treasure hunts.[12]

The boys were soon exploring the hills and woods around the two-hundred-acre campsite. It was humid and uncomfortably hot, but the group soon found a perfect spot in which to swim. They decided to build a causeway and a diving board, and worked together to carry rocks in a human chain, alternating their sweaty toil with dips in the cool of the river. They cooked hamburgers outside at their hideout rather than returning to the campsite mess hall. To help the boys who were nervous swimmers or divers, the group would form a ring of swimmers around the board to support their anxious friends. Soon, the group vowed, "We will *all* be able to swim." Working together, they carried a canoe up to the swimming hole, dug a latrine nearby, pitched tents as a storm approached, spotted a rattlesnake, and planned an overnight hike.

The counselors occasionally stepped in with a task for the group, such as a treasure hunt with a cash prize for the group to spend together. But these interventions were rare: the adults tended to watch from the sidelines, giving the boys space to make their own decisions.

What the boys did not realize was that each decision, comment, or disagreement was being painstakingly recorded by the apparently inattentive adults. They jotted notes down in shorthand and completed them in the evening after the boys had gone to sleep. The group was part of an experiment, a masterpiece in manipulation and one that would later be called the "forgotten classic" of social science.[13] The experiment was being supervised by a group of researchers led by a social psychologist, Muzafer Sherif.

There was something else that the boys hadn't realized. A day after they had arrived at Robbers Cave, another group of boys very much like them had arrived and set up camp on the other side of a hill. The second group was having just as much excitement, building a rope bridge over their swimming hole, performing campfire skits, solving a treasure hunt, and—with the help of adults—killing a poisonous copperhead snake that slithered into their camp. Despite occasional disagreements, most of the boys were having a glorious time. But the two groups were unaware of each other's existence.

Both groups had decided to give themselves a name and a flag. The first group were the "Rattlers" and the second, the "Eagles." After a few days, some Rattlers heard the Eagles playing baseball on "their" ball field. The staff explained to each group that there was another group of boys in the camp, and soon the Eagles and the Rattlers were eager to compete with each other on the baseball field. The camp staff suggested a series of contests—baseball, tug-of-war, tent pitching, a talent show—with a trophy, medals, and much-coveted Swiss Army knives for the winners.

The trouble began almost immediately. The Rattlers arrived early for the game, considering themselves the home team. They planted a "Keep Off" sign and a Rattler flag on the baseball diamond. Dark threats of revenge were muttered against any Eagle who disturbed the flag. Then the Eagles approached, carrying their flag on a pole and singing the ominous notes of the theme from *Dragnet*, a popular TV show of the day. The groups sized each other up, and then the name-calling and jeering began, followed by the chanting of insulting songs about the other group. "You're not Eagles, you're pigeons!" yelled one Rattler, and the Rattlers went on to win the game. Smarting from the defeat, one Eagle stole a glove that a Rattler had left on the field and threw it in the river.

A bitter rivalry developed. Occasional displays of sportsmanship became less and less frequent, replaced by jeers and insults. The Eagles and Rattlers ate together in the mess hall, but they segregated themselves and threw food, paper cups, and taunts at each other.

The experimenters had been planning to create some artificial friction between the groups, but they abandoned that plan. It wasn't necessary: the boys needed no provocation to go to war.

After supper on the first day, the Rattlers defeated the Eagles at tug-of-war. The Eagles were despondent until someone noticed the Rattler flag on the ball field. Without delay, the Eagles ripped it down, tore it up, burned it, and rehung the charred rag. When the Rattlers discovered their desecrated flag, brawling began, and the adults had to intervene to break up the fight and persuade the boys to play another game of baseball.

This time the Eagles won. They celebrated with supper, comedy skits around the campfire, and then a well-earned sleep. But before midnight, the Eagles were shocked awake by the revenge of the

Rattlers, who burst into their hut, overturned their beds, ripped down the window screens, and stole comic books and a pair of jeans belonging to the de facto leader of the Eagles. (The next day, the jeans appeared on a flagpole, daubed with insulting slogans in bright orange paint.)

More raids followed from each side, and with the Eagles wielding socks stuffed with stones, the staff had to step in to prevent serious violence. The staff fudged some of the competitions to keep the series of contests close, but beyond that, no manipulation was needed: the two groups had grown to loathe each other.

When the Eagles won the overall contest—with a trophy, medals, and much-prized pocket knives—at least one of them was so happy that he wept. The Eagles ran to their swimming creek and leaped into the water in celebration. This was a mistake: the Rattlers raided again in their absence, overturning beds, heaping personal possessions in a mess, cutting boats loose to send them floating down the river, and stealing the precious pocket knives and medals. Confronted later by the furious Eagles, the Rattlers announced that they would gladly return the knives and medals to their opponents.

All the Eagles had to do was to get down on their bellies in the dirt and crawl.

We now have the answer to an old question. Are children vicious and violent, as portrayed in William Golding's unforgettable *Lord of the Flies*? Or are they the cheerful do-gooders portrayed in Enid Blyton's Famous Five books? Muzafer Sherif discovered that children are both. The boys were creative and mutually supportive, until confronted with a competitor group. Then they became insular, violent, and cruel.

Now, children are not adults, and one would not expect adults to fall out over a mere game.* But it is striking how easily tribal loyalties emerge in adult contexts. Sometimes the consequences are far graver

*Unless the game was between Manchester United and Liverpool, or Barcelona and Real Madrid, or the Yankees and the Red Sox, or . . . you get the idea.

than anything a group of boys could produce: What are most genocides if not tribal conflict carried to the worst extremes? But more often, we grown-ups suppress our tribal feelings. We naturally divide ourselves into tribes (we're the marketing department, they are the accounting department). Even if we rarely steal from these rival tribes or insult them to their faces, the annoyance we feel is quite real, and often owes more to our tribal feelings than to any genuine offense the accounting team may have committed.

One instructive study was conducted by the legal scholar and policy wonk Cass Sunstein, with two social psychologists, Reid Hastie and David Schkade. The three researchers assembled participants from two quite different cities: Boulder, Colorado, where people often lean to the left (it's known jokingly as "The People's Republic of Boulder") and Colorado Springs, which is well known as a conservative stronghold. Participants were privately asked their views on three politically heated topics: climate change, affirmative action, and same-sex partnerships. Then they were put into groups with others from their town, and asked to discuss the issues as a group.[14]

Before these discussions, as one might expect, the people from Boulder tended to espouse left-wing views while the citizens of Colorado Springs tended to favor the views of the right. But there was a broad spread of views among each town's citizens, and a substantial overlap between the groups: some people from liberal Boulder were to the right of some people from conservative Colorado Springs.

After the discussions, the range of political views sharply changed. First, people were emboldened after discussing controversial issues with people who tended to hold similar views, and their views became more extreme. The Boulder groups moved a long way further to the left, and the Colorado Springs groups moved a long way further to the right. This was true not only of what people said in public, but also of what they told the researchers in private. Second, the diversity within each group was suppressed, so the spectrum of opinion was much narrower. The Boulder groups converged on left-wing views, of course, and the Colorado Springs groups converged on right-wing views. Given these two shifts in the groups' views—more extreme, with less internal variety—the inevitable result was that the groups became sharply divided from each other. Where once there had been a substantial overlap between the residents of Boulder and Colorado Springs, now that overlap was much reduced. Adults can be tribal, too.

In one way, the Eagles and the Rattlers had a big advantage over many adults seeking to work together: they were homogenous. They were from the same city and the same race, religion, and class—and of course they were all eleven-year-old boys, with all that that implied about a shared love of baseball, hamburgers, and exploring. Many adults need to find a reason to cooperate based on far less common ground.

It's now widely recognized that cognitive diversity is a recipe for creativity and an antidote to groupthink. Indeed, the very word "groupthink" was popularized by a psychologist, Irving Janis, to describe a process whereby like-minded people make bad decisions without seriously examining them. Keen to maintain a friendly atmosphere within the group, they self-censor their own doubts and do not challenge each other. Since the group is full of smart people, each one feels confident that the group must be making a smart decision. Each one abdicates his own responsibility to think critically, assuming that others are doing the hard thinking for him.[15]

Back in 1951, two decades before Janis published his ideas on groupthink, another psychologist, Solomon Asch, had carried out a famous set of experiments exploring conformity and dissent. Asch found that people would sometimes suppress their own judgments in order to agree with a unanimous group, even though the group was clearly in the wrong. (The group was made up of actors working for Solomon Asch, surrounding a single, rather confused participant, unaware that he was being set up.) The cure for this groupthink? Even a single dissenting voice broke the spell, and the experimental subjects felt much more able to express their own dissent.[16]

More recently, complexity scientist Scott Page published *The Difference*,[17] a book that uses a mathematical rather than a psychological framework to explore similar questions. Page showed that in many problem-solving contexts, "diversity trumps ability." For example, if you already have four brilliant statisticians working on a policy problem, even a mediocre sociologist or economist may add more to your team than another brilliant statistician. If you're trying to improve your tennis game, you may do better working with a tennis coach, a nutritionist, and a general fitness trainer rather than three tennis coaches. And, adds Page, "There's a lot of empirical data to show that diverse cities are more productive, diverse boards of directors make better decisions, the most innovative companies are diverse."[18]

The logic behind these results is that when dealing with a complicated problem, even the smartest person can get stuck. Adding a new perspective or a new set of skills can unstick us, even if the perspective is off-the-wall or the skills are mediocre. The fresh input works much like the Oblique Strategies employed by Brian Eno or the random leaps used by silicon chip algorithms. It's the difference itself that helps.

"If we're in an organization where everyone thinks in the same way, everyone will get stuck in the same place," says Scott Page. But people with different problem-solving skills will get stuck in different places. "One person can do their best, and then someone else can come in and improve on it."

While this all sounds very reasonable, the truth is that facing up to these different views can be messy and awkward. For example, in

2006 the psychologist Samuel Sommers examined the decision-making processes of juries, some all-white and some racially mixed. (These were mock trials based on real cases.) Deliberating the case of a black defendant, the mixed juries did a better job of working through the information presented to them. This wasn't just because the black jurors brought a fresh perspective to the deliberation room. It was also because white jurors were less lazy in their thinking when black jurors were present, citing more facts about the case and making fewer mistakes.[19] People think harder when they fear their views may be challenged by outsiders. Other researchers have found similar effects. For example, when experimental subjects are challenged to write an essay, they write better, more logical prose when told their work will be read by someone with different political beliefs rather than someone like-minded.[20]

When deliberating with a group, then, we should be seeking out people who think differently, who have different experiences and training, and who look different. Those people may bring fresh and useful ideas to the table; even if they do not, they'll bring out the best in us—even if only by making us feel awkward and forcing us to shape up. That messy, challenging process is one we should embrace.

Unfortunately, this is not something that comes naturally, as demonstrated by three psychologists who recently published a fascinating study of group dynamics. Katherine Phillips, Katie Liljenquist, and Margaret Neale challenged students to work together in groups to solve a murder mystery problem.[21] The groups were given various materials about a murder—witness statements, alibis, and a list of three murder suspects. Their task was to figure out who committed the crime. In some cases the groups comprised four friends—members of the same college fraternity or sorority. In other cases the groups were made up of three friends and a stranger.

Given what we've been discovering about the advantages of

cognitive diversity, it may not be a surprise to hear that the groups that included a stranger did a better job of finding the murderer. As with the diverse juries or the essay writers who expected a political challenge, the stranger provoked the friends to raise their game. The friends were more careful about exploring their own conclusions, paid more attention to the newcomer and to the task at hand, and were more willing to change their views. Assumptions that might have been allowed to ride among friends had to be examined carefully under the scrutiny of a stranger.

What is more, this effect was large: groups that had to accommodate an outsider were substantially more likely to reach the correct conclusion—they did so 75 percent of the time, versus 54 percent for a homogenous group and 44 percent for an individual.

The problem comes when we ask a different question—not how well the group did, but how well the members of the group thought they'd done. The answers are remarkable. Members of diverse teams didn't feel very sure that they'd gotten the right answer, and they felt socially uncomfortable. The teams made up of four friends had a more pleasant time and they also tended to be confident—wrongly—that they had found the right answer.

When it comes to picking our own dream team, we seem incapable of figuring out what's good for us. The diverse teams were more effective, but that is not how things seemed to people in those teams: team members doubted their answers, distrusted their process, and felt that the entire interaction was an awkward mess. The homogenous teams were ineffective and complacent. They enjoyed themselves and wrongly assumed that because their friendly conversation was smooth and effortless they were doing well.

Observing small groups in the real world points to similar conclusions. Consider the research of sociologist Brooke Harrington, who studied the stock-picking investment clubs of 1990s California much as an anthropologist might study the wedding customs of Uzbekistan. This was a fascinating time, when world stock markets were booming, media coverage was fervent, and people clubbed together to learn about investing in stocks and to invest money as a group. These investment clubs weren't purely social, like book clubs; with substantial sums of money invested, the clubs were often incorporated and had formal rules of governance.[22]

Unfortunately, the clubs were often fun. Clubs of friends made far worse decisions than clubs formed—for example—through the workplace, where club members do not necessarily know one another outside the monthly club gatherings. As Harrington zoomed in on a small number of clubs, sitting in on month after month of investment meetings, it became clear why this was. The "friendly" clubs would make decisions aimed at preserving those friendships rather than picking the best stocks.

For example, one friendly group decided not to invest in Bombardier simply because one member thought the company was an arms manufacturer. In fact, the company largely makes trains and civilian planes, but the group wasn't prepared to even discuss whether Bombardier was or was not in the arms business. "Why run roughshod over the feelings of members?" said one member of the club. "If there's strong opposition, we can't push."[23]

Harrington noticed that the groups of friends made poor financial decisions in order to keep the group itself running smoothly. While the less social investment clubs would have voted down unappealing investment proposals, the sociable clubs would postpone sensitive decisions to avoid hurting anyone's feelings. Cash accumulated rather than being profitably invested, because when faced with a tough choice, the group's decision would be: "Let's discuss it another time."

Here's an example of the kind of conversation they were avoiding, which took place at a meeting of a non-sociable investment club,

Portfolio Associates. A club member was doing a poor job of explaining the strengths and weaknesses of his recommended investment. "We're falling short of our mission—we need data and analysis," commented another member. "You're being kind of picky—I worked hard on this," was the defensive response, and the conversation grew tense. The idea was promptly voted down, and one member muttered, "This used to be fun."[24]

Harrington witnessed the entire discussion and noted the sour mood. But Portfolio Associates had superb financial results. As with the mixed student teams working on murder mysteries, Portfolio Associates did brilliantly and had a miserable time.

It makes sense that for most teams, there must be a trade-off between the cohesion of a rowing team and the radical openness of an Erdős network. The trouble is that we systematically get the trade-off wrong. Faced with a choice of more cohesion versus more openness, our temptation to be tidy-minded means we'll go for cohesion every time. Cohesion makes us feel more comfortable. We mistakenly think that diversity is getting in the way even when it's helping. Like Carlos Alomar in Berlin, we don't enjoy the disruption, we don't believe the disruption is useful, and it may be months or years before we finally realize how much we gained from what seemed at the time to be an awful mess.

The modern world is full of opportunities to meet new people. We rarely take them. We're timid about whom to date, whom to hire—even whom to schmooze with at corporate networking events. A clever study by two psychologists, Paul Ingram and Michael Morris, was built around just such an event. It was a mixer, an evening of drinks and chat for executives. Ingram and Morris invited a range of high-powered consultants, entrepreneurs, bankers, and other businesspeople to the event in New York. About a hundred showed up.

Almost all had emphasized that their aim was to meet new people rather than hang around with old associates; they told the researchers they wanted to build new ties, or expand their social network.[25]

What they actually did was rather different. The scientists were able to track exactly where people went and whom people chatted with during the party, thanks to a digital tag that each attendee had been given to wear. The tags revealed that people were making a beeline for people they already knew and then staying close to them. When they did meet strangers, they did so because those strangers were friends of friends. As a result the new acquaintances tended to be from the same industry.

(No wonder that two other researchers, sociologists Howard Aldrich and Martha Martinez-Firestone, recently concluded that contrary to their reputation, most entrepreneurs aren't terribly creative. One reason: most entrepreneurs hang out with other people who are exactly like them.[26])

Of course it's human nature to spend time with your friends. But what's striking about this research is that people said they intended to do exactly the opposite. People went to a networking event with the expressed intention of expanding their social networks, and they didn't even try. Those that did meet new people encountered only friends of friends, perpetuating old cliques.

In principle, the modern world gives us more opportunities than ever to forge relationships with people who do not look, act, or think the same way that we do. Travel is cheaper, communication is free and instantaneous, and a host of tools exist to help us reach across previously unbridgeable social divides. But what do we do with these opportunities? We keep our social networks nice and tidy by seeking out people just like us.

Consider a study of college friendships conducted by Angela Bahns, Kate Pickett, and Christian Crandall.[27] These psychologists compared the way students formed friendships at small college campuses, of around five hundred students apiece, with the friendship structure at the University of Kansas, which has a student population of a medium-sized town. The researchers sought out pairs of people who were chatting in the student union or cafeteria, and gathered details about students' age, sexual orientation, and ethnicity along with more fine-grained information such as how much they drank, smoke, or exercised, and what they felt about issues such as abortion, and their attitudes to Arabs, gay men, and black people. And they were asked about their friendships.

With twenty-five thousand students to choose from, the University of Kansas offered a far greater range of views and lifestyles than the smaller colleges did. In principle, then, friendship networks at the large campus should be far more diverse. They weren't. On the larger campus, students were able to seek out their ideological twins; on the smaller campuses, people made friends with people very different from them.* Forced by circumstance to befriend people at least somewhat different from themselves, they did so. And they made the friendships work: friendships at the smaller colleges were actually closer and lasted longer than those at the larger university. Offered a wider choice of friends, students at larger schools chose sameness. It's astonishing how widespread this tendency to homophily can be, and it can be both deep-rooted and absurdly superficial.†

But while our attraction to people who share our outlook is not new, what is new is that we're far more able to indulge that desire. Women are now far freer, better educated, and better paid, which is

*It's theoretically possible that causation ran the other way: students who wanted a homogenous friendship group sought out larger colleges. But several pieces of indirect evidence suggest otherwise, most obviously that the large college was objectively more diverse, not less diverse.

†One study used personality tests and careful observation to rate the subjects for age, status, bravery, curiosity, and the tendency to solve problems independently versus by observing and imitating others. The experimental subjects sought out others like them: the curious spent time with the curious, the brave with the brave, the young with the young, and the old with the old, while the high-status types strutted around together. The only unusual thing about this research? It was carried out not on humans but on baboons.

good news. But one unintended consequence of that freedom is what economists call "assortative mating." Executives with MBAs used to marry their secretaries; now they marry other executives with MBAs.[28] And just as people choose ever more similar spouses, they also choose ever more similar neighborhoods in a process called "assortative migration." In the United States, neighborhoods are increasingly segregated—economically, politically, almost any way one cares to look at the data.[29] We have an unprecedented choice of news outlets. Americans, Canadians, Australians, and Brits can easily read *The Times of India* or *The Japan Times*. But we don't. Instead, conservatives watch Fox News and liberals watch MSNBC.[30]

There's the Internet, of course, a cornucopia of news and opinion, but we sample its riches selectively—often without realizing how the selection is made. Consider the way that the troubles of Ferguson, Missouri, were covered by social media in the summer of 2014 after a police officer, Darren Wilson, shot and killed a young black man, Michael Brown. Night after night of confrontation between police and protesters barely made a ripple on Facebook. The most likely explanation for that is that Facebook is set up for sharing good news. You signal your approval of a post by clicking "Like," which feels like an inappropriate response to a photograph of a masked protester or a line of riot cops. Because such photographs aren't "Liked" much, Facebook's algorithm doesn't tend to display them much; Facebook users might also self-censor, avoiding grim and controversial topics.

In contrast, Ferguson did trend widely on Twitter, which posts an unfiltered feed and offers "retweets" instead of "likes." But the story here is not much more cheerful. Emma Pierson, a young statistician based at Oxford University, dug into the data and found that tweets about Ferguson were clearly divisible into two groups, the "blue tweets," which claimed that Brown's death was an outrage and the police response to protesters was oppressive, and the "red tweets," which claimed that police officer Wilson was being scapegoated and the protesters were looters. (Many of the tweets made false claims, which were rapidly retweeted.)[31] Pierson's analysis showed that the two groups, with very different views of the world, barely interacted.[32]

From the middle of one of these groups, surrounded by outrage expressed by like-minded people, it is easy to believe that the world agrees with you. Of course the Internet is full of contrary viewpoints that might challenge our assumptions and encourage us to think more deeply, but few of us realize that we might have to get out and look for those viewpoints. In the words of author and digital activist Eli Pariser, a "filter bubble" exists to give us more of what we already believe. It is sometimes hard to see that bubble for what it is. When our stream of social media updates fits tidily into our preconceptions, we are hardly likely to mess it up by seeking out the people who disagree.

The pattern repeats endlessly: we gain new choices about whom to listen to, whom to trust, and whom to befriend—and we use those new choices to tighten the circle around us to people who are more and more like us. Given a larger social map to explore, we pick the tidiest corner we can find. We use a large, diverse campus to meet people exactly like us. At a networking event, we stick with old friends even though our explicit aim was to meet new people. And when we are forced into the discomfiting position of working with strangers, we disparage the very team dynamic that is bringing us success.

Traditionally, corporate attempts to promote collaboration have emphasized "team building." These efforts are fine up to a point, but we can't expect too much from them. Most team-building attempts simply involve hanging out together, or participating in some fairly trivial activity. That didn't help at Robbers Cave. Muzafer Sherif arranged for the Eagles and the Rattlers to play games together, watch films together, and eat together. None of this activity broke through the atmosphere of mutual loathing. In each case, insults were hurled (followed by chunks of mashed potato, when available).

So if we want to embrace a messier social setting, to get out of our bonding comfort zones and start bridging, too, what do we need to do? Four lessons suggest themselves.

The first, and most straightforward, is to recognize this tendency in ourselves to spend time with people who look and sound just like us. Instead we need to find the social equivalent of Brian Eno's Oblique Strategies: people with whom or places or situations where we won't be able to avoid new kinds of interactions. Perhaps it's as simple as joining a new group, learning a skill, or engaging in a pastime with strangers. Perhaps it's taking an extended trip to a distant city, a place where everyone is a stranger. Or perhaps it is being a little braver at the next networking event.

A second lesson emerges from the work of de Vaan, Stark, and Vedres on how networks of different teams were able to come together and produce excellent computer games: we should place great value on the people who connect together disparate teams. These are not just Erdős-style free spirits, but people who have worked intimately with more than one group, whom several teams regard as "one of us." Rather than play a mere bridging role, they sit in the intersection of the Venn diagram. They are both bridging and bonding simultaneously. "The role of these people is to knit together the teams and to build trust," says Balázs Vedres.[33]

This is a tough and undervalued role. Says Mathijs de Vaan, "there is a lot of pressure on these people."[34] And Vedres adds, "It is hard to be a double insider." It is, however, essential.

A third lesson is to constantly remind yourself of the benefits of tension, which can be easy to forget when all you want is a quiet life. When Samuel Sommers studied jury deliberations, he found that it was the presence of the black jurors that prodded the white jurors into thinking more carefully about the case. De Vaan, Stark, and Vedres argue that creative collaboration is all about a sense of dissonance. You don't just take a nice, neatly packaged idea from a stranger and put it into a fresh context. It is the ill-matched social gears grinding together that produces the creative spark.

The Sky cycling team won the 2012 and 2013 Tour de France, but then underperformed in 2014. The team's manager, Dave Brailsford, was wise enough to identify the problem: "We'd been becoming pretty aligned over the last six years working together," he said of the core team around him. "If you gave us a problem we'd come back with the same answer, [we had lost] the cognitive diversity we had as a group. [Before] when I would say something, they would say 'bollocks,' we'd argue a lot, there would be tension but we'd come up with some good ideas, constantly pushing forward."[35]

Brailsford also knew what he had to do: rock the boat. "It's a pain in the arse to do it. It's going to be stressful, it's not going to be pleasant, but ultimately you have to rock it from side to side, bring new people in who will question everything, ask why we are doing this, take us forward." Sky bounced back and won the Tour de France again in 2015.

A final lesson is that we have to believe the ultimate goal of the collaboration is something worth achieving, and worth the mess of dealing with awkward people. Brailsford says that "team harmony" is overrated: he wants "goal harmony" instead, a team focused on achieving a common goal rather than having members get along with one another. When Brooke Harrington watched friendly investment clubs underperforming, she was watching people more interested in staying friends than in achieving financial goals. Brailsford doesn't seem to be interested in staying friends; he is interested in achieving goals.[36]

• • •

Muzafer Sherif and his colleagues had provoked a war between two tribes of boys, and some popular approaches to peacemaking—arranging ways for the tribes to spend some time together and get to know each other, like playing games and sharing meals—weren't working.

So Sherif took a different route to peace, one that began with the camp's water supply. Water from a reservoir was pumped to a large water tank a little over a mile outside the camp. The camp staff quietly went up to the tank and blocked the flow of water down to the camp by closing a valve and covering it with large rocks; they also prevented water from being drawn directly from the tank by stuffing sacking into a tap. The boys were then informed that there seemed to be some problem with the camp's water supply—possibly the fault of vandals who, it was said, had caused problems in the past.

As every faucet in the camp ran dry and the boys grew thirstier, the staff led four groups to scour the area for possible faults. Having eliminated alternative explanations, the four groups converged on the water tank and quickly began to figure out the problem: yes, the tank was still full of water; no, the tap didn't work; yes, the valve had been closed and blocked. Eagles and Rattlers shared tools and took turns and eventually the valve was open and the tap unblocked. The Eagles didn't even have water bottles with them and were especially thirsty, and the Rattlers allowed them to drink first without protest.

Solving the water shortage did not bring peace overnight—the two groups continued to bicker and throw food at supper—but there were several small gestures of friendship. The way ahead seemed clear: when the two tribes had to work together to solve a mutual problem, relations improved. And so the experimenters continued to manufacture problems large and small, most notably a truck "breakdown" that soon had all the boys tugging on a length of rope to get it started again. The self-segregation that had been such a feature of their meals quickly broke down as the boys mixed together to win their tug-of-war with the truck.

Peace was beginning to break out; soon the tribal identities themselves were blurring. The two groups had agreed to take turns to cook for each other, but then everyone joined in to cook together. When the boys had to pitch tents and each group discovered missing equipment, they turned to each other and swiftly—almost wordlessly—exchanged gear so that both tents went up smoothly.

The message of Muzafer Sherif's work is that when you give people an important enough problem to solve together, they can put aside their differences. A good problem contains the seeds of its own solution. Rather than lubricating people with drinks at a networking reception, or getting them to play silly games at a team-building event, the way to get conflicting teams to gel is to give them something worth doing together—something where failing to cooperate simply isn't an option.

At the end of three weeks—one week of tribal bonding, one of tribal conflict, and one of tribal reconciliation—the boys returned home on a single bus at their own request. They mingled together without regard to their old group identities. When the bus stopped at a refreshment stand, the Rattlers remembered five dollars that they had won by vanquishing the Eagles in a "bean toss" contest. They decided that this prize fund would be used to buy milk shakes for both groups. Individual boys paid for their own sandwiches and treats, but those with spare money chipped in to help those who lacked funds.

The distinction between Eagles and Rattlers had been forgotten. All that was left was a bus full of boys who had shared an unforgettable summer vacation.

3

Workplaces

"Nobody cares what you do in there."

Where Steve Jobs Went Wrong, and Why It's Nobody Else's Business Whether You Tidy Your Desk

In 1923, Henry Frugès, a French industrialist, commissioned a rising star in the field of architecture to design some homes for the workers who labored to build packing cases in his factories in Lège and Pessac, near Bordeaux. The brightly hued houses were pieces of pure modernism, concrete cuboids shorn of decoration. They were starkly beautiful, in the way that modern architecture at its best can be. The architect's name was Charles-Édouard Jeanneret-Gris. Today we know him as Le Corbusier.

Le Corbusier admired the energy of modern industry and scorned the messy rural vernacular of French peasant architecture. Where was the beauty in that? Le Corbusier loved straight lines, elegant curves, and smooth planes: "These things are beautiful because in the middle of the apparent incoherence of nature of the cities of men, they are places of geometry, a realm where practical mathematics reigns," he once wrote. "And is not geometry pure joy?"

Reasonable people may disagree with that, and there was one group that did not care much for Le Corbusier's geometry: the humble French workers who lived in his joyful cubes at Pessac, trudging home each night after a tough day of work in a factory. As writer Alain de Botton observes in *The Architecture of Happiness*, "At the end of a shift in the plant, to be further reminded of the dynamism of modern industry was not a pressing psychological priority."[1]

The families who occupied Le Corbusier's homes defied his designs in a simple and practical fashion. They added old-fashioned shutters and windows; they erected pitched roofs over the flat ones; they put up flowery wallpaper over the uninterrupted monochrome walls, and marked out little blocks of garden with wooden picket fences.

Their gardens were decorated with gnomes.

Steve Jobs, one suspects, would not have approved of the gnomes. Jobs, like Le Corbusier, loved simplicity and clean modern lines—although unlike Le Corbusier, Steve Jobs had a gift for making things that people loved.

Jobs is most famous for his work on computers, phones, and tablets, galvanizing outstanding designers for three decades to produce some of the most beautifully crafted technology in the world. But Jobs also designed a building—the headquarters of Pixar, the animation studio that produced films from *Toy Story* to *Inside Out*. Jobs was Pixar's majority shareholder.[2]

There can be no doubt that Steve Jobs was just as committed to the ideals of beauty as Le Corbusier had been, and he could be just as controlling. One of the saddest and most eloquent anecdotes in Walter Isaacson's biography of Jobs describes him, semiconscious after receiving a liver transplant, ripping off his oxygen mask because it was ugly, and demanding that the medical team bring him five alternative designs so that he could pick the best.[3]

In happier days Jobs focused this fierce love for design on Pixar's headquarters. In the wake of the smash hit *Toy Story 2*, he commanded a bigger budget than Le Corbusier. There was no need to save money using thin concrete walls. The Steve Jobs Building, named after Jobs's death, is crafted of steel and glass, wood and brick, and Jobs obsessed over every detail. (It is easy to forget that the building also had an architect: Peter Bohlin, who designed the Apple stores.) Huge, beautiful steels were chosen after Jobs had pored over samples from across the country and selected a particular steel mill in Arkansas. He insisted that the girders were bolted rather than welded.[4]

And like all good designers, Steve Jobs cared about function as well as form.

"Steve had this firm belief that the right kind of building can do great things for a culture," says Ed Catmull, Pixar's president. "Steve wanted the building to support our work by enhancing our ability to collaborate."[5]

Jobs had become fascinated by the idea of serendipitous interactions. How to make sure that everyone mingled together? He hit upon a plan: Pixar's headquarters should have just a single pair of large restrooms off the main lobby. People would make new connections or revive old ones, because everybody would have to head to the lobby, brought together by a shared human need to urinate.[6]

Le Corbusier and Jobs were cultural giants, two of the most influential tastemakers of the last hundred years. But while they were unique, their love of tidy, minimalist spaces is common in the corporate world.

The "5S" system of management—Sort, Straighten, Shine, Standardize, and Sustain—has long stood for efficiency through tidiness and uniformity. The 5S system began in precision manufacturing spaces; clutter was discouraged because it might cause errors or delays, as were distracting personal effects. But 5S has somehow begun to bleed from car assembly lines and operating theaters and semiconductor manufacturing plants, where it might make sense, to the office cubicle, where it does not. Management gurus sing the praises of the "lean office."

As *The Wall Street Journal* explained back in 2008, adherents of 5S at organizations such as Kyocera "are patrolling to make sure that workers don't, for example, put knickknacks on file cabinets." When the *Journal* went to Kyocera's San Diego offices and followed the "5S inspector" around (he was a gently spoken middle manager by the name of Dan Brown), he was armed with a checklist and a digital camera as he cajoled his colleagues into removing illicit hooks from cubicle walls. He refused to be deflected by a clutterbug who had swept his junk into boxes and stored them in a closet. The closet was opened, the boxes inspected and photographed.[7]

This might seem intrusive, but as a management consultant breezily explained, "If managers clearly explain why they're doing something, I think most people will understand the rationale."

Perhaps. But then what *is* the rationale? The closest the *Journal* got to an explanation was that "to impress visitors, the company wants everything to be clean and neat." This is why "sweaters can't hang on the backs of chairs, personal items can't be stowed beneath desks and the only decorations allowed on cabinets are official company plaques or certificates."

Clear enough: things must look tidy to put on a good show for visitors. But will visitors really be won over by cabinets decorated with Kyocera's own self-congratulatory plaudits? And if the aim is to impress visitors, why was Dan Brown earnestly examining the inside of filing cabinets and closets?

Le Corbusier's vision was revolutionary; Steve Jobs's was exacting; Kyocera's was petty. But in all three cases one can see a very simple mistake being made. Each had failed to realize that what makes a space comfortable and pleasant—and, to turn to the concerns of modern business, inspiring and productive—is not a sleek shell or a tastefully designed interior. Indeed, it may have very little to do with how a building looks at all.

In 2010, two psychologists at the University of Exeter, Alex Haslam and Craig Knight, set up simple office spaces. Some were in a psychology lab, and some in a commercial office. Haslam and Knight recruited experimental subjects to spend an hour on administrative tasks such as checking documents. The idea was to see how the office environment affected how much people got done, and how they felt about it.

There were four different office layouts. The first was the *lean* office, a clean and spartan space with a bare desk, swivel chair, pencil, and paper. It reflected a Corbusian love of undecorated functionality, but the name "lean" was also inspired by the Japanese ideas of 5S that companies such as Kyocera had been pushing. It was Sorted, Straightened, Shined, and Standardized—although whether it could be Sustained was another question. It quickly became clear that the sheer tidiness of the space felt oppressive. "It just felt like a show space with nothing out of place," commented one participant, adding, "You couldn't relax in it." Perhaps that is what proponents of office neatness intend.[8]

The second office layout *enriched* the lean office with some decorative elements. Large prints showing close-up photographs of plants hung on the wall. (One of the experimenters, Craig Knight, told me they reminded him of Georgia O'Keeffe paintings.) There were several potted plants, too. It may surprise modernists and fans of the 5S system to hear that workers got more done in the enriched office, and more accurately, while feeling better about their experience. It will not surprise anyone else.

The final two office layouts used the same components as the enriched office. Visually, they seemed much the same. In fact there was no visible difference at all between the pleasing and productive enriched office, and a space that was despised by all those who had the bad luck to have to work there.

The distinction in both cases was not how the office looked, but who got to decide its appearance. The most successful office space was called the *empowered* office. Like the enriched office it offered the same tasteful prints and the same little shrubs, but participants were invited to spend some time arranging those decorations however they saw fit. They could even have asked for them to be removed entirely, perfectly mimicking the lean space, if they wanted. The empowered office could be lean, or enriched, or something else; the point was that the person working in the office had the choice.

To produce the hated environment, the experimenters followed the same procedure, inviting participants to take time to arrange the prints and the plants however they wished. Once that had been done, the experimenter returned and began rearranging everything until the office precisely matched the enriched setting. The scientists called this condition the *disempowered* office, though that may be too mild a term. "I wanted to hit you," one participant told the experimenter later, after the trial had been explained.

The empowered office was a great success—people got 30 percent more done there than in the lean office, and about 15 percent more than in the enriched office. These are large effects; three people in empowered offices achieved almost as much as four people in lean offices. The enriched office was a modest success, but the disempowered office, which offered exactly the same physical amenities, produced low productivity and low morale.

Haslam and Knight asked their participants a variety of questions about how much they rated the office they had been working in. They loved the empowered office and hated the lean and disempowered ones, complaining of being bored or even of physical discomfort such as feeling too hot. And their feelings of despair were all-embracing: if they disliked the office space, they also disliked the company that was hosting it, and disliked the task they were doing in it.

The physical environment certainly mattered, and—contrary to what Kyocera or Le Corbusier might believe—decorations such as pictures and plants tended to make workers happier and more productive. But there was much more to the environment than its design—equally important was who had designed it. The best option was to let workers design their own space. (At that point, it made no difference whether the space they created for themselves was sparse or enriched—presumably because each worker chose a space that worked for her.) The very worst was to give them the promise of autonomy, and then whisk it away.

But who would do such a thing? Let's see how things are going over at Kyocera:

> Mr. Scovie proudly showed Mr. Brown his tidy desk, which back in June could barely be seen for all the clutter, he admits. When asked for a peek inside his drawers, Mr. Scovie tried to steer the conversation to the placement of a desk blocking his access to some filing cabinets. Pressed, Mr. Scovie reluctantly agreed to open his drawers, one of which he warned was "really nasty."[9]

The humiliation is palpable. The description evokes a parent nagging a child to tidy her room, or airport security patting down a suspected hijacker. One perfectly competent employee is being harassed by another perfectly competent employee to satisfy the pointless demands of a company rule book.

Haslam and Knight carried out the most explicit test of the importance of giving workers freedom to control their workspace, but other researchers have also pointed in that direction. In one study, NASA sent marine biologists to work for weeks on end in a tiny undersea lab—a truly tough environment, but the biologists loved it. However, they preferred to cook their own basic food from tins rather than eat elaborate food that had been prepared for them in advance.[10] Robert Sommer, a psychologist at the University of California, Davis, spent years comparing "hard" and "soft" architectural spaces—those that people couldn't change, and those that they could. Examples of "hard spaces" include those where the windows don't open, the lights or air-conditioning cannot be changed, or the chairs are bolted to the ground. The quintessential hard space is a prison—but these prison-like features have spread to schools, public spaces, and the office. Sommer repeatedly found that apparently trivial freedoms, such as the right to paint your own wall, help people define personal space, and make people happier and more productive.[11]

Unfortunately, 5S enthusiasts at the Virginia Mason Medical Center in Seattle didn't get the memo. Doctors and nurses there were in the habit of hanging a stethoscope on a hook, but management came up with a tidier solution: a drawer marked "stethoscope." The medical staff kept on hanging the stethoscope on the hook. What to do? "Eventually," said a supervisor, "we had to remove the hook."[12]

The tidiness craze is global. At Her Majesty's Revenue & Customs, the UK's tax collection agency, staff were instructed in late 2006 to remove family photographs and souvenirs from their desks.[13] At BHP Billiton, a vast mining company based in Australia, staff were ordered to maintain a clear desk as defined in an eleven-page instruction manual:

"Clear desk means that at the end of each day the only items remaining will be monitor(s), keyboard, mouse, mouse pad, telephone handset and headset, one A5 photo frame and ergonomic equipment (ie footstool, gel wrist pad etc)."[14]

If you wish to display an award, that's okay—but only if you remove the A5 photograph. No plants allowed. And don't think about ignoring the rules: "Facilities Management will consult with team managers about lapses." All these anal-retentive rules are justified with much the same circularity as at Kyocera: clear desk policies are useful because they will keep things tidy, "to create and maintain a workplace that is clean, organised, and professional."

It is one thing to sharpen and straighten all the pencils on one's own desk, metaphorically or otherwise. To order someone else to sharpen and straighten the pencils on their own desk displays a curious value system in which superficial neatness is worth the price of deep resentment.

Use a spiral slide to get to the lobby! Have a team meeting in a pod shaped like a clown car! Enjoy risqué art installations! The business world is capable of embracing more than one fad for office design. While Kyocera, BHP Billiton, and the UK's Revenue & Customs agency apparently favor the lab-rat chic of minimalist desks and bare cubicle walls, trendier companies prefer crazy materials and bright colors. And no company is or ever will be as with-it as the advertising agency Chiat/Day, creators of "1984," the advertisement that launched the Apple Mac.

Amid gushing newspaper write-ups about the "workforce of the future," Jay Chiat announced a radical plan to sweep away cubicles and offices and even desks. Armed with the best mobile technology available—in 1993—Chiat/Day employees would roam free in open spaces, winning sales and creating great ads wherever they wished. What's more, those spaces would be playful, zany, and stylish. The agency's new Los Angeles offices, designed by Frank Gehry and Claes Oldenburg, boasted a four-story sculpture of a pair of binoculars, and curvaceous two-seater pods from fairground rides were installed with the hope that people would sit together in them and think creative thoughts. The New York office, designed by Gaetano Pesce, had a mural of a vast red pair of lips, and a luminous multicolored floor with hieroglyphs all over it. Pesce had a boyish sense of humor: the floor in front of the men's room had an illustration of a man urinating; his chairs had springs instead of feet, and would wobble and tip back so that when a woman sat on them, her colleagues could admire the view up her skirt; his conference tables were made of a silicone resin that would grab and hold important papers during meetings, with hilarious results. (It is not clear how many of these jokes were intentional.) The architect Frank Duffy, while admiring the daring of the project, comments, "Perhaps its gravest weakness is that it is a place where 'play' is enforced on everyone, all the time."[15]

Jay Chiat saw himself as a revolutionary figure, a man chosen by destiny to tear down the conventions of office life. And, in some ways, his plans did prove visionary. Hiring Gehry showed impeccable taste; this was several years before the Guggenheim Bilbao would make Gehry the most famous architect on the planet. The bright colors, different architectural zones, clusters of couches interspersed with large tables, and use of mobile technology to free workers have all been widely copied. Chiat's desire to make the office more like a university campus—"The idea is, you go to lectures, gather information, but you do your work wherever you like"—was also ahead of its time. Microsoft and Google each now refer to their corporate headquarters as a campus.

Overall, however, Chiat's farsighted experiment was not a success. The results—as described in a superb article by Warren Berger—were "petty turf wars, kindergarten-variety subterfuge, incessant griping, management bullying, employee insurrections, internal chaos, and plummeting productivity. Worst of all, there was no damn place to sit."[16]

Part of the problem was Chiat's familiarly Kyocera-esque impatience with personalized workspaces. Chiat's homes were decorated with modernist art rather than family photographs or souvenirs. He spent much of his time on airplanes, in any case. The idea that someone might want a desk cluttered with knickknacks was puzzling to him. Chiat dismissively commented that his staff could be given tiny lockers as a place to "put their dog pictures, or whatever."

Chiat's tidy-minded sensibilities went further than dog pictures: he tried to insist on an entirely digital, paperless office. If he saw storyboards taped on walls, or proofs of advertising posters, he'd demand that they be removed. What part of "paperless" didn't people understand? Unfortunately, back in 1993, cell phones were temperamental and laptops were clunky, and both were expensive. Rather than own these essential tools, staff would sign them out each morning and return them to a concierge when they went home at night. The agency hadn't bought enough for everybody, and this proved to be a false economy. Ill-tempered queues formed like breadlines each morning at the concierge desk. Staff who lived near the office would show up at six a.m., sign out a precious computer and phone, hide them somewhere, and then go back to bed for a couple of hours. Senior staff would order their assistants to rise early and secure their kit. Civil war broke out as each department claimed its work had priority over the others. Who would rely on digital documents if they couldn't count on access to a computer?

With no personal workspace to call their own—Chiat would

personally prowl the open-plan space, remembering where people had sat the day before and haranguing them not to "nest" in the same spot—Chiat's employees had to improvise ways to keep hold of the paper copies of their contracts and storyboards and concept art. The personal lockers, intended for their dog pictures, were no good—they were too small to fit a standard binder. Some staff stashed binders in heaps in the corner. Others used their cars as storage, heading to the parking lot to file and retrieve important documents. One employee journeyed across the open prairie of the office with a little red wagon piled with her binders and papers. Not long after this story was reported, the *Dilbert* cartoon featured Wally pushing his work around in a shopping cart, tagging the office with graffiti and pondering joining a gang to give him a sense of identity.[17]

Playful offices such as Chiat/Day are often presented as radically different from traditional offices or cubicles. It is true that they reflect a different aesthetic, but Craig Knight—one of the scientists behind the research on workplace "enrichment" and "disempowerment"—points out that if the playfulness is inescapable, the philosophy ends up being much the same: management is the business of managers, design is the business of designers, and office serfs should simply accept what has been assigned to them. The tales of Chiat devoting some of his own scarce time to enforcing the rules is reminiscent of the researcher in Knight's "disempowerment" setup driving an experimental subject to such rage that she wanted to hit him.

Chiat's gaudy, postmodern tastes in architecture may be a world away from Le Corbusier's simple modernist sensibilities, yet one similarity with Le Corbusier is striking: both men were unafraid to dream big dreams on behalf of other people. As the boss, Chiat insisted that his was the only vision that mattered. As one of Chiat's top lieutenants, Bob Kuperman, summarized the matter: "Jay didn't listen to anybody, he just did it."

The story of Chiat/Day has a happy ending, after a fashion. Though the office makeover was dysfunctional, it looked fabulous in photo spreads, and design magazines went wild for it. Chiat/Day even started hosting paid tours of their office space. Having wrenched the spotlight onto his agency, Jay Chiat cashed in by selling his stake in the firm to Omnicom. Before long, the individual workspaces, paperwork, and dog pictures were back.

While Chiat/Day's Gehry-designed headquarters were built to symbolize creativity, truly creative spaces often look very different. If you ask the veterans of MIT what a creative space looks like, one building comes to symbolize all that's best at the university. This building, which was demolished a few years ago, didn't even have a proper name—it was known only as Building 20—and it could hardly have been more different from the kind of structure that star architects put together.[18]

Building 20 was, quite literally, designed in an afternoon. In the spring of 1943, Don Whiston, a young architect and former MIT student, received a call from the university asking for preliminary plans and building specs for a 200,000-square-foot building by the end of the day. Whiston delivered. So did the builders who erected this squat, ugly, sprawling structure in plywood, cinder block, and asbestos with remarkable speed.

"I watched them put up Building 20," one MIT professor recalled over half a century later.[19] "You know those time-lapse photographs they make of construction of skyscrapers? Well, Building 20 went up like that—almost like that—in real time."

There was a war on, after all. Building 20 was thrown together to house the Radiation Laboratory, or Rad Lab, a secret project that turned the primitive radars of the day into essential weapons of war. It was a vast research effort, and arguably more significant than the more celebrated Manhattan Project.

Unsurprisingly, given the hasty design and construction, Building 20 was a spartan, uncomfortable place to work. It was too hot in summer and too cold in winter. It was filthy with the dust of the just-finished building work. From the outside, it was a long, crude, three-story building, a cross between an army barracks and a garden shed. From the inside, it was a confusing, badly signposted labyrinth. And it was a firetrap: permission to build it was granted only on condition that it was pulled down within six months of the end of the war.

For two short years, Building 20 housed an astonishing cluster of researchers: one-fifth of the physicists in the United States passed through Rad Lab, which absorbed $2 billion of military funding—only $848,513 of which was spent on Building 20 itself. Nine Nobel Prize winners emerged from the Radiation Laboratory, and the technology they and their colleagues developed was an unqualified success: radars to allow planes to find U-boats; radars to provide early warning of V-1 attacks on London; radars to allow planes to land blind; radars to guide bombing raids; and more. The radar systems developed in Building 20 made previous technologies obsolete. The saying went that the atomic bomb may have ended the war, but it was radar that won it.

Given the temporary nature both of the Rad Lab wartime push and the building that housed it, you might imagine that Building 20's triumphs were fleeting—a glorious moment in the history of applied science. And you might also assume that those triumphs took place despite the crude design and hasty construction of Building 20, not because of it. The authorities at MIT would have agreed with you. As promised, preparations were made to pull down the ugly, dysfunctional, and unsafe structure. The radio towers on the roof were removed; Rad Lab's offices were dismantled. Building 20 would be replaced, in due course, with something more carefully designed and, well, a bit tidier.

Then came a stay of execution. The GI Bill of 1944 subsidized veterans to go to college. MIT was suddenly swamped by new students and desperately short of space. Building 20 was spacious and ready to be pressed into use. And so a temporary structure designed in an afternoon began a final act that was to last for decades.

It was quite a swan song. While we might assume that Rad Lab, the fruit of an extraordinary war effort, would have succeeded anywhere, the flow of ideas from Building 20 simply didn't stop. It was the birthplace of the world's first commercial atomic clock. One of the earliest particle accelerators was also constructed there. The iconic stop-motion photographs of a bullet passing through an apple were taken in Building 20 by Harold Edgerton. It was home to MIT's Tech Model Railroad Club, a wellspring of hacker culture—hacks being skillful, innovative, and, yes, messy improvisations in pursuit of no goal other than the sheer joy of it. (In the 1950s, the hackers ran the model railway using components from the telephone exchange system.) From Building 20 emerged Spacewar, the first arcade-style video game. Meanwhile, from his office in Building 20, Jerry Lettvin was working on one of the most influential papers in cognitive science, "What the Frog's Eye Tells the Frog's Brain." Noam Chomsky and Morris Halle revolutionized linguistics in Building 20.

It was in Building 20 that Leo Beranek built one of the first anechoic chambers, a room that swallows sound waves. The composer John Cage visited Beranek's chamber and realized that, even there, he could hear his own blood being pumped around his body. This realization that there would always be ambient noise prompted him to compose *4′33″*, his infamous four and a half minutes of silence.* Meanwhile, Beranek founded the company Bolt, Beranek and Newman,

---

*Sources differ as to whether Cage visited the anechoic chamber in Building 20, or another one across town at Harvard University. Building 20 can claim so many other milestones that perhaps this one can be generously ceded to Harvard.

which moved from developing acoustic-processing computers to building some of the first Internet networks and inventing e-mail as we know it today. Leo Beranek wasn't the only acoustic pioneer at Building 20: a young electrical engineer named Amar Bose, dissatisfied with a piece of hi-fi equipment he'd purchased, wandered down the corridor to the acoustics labs to see whether anything better could be created. There, he revolutionized the speaker, and established the Bose Corporation. DEC, the Digital Equipment Corporation, a major force in the pre-PC era of computing, was another significant technology company incubated in Building 20.

All this took place in an atmosphere of chaos and neglect—to the extent that a storeroom in Building 20 was taken over by a homeless botanist who haunted the corridors in the 1960s and 1970s. MIT tried to evict him, and lost the case. Surely a myth? And yet both Jerry Lettvin and Morris Halle testified to his existence. "He turned down a job at the Field Museum in Chicago in order to remain a phantom in Building 20," Lettvin told *The Boston Globe*.

Building 20 was ugly and uncomfortable but its occupants loved it. MIT's president during the 1970s, Jerome Wiesner, described it as "the best building in the place," while Jerry Lettvin said it was "a building with a special spirit, a spirit that inspires creativity and the development of new ideas," adding that it was the "womb of the Institute. It is kind of messy, but by God it is procreative!"

The question is, why?

When people praise Building 20, they often point to something that Steve Jobs himself would have admired: the building's propensity to throw people together at random. This was as much by accident as anything; for instance, Building 20 had a baffling system of office numbering. If you wanted to find the Office of Naval

Research—a descendant of Rad Lab—it was in Room 20E-226. But where exactly was that? The 20 of 20E-226 was clear enough: it referred to Building 20. The "E" referred to E wing, which was parallel to and sandwiched between A wing on one side and D wing on the other. C wing was farther along. B wing was the spine that linked all the other wings together. (In a more logical world, B should have been A, A should have been B, E should have been C, and C should have been E.) The 226 meant room 26 not on the second story but on the third, Building 20 being one of the few buildings in America to have unilaterally adopted the British system for labeling floors.

This absurdly inefficient way of organizing a building meant that people were constantly getting lost and wandering into places they didn't intend to go. Better still, because Building 20 was low-rise and sprawling, when chance meetings occurred, they didn't happen in elevators, the eternal home of the glib, tidy monologue we call the "elevator pitch." They began in long corridors, where a genuine conversation could develop.

More important, the combination of people who could have those conversations was strange and wonderful. In the early 1950s, Building 20 contained departments that were wartime holdovers—nuclear science, flight control, the "Guided Missiles Program Office"—but also plastics research, the adhesives lab, the acoustics lab, the electronics lab, and even an outpost of the architecture department: a lighting design shop. Over the next ten years, MIT's data processing group was added, along with the ice research lab, MIT Press, and the student hackers at the Model Railroad Club. Into the mix were stirred machine shops for the nuclear scientists and for the electronics research lab, the photography labs, a materials lab for the anthropologists, and solar car researchers who would use the building's corridors as driveways and parking lots. The building even hosted a piano repair shop (a "computer free" zone, warned a sign on its wall) and the Reserve

Officers' Training Corps (ROTC) offices, right next to the office of the anti-establishment linguist Noam Chomsky.*

This unlikely mess made possible chance interactions among innovative researchers that paid such spectacular dividends. Who would have guessed that throwing the electrical engineers in with the Model Railway Club would result in hacking and video games? Or that the electronics specialists, the music department, and the acoustics lab would end up spawning technology pioneers such as the Bose Corporation and Bolt, Beranek and Newman?

Nobody would have guessed, and nobody tried to guess, either. The hodgepodge of Building 20 was the result of simple expedience and neglect. Where did MIT put disciplines that didn't fit, researchers who had no clout, projects that made no money, student hobbyists, and anything and anyone else that just didn't seem to matter? In the cheapest, nastiest space they could find. If Building 20 hadn't been a mess, these strange collaborations might never have happened.

Another key element of Building 20's success was that the space was easy to reconfigure. Its services—water, phones, electricity—were exposed, running along the corridor ceilings, supported by brackets. This was ugly but convenient. Researchers thought nothing of tapping into them directly for whatever experimental needs they had. Paul Penfield, a longtime occupant of Building 20, recalled: "You know that if you want to run a wire from one room to another, you don't call Physical Plant, you don't plunk down a thousand dollars to call an electrician and a carpenter, instead you get out a power drill or a screwdriver, and you jam it through the wall, and you string the wire, and you take care of things right away, and you do it in one afternoon, rather than waiting six months for a purchase order to come through."

*During protests against the Vietnam War, a notice was circulated pointing out how close the ROTC was to the linguistics department, and slyly advising antiwar campaigners, "Please trash selectively."

Can you imagine what the clean-desk brigade at Kyocera would have made of that?

In some ways, a modern office designer would approve of Building 20: contemporary office buildings today are routinely designed so that partition walls can be added or removed to make whatever space is necessary. But few modern offices boast the extreme reconfigurability of Building 20: when the atomic clock was being developed by a team led by Jerrold Zacharias, the group simply removed a couple of *floors* from their laboratory to accommodate it.

And Building 20's true advantage wasn't so much that it was reconfigurable by design, but that the building's inhabitants felt confident that they had the authority (if only by default) to make changes, even messy changes. It was that it was so cheap and ugly that in the words of Stewart Brand, author of *How Buildings Learn*, "Nobody cares what you do in there."

Unlike at Kyocera or Chiat/Day, Building 20's inhabitants were in control. Heather Lechtman, professor of material science and archaeology, told Brand: "We feel our space is really ours. We designed it, we run it." After Jerome Wiesner became president of MIT in 1971, he kept a secret office tucked away in Building 20. Why? Because "nobody complained when you nailed something to a door."

A university or corporate research center can and should create interdisciplinary spaces in which well-established teams seek common problems to work on. But the anarchy of Building 20 went way beyond what any official effort at cross-cultural collaboration is ever likely to tolerate. It would be a brave CEO who'd play host to model railway enthusiasts and homeless botanists.

When Building 20 was at last demolished in 1998, MIT held what could only be described as a wake. Engineering professor Paul Penfield organized the commemoration "to help each other through the grieving process."

Building 20 was replaced by the ultimate architectural status symbol—a building designed, like the Chiat/Day headquarters, by Frank Gehry. Gehry's Stata Center, which opened in 2004, is designed as a symbol of creativity. Imagine one of Dr. Seuss's architectural fantasies bursting fully formed onto the campus of the Massachusetts Institute of Technology, and you begin to get the picture. The architecture critics loved the center's messy appearance. In *The Boston Globe*, Robert Campbell gushed, "The Stata's appearance is a metaphor for the freedom, daring, and creativity of the research that's supposed to occur inside it."[20]

But being a metaphor for freedom, daring, and creativity is not the same as actually being conducive to it. The cheap and cheerful Building 20 was a proper mess. But its computer-modeled replacement, painstakingly constructed at the cost of $300 million, was more of a tidy-minded person's idea of what a mess looks like. The Stata Center soon developed problems, including a tendency for snow to build up on the building's wacky windows and then cause damage by sliding off. MIT administrators were sufficiently irked to take Gehry, and the building contractors, to court.[21]

But the real problem with the structure wasn't a buildup of snow. Shortly before the Stata Center was due to be occupied, *Wired* magazine caught up with one of the MIT greats, the computer guru Gerald Sussman, and asked him what he thought of the new building.

With a thin smile of contempt, he said all that needed to be said: "I didn't ask for it."[22]

It is still fashionable, especially in creative industries, to follow the Chiat/Day example and install playground equipment and quirky decorations in the office. For the past decade, the most-written-about corporate headquarters has been Google's "Googleplex" in Mountain

View, California, with its Ping-Pong tables and slides. The media remain as giddy as ever about unusual corporate environments.

But it is easy to fall victim to a logical error here. Google wasn't successful because it built the toy-filled Googleplex. It built the toy-filled Googleplex after it had already become successful, just as Chiat/Day commissioned Frank Gehry after being the most admired advertising agency of the 1980s.

A closer look at the history of Google's headquarters suggests a closer resemblance to MIT's Building 20 than to Chiat/Day's hot-lipped theme park. For the first two years of Google's gestation, while Sergey Brin and Larry Page were making some of the foundational breakthroughs, there were no headquarters at all: Brin and Page were studying at Stanford University.[23]

In September 1998, Google moved to the clichéd start-up location: a garage. They rented some rooms, too, in a house on Santa Margarita Street in Menlo Park. One room contained Sergey, Larry, and two other engineers. The garage itself was packed with servers. Desks were the simplest possible design: a door placed horizontally across a pair of sawhorses. Nothing could be cruder or easier to put together and take apart, or easier to hack about. One day the house's owner, Susan Wojcicki, was expecting delivery of a refrigerator. She returned home to find that the Googlers had commandeered it, moved it to their part of the house, and filled it with drinks and snacks. This was the typical "anything goes" scavenger mentality of early Google. Wojcicki didn't seem to mind—she later joined the company and ended up running YouTube.[24]

In any case, by the spring of 1999, Google had moved again, to an office over a bicycle shop. The desks, again, were doors on sawhorses, and the engineers had decided to bring up a Ping-Pong table. Larry and Sergey left red and blue inflatable gym balls around, less as an aesthetic statement and more because they liked to work out with them.[25] Google soon moved again, to an office-park facility in Mountain View. This office space later became known as the NullPlex, the space before the Googleplex itself. But again, the space was crude—a "mishmash," said the facilities manager, George Salah. A "mongrel style," said Steven Levy, journalist and unofficial historian of Google. One of the first high-priority projects to be tackled in the new space was the problem of how to make searches more responsive to the latest news. Google set up a war room, and again, it was a straightforward, unassuming space. Half a dozen engineers grabbed a conference room, set up their computers the way they wanted, and got to work.

Then there was the time that one Google engineer decided he didn't like the wall of his office. When Google's facilities manager came in the next morning, he was surprised to discover that the engineer and his colleagues had knocked it down. But he didn't complain. Neither did he complain when the engineer later changed his mind and decided he'd like to put the wall back again; instead, he mused that the process had "made it a more Googley environment."

Any veteran of MIT's Building 20 would recognize the thought process. And when the suit-and-tie executive Eric Schmidt joined Google as the new boss in 2001, he reassured Salah, "Don't change a thing. Make sure it looks like a dorm room."[26]

"No matter what happened," writes Steven Levy, "engineers would have the run of the place."[27]

The offices at Chiat/Day may have looked superficially different from the offices at Kyocera, but they were managed with fundamentally the same tidy-minded aesthetic: *This place should look the way the boss wants it to look.* Google's offices, like Building 20 at MIT, have been managed very differently: *It doesn't matter how this place looks.* The denizens of Building 20 had tremendous power over their environment, even by the standards of tenured academics. This wasn't because of their high status. If anything the opposite was true: the higher-status academics were placed in high-status spaces that were too beautiful, expensive, and historically significant to tinker with. (No wonder Jerome Wiesner, MIT's president, felt trapped by the magisterial perfection of his office, and kept a messy bolt-hole in Building 20.) The lower-status academics were placed in low-status spaces, and that meant they could do whatever they wished. Nobody cared.

People flourish when they control their own space. But if it causes so much damage to impose a rigid aesthetic on workers, why are bosses so keen to keep everything shipshape? It seems as though actively encouraging staff to take control is far scarcer than the benign neglect of Building 20. Why is creativity something that happens only when the boss isn't looking?

Some clues come from the remarkable career of Robert Propst. Propst was a sculptor, painter, art teacher, and inventor of devices as varied as a vertical timber harvester and a machine-readable livestock tag. A trained chemical engineer, he'd spent the Second World War managing beachhead logistics in the South Pacific. In 1958, he was hired by the Herman Miller company, a manufacturer of office furniture. Herman Miller's managers thought Propst was a genius.[28]

He was certainly an independent spirit: he stayed in Ann Arbor, Michigan, 150 miles away from Herman Miller's headquarters in Zeeland, later persuading the company to set up a research division there to accommodate him. Propst continued his inventions, and in office furniture circles he is famous for creating the "Action Office II." Launched in 1968, this modular system of parts could be clipped together at funky angles, allowing office workers to craft an environment suited to their own needs, like children tinkering with Legos. Propst imagined a free-flowing office environment with an egalitarian ideal. Good-bye to a boss's desk that looked like a mahogany altar, and to the interchangeable serfs of the typing pool; hello to autonomy, to workers who could "behave like a manager at every level."

But then America's office managers made a few modifications. Propst's original dividers clipped together at an angle of no less than 120 degrees, providing a fanned-out space on which to pin working documents. Managers demanded dividers with 90-degree angles, allowing micro-office after micro-office to snap together in regimented lines. They loved the fact that Action Office II's partitions didn't count as walls, but as furniture, which earned a more generous tax treatment. And so the office cubicle was born.

Robert Propst had been committed to the idea of the empowered worker. He knew that good design meant giving workers control over their own environment. But he was helpless in the face of corporate bosses more interested in saving money than in his progressive design ideals. Propst was left to condemn the perversion of his ideas as "monolithic insanity," "hellholes," "egg-carton geometry," and "barren, rat-hole places."

When the father of the cube farm died in 2000, workplace cubicles had never been more ubiquitous. Empowerment is all very well, but never underestimate what managers will inflict on workers in an effort to avoid tax and minimize rents.

If cubicles are attractive because they are cheap, Propst understood that other forces are also at play. Managers could be tidy-minded simply because tidiness seems like the right and proper way to be. "We all have this desire for formal order," Propst had written in 1968. "The only problem is that it conflicts severely with the more organic kind of spatial order human interchange uses best."[29]

So far, the desire for formal order is winning. We like tidiness to the point of fetishizing it; we find clutter and irregularity disturbing and don't notice when it is doing us good.

T George Harris, a veteran journalist and editor of *Psychology Today*, put his finger on the problem back in 1977:

> The office is a highly personal tool shop, often the home of the soul . . . this fact may sound simple, but it eludes most architects, office designers, and thousands of regulations writers in hundreds of giant corporations. They have a mania for uniformity, in space as in furniture, and a horror over how the messy side of human nature clutters up an office landscape that would otherwise be as tidy as a national cemetery.[30]

Harris details some of the fussier corporate policies of the day—at CBS, where "a producer could not look at film slides in his office without first nursing two interoffice memos up through the facilities hierarchy—one memo to dim overhead lights, the other to move a chair." Harris sounds like he's joking, but he isn't. Another supposedly creative business, the publisher McGraw-Hill, "set up a Deviation Committee to rule on any request to make any change in the physical setup specified in a positive blizzard of advance memos."

Consider the following piece of well-worn advice from fifty years ago, in *The Business Etiquette Handbook*:

> *Avoid over-decorating your desk or area.* When your desk, shelves, and wall space are covered with mementoes, photographs, trophies, humorous mottoes, and other decorative effects, you are probably not beautifying the office; rather you may be giving it a jumbled, untidy look . . . The proper atmosphere for a business office is one of neatness and efficiency, not hominess.[31]

The unexamined assumption is that this jumbled untidiness is bad, and that if the office looks streamlined then it will also be more productive. But the evidence suggests the opposite. Yet fifty years later, bureaucrats at Kyocera and BHP Billiton are continuing with these tidy traditions.

Is there any evidence that neat environments really help? The longer T George Harris chased credible research into the impact of "good design" on employee productivity, the more elusive that research seemed. "People suddenly put into 'good design' did *not* seem to wake up and love it," he wrote. What they loved instead was control over the space in which they had to live or work.

And that control typically leads to mess. The psychologist Craig Knight admits that a space that workers design for themselves will almost always look rather ugly. "It doesn't look as good as something a designer would have chosen, and it never will."[32]

The management theorist A. K. Korman vividly recalls visiting one factory where the mess had been embraced:

> I was assaulted with a kaleidoscope of orange, blue, pink, yellow, red and multi-colored machines. My host laughed at the expression on my face and then went on to tell me that the management of the company had told the workers they could paint the machines any color they wanted and the company would furnish the paint if they furnished the manpower. The result was a very unusual looking factory to me, although it was a pleasing work environment to those who worked there every day.[33]

From the vantage point of a nice corner office, someone else's messy desk is an eyesore. The clutter is visible, but the resulting sense of empowerment is not. For the senior manager, the lesson is simple: Resist the urge to tidy up. Leave the mess—and your workers—alone.

• • •

When Steve Jobs got an important idea in his head, it wasn't easy to dissuade him. His plan to impose a single pair of serendipity-inducing über-bathrooms on Pixar seemed to be a very important idea indeed. Random connections mattered, thought Jobs, and he was right. And what better way to promote random connections than by forcing people to go through the lobby several times a day, at intervals governed by the call of nature?

"He felt that very, very strongly," says Pam Kerwin, Pixar's general manager.

So Jobs explained his idea to Pixar's staff at an off-site meeting to discuss the plans, and the staff didn't like it at all. As Kerwin recalls, "One pregnant woman said she shouldn't be forced to walk for ten minutes just to go to the bathroom, and that led to a big fight."

John Lasseter, Pixar's creative director, stood up for the pregnant woman. Jobs was frustrated. People just didn't understand the vision. They didn't get it.

But then Jobs did something extraordinary and out of character. He backed down. The Steve Jobs Building contains not one, but four pairs of bathrooms.[34]

There is still plenty of opportunity for serendipity, thanks to an atrium that focuses activity, with the main doors of the building, a café, a game area, the mailboxes, three theaters, conference rooms, and screening rooms all spilling into it. John Lasseter says that Jobs's basic instincts had been correct: "I kept running into people I hadn't seen for months. I've never seen a building that promoted collaboration and creativity as well as this one."

Pixar's boss Ed Catmull agreed. "People encountered each other all day long, inadvertently, which meant a better flow of communication and increased the possibility of chance encounters. You felt the energy in the building."[35]

No doubt that is true. But something else matters just as much as serendipity: autonomy. Junior staff were able to stand up to Steve Jobs, the owner, the legend, the control freak's control freak—and to get their own way about something that mattered to them. That was more important than all the riveted steel and elegant brickwork Pixar's success could buy.

One day, Catmull found himself reflecting on a gorgeous table in Pixar's main conference room. It was long and elegant, chosen by one of Jobs's favorite designers. It reminded Catmull of a comedy sketch in which a wealthy couple sat down for a dysfunctional dinner, the man at one end, the woman at the other, a vast candelabra in the center, and no possibility of having a conversation. Catmull realized that although the table was beautiful, its long, thin design was dysfunctional when it came to the open, egalitarian discussions Pixar claimed to value.[36]

At meetings, thirty people faced off against each other in two lines, and if they were to hear everyone, the high-status people had to cluster around the middle. That would be Catmull, Lasseter, and the director and producer of the film in question. There was an informal but perfectly real hierarchy, as lesser people had to sit farther and farther away from the conversation and found it hard to get a word in. The hierarchy was gradually formalized with the introduction of place cards.

Catmull admits he didn't notice for over a decade—after all, the conversation seemed fine to *him*. Eventually he realized the problem after having a much better discussion sitting around a less elegant table in a different room. In a couple of days, the beautiful table in the main conference room was gone. There is more to creativity than elegance.*

---

*At the next creative meeting, senior director Andrew Stanton made a big play of picking up the place cards, shuffling them—echoes of the Oblique Strategies—and dealing them in random order. It's often tempting to stack the deck in a convenient order, but sometimes we need to shuffle it.

Staff autonomy continues to flourish at Pixar. The most famous example is a concealed room that can be reached only through a crawlway and which was originally designed merely to provide access to the air-conditioning valves. Once a Pixar animator discovered the secret panel into the space, he installed Christmas lights, lava lamps, animal print furnishings, a cocktail table, a bar, and napkins printed up with the logo "The Love Lounge." When Steve Jobs found out about the Love Lounge, he loved it.

"The animators who work here are free to—no, encouraged to—decorate their work spaces in whatever style they wish," explains Catmull. "They spend their days inside pink dollhouses whose ceilings are hung with miniature chandeliers, tiki huts made of real bamboo, and castles whose meticulously painted, fifteen-foot-high Styrofoam turrets appear to be carved from stone."[37]

It sounds like a mess.

4

Improvisation

"You ain't got much time to think, 'cause you in the chair from now on."

Martin Luther King, the Help Desk, and the Unexpected Benefits of Letting Go of the Script

In 1963, defying the wet-velvet heat of a Washington, D.C., summer, thousands upon thousands of people gathered to march in America's capital. They were there for "jobs and freedom," to show the Kennedy administration that civil rights legislation must be pushed through Congress—and to hear Martin Luther King, Jr., speak.

The official program had been long, packed with speech after speech. The damp heat was oppressive. A few people began to drift away in search of shade. But a quarter of a million remained. They stretched back from the Lincoln Memorial, packing the sides of the famous reflecting pool, swirling around the base of the Washington Monument and extending toward the intransigent Capitol itself. The Mall usually dwarfs anything on a human scale; not that afternoon.

The gospel singer Mahalia Jackson sang "I've Been 'Buked and I've Been Scorned." Anticipation built in the crowd. All three television networks switched to live coverage of the event. Dr. King stepped forward to speak, to address not only the sweltering crowd but also a national audience he had never had before and might never have again. It was his moment, and he knew it had to be perfect.

Dr. King had spent the night laboring on his speech with a few trusted aides, weighing every word of what he would say. He knew that he would be speaking with the monumental statue of Abraham Lincoln behind him, and a hundred years after Lincoln's Emancipation Proclamation had declared that the slaves of the U.S. South were free. So King decided to open with an artful echo of Lincoln's great Gettysburg Address. King's text began, "Five score years ago, a great American, in whose symbolic shadow we stand, signed the Emancipation Proclamation. This momentous decree came as a great beacon light of hope to millions of Negro slaves who had been seared in the flames of withering injustice."

Martin Luther King could draw on long experience of carefully crafting his speeches. His memory had always been prodigious; at the age of five he was learning Bible passages by heart. He told his parents that when he grew up, he was going to get some "big words."[1]

So he did. Martin's father was a preacher and the boy took to the craft of speechmaking early. At the age of fourteen, Martin traveled across Georgia on a bus to compete in a public-speaking contest. On the way home to Atlanta, the white driver ordered Martin, a "black son-of-a-bitch," and his teacher Sarah Bradley to give up their seats when whites got on the bus. Bradley eventually persuaded Martin to comply. The night stayed with King, who later recalled that he had never in his life been more angry.[2]

But while the journey home was an unforgettable insult, the day had been a triumph. King had won a prize at the contest, delivering his speech, "The Negro and the Constitution," entirely from memory. That was the teenage King's approach: rigorous research, careful drafting and redrafting, memorizing the beautiful script, and then delivering it with passion.

King used the same principles three years later, preaching for the first time in a small meeting room at his father's church. He was spectacular. "The crowds kept coming," his father recalled. "We had to move to the larger auditorium."[3] He won an oratory prize in college, where with thoughts of becoming a lawyer he practiced court testimony in front of a mirror. And when King applied for his first job as a minister, at a Baptist church in Montgomery, Alabama, he used a sermon he'd preached several times before.[4] Once he secured that job, he lavished enormous effort on his sermons, despite weighty obligations elsewhere. King was still finishing his doctorate in theology, rising at half past five each morning, making coffee, shaving his stubborn bristles into a neat mustache, and then working for three hours before his pregnant wife, Coretta, woke to join him for breakfast.[5]

His Sunday sermons mattered enormously to King. He began drafting on Tuesday, and continued to research and draft throughout the week, drawing ideas from Plato, Aquinas, Freud, Gandhi. As Sunday approached, he would write it all out on yellow lined paper and commit it to memory. He would bring the script to church with him, but as he ascended to the pulpit he would leave it in his chair and speak without notes for half an hour or more. The congregation adored him, and the way he spoke stylishly about matters of substance. "He was fantastic," recalled one of his staff. And to achieve this mastery, the young Reverend King spent fifteen hours crafting each sermon.[6]

Martin Luther King, Jr., was one of the greatest speechmakers to grace the English language, and at first it might seem obvious why. As well as being educated and prodigiously talented, the young reverend left nothing to chance. Every syllable of his oratory was meticulously prepared.

By contrast, consider the fate of those who do not seem to have prepared. Rick Perry, then the governor of Texas, was once the favorite to be the Republican presidential nominee for the 2012 election. His chances ebbed because his performance in debates was excruciating. During one debate, a journalist tweeted, "I think Rick Perry just had a stroke."[7] In another, Perry confidently began to list the three government departments he'd abolish if he were president—but couldn't remember the third item on the list. The moment fifteen minutes later when he piped up to add that he'd remembered the third one is so embarrassing it makes you want to disappear.[8]

In 2014, Ed Miliband, leader of the UK's Labour Party, gave a speech to make the case that he should be the next prime minister. Not for Mr. Miliband the countless hours committing the speech to memory, nor the more obvious routes of the teleprompter or script.

"What I try and do is I try and write a speech and then I use it as the basis for what I want to say to the country," he explained in a TV interview the morning after. "I like it as a way of engaging with people. And, of course, it's one of the perils of it that there are bits that get left out, bits that get added in. It sort of comes with the territory."[9]

It sort of does. Mr. Miliband duly forgot to deliver the section of his speech that discussed a key electoral battleground, the budget deficit. Mr. Miliband's opponents had been trying to focus on the deficit and to paint him as someone who simply didn't take it seriously. His carelessness seemed to confirm that the critics were right. After a bruising election defeat a few months later, Ed Miliband's career as Labour leader was over.

Entrepreneur Gerald Ratner managed to self-destruct more quickly. Ratner had spent the 1980s building the largest jewelry chain on the planet. He destroyed it with a couple of jokes.[10] Speaking to a prestigious audience of business leaders in 1991, Ratner joked that one of his products—a crystal decanter—was "total crap," and that a set of earrings he sold were cheaper than a shrimp sandwich, "but probably wouldn't last as long." The comments hit the front pages of the newspapers and sales at Ratners collapsed. Ratner was defenestrated; the company even jettisoned his now toxic name. The cost of his slip was estimated at half a billion pounds—three-quarters of a billion dollars. Gerald Ratner himself lost everything.

Who would want to risk the fate of a Gerald Ratner when they could follow the meticulous example of the young Martin Luther King? It seems obvious that when speaking in public we should prepare as diligently as Martin Luther King did when he drafted and memorized his sermons.

But what if that's wrong? What if we should improvise more, taking risks and saying what comes to us on the spur of the moment? Because while the stories of Dr. King, of Ratner and Miliband and Perry, appear to suggest that careful preparation is essential, there are also times when it makes sense to embrace the messy process of improvisation. And there's an obvious place to start.

On March 2, 1959, a group of jazz musicians assembled at East Thirtieth Street in Manhattan, in a church that had been converted into a recording studio.* [11] Miles Davis, the group's leader, had brought with him the vaguest sketches of melody lines. And the session started awkwardly, since Davis had drafted in a new pianist, Bill Evans, without troubling himself to warn the incumbent, Wynton Kelly.

Although jazz is famous for its spirit of improvisation, usual

*The word "converted" may suggest more effort and expense than had actually been involved. Studio engineer Fred Laico recalls that the record company "was not going to go in there and clean it up and make it look pretty. We didn't change a thing: for years we had drapes from the old church hanging askew and dust all over." It was a truly magnificent recording space, but it was something of a mess.

practice was to record each song several times, and it was common to splice together tape from the different takes. But as Bill Evans explained to the jazz writer Ashley Kahn, Miles had a different approach: "The first complete performance of each thing is what you're hearing . . . I think that is what accounts for some of the real freshness. First-take feelings, if they're anywhere near right, they're generally the best. If you don't take that one, generally, you take a dip emotionally."[12]

One of the pieces was "So What." The recording began with a few takes aborted almost immediately: there was paper rustling in the studio in a couple of them. But when the producer worried that the microphones were picking up Jimmy Cobb's snare drum vibrating in sympathy with the bass and piano, that didn't worry Miles: "All that goes with it," he said. It was part of the music.

Then a new attempt on the piece begins with a soft, suspenseful duet between Bill Evans on piano and Paul Chambers on bass. It's *rubato*, played in a loose, flexible tempo different from the rest of the piece, and with the bass carrying the tune, it sounds like very little that has ever been done before. Davis, John Coltrane, and Cannonball Adderley join in on brass with a more traditional call-and-response and the take builds toward the solos.

After ninety seconds comes a critical moment. Jimmy Cobb, hastily switching his brushes for sticks, gives his cymbal a whack that's just a little too hard. Cobb expects Miles Davis to call a halt—but instead the trumpeter launches into what is to become one of the most famous solos in jazz, with Cobb's cymbal resounding and fading in the background. It's an electrifying combination; but at the instant the cymbal splash happened it must have seemed like a mistake.

After two recording sessions, Miles Davis had a record that would change the course of twentieth-century music—*Kind of Blue*.[13] Quincy Jones, the revered producer of Frank Sinatra and Michael Jackson, said, "I play *Kind of Blue* every day—it's my orange juice. It still sounds like it was made yesterday." Another legend, jazz fusion pioneer Chick Corea, said that while it's one thing to play a new tune, "it's another thing to practically create a new language of music, which is what *Kind of Blue* did."[14]

And yet Miles Davis and his band improvised this musical revolution from moment to moment.* That seems little short of a miracle.[15]

And the most striking fact about *Kind of Blue* is this: It wasn't the record that Miles had been hoping to produce.

"When I tell people that I missed what I was trying to do on *Kind of Blue*, that I missed getting the exact sound of the African finger piano up in that sound, they just look at me like I'm crazy," he wrote in his autobiography. "Everyone said that record was a masterpiece—and I loved it, too—and so they just feel I'm trying to put them on. But that's what I was trying to do on most of that album, particularly on 'All Blues' and 'So What.' I just missed."[16]

He just missed. Not to worry, though—there will be other days, and other studio sessions. Sometimes the mess produces something worth having—even, or especially, if it wasn't what you were aiming for.

Like pianist Keith Jarrett and guitarist Adrian Belew, Miles Davis and his group were touched by musical genius. Their exploits can seem remote from our everyday achievements. Yet we can learn from

---

*Of course, *Kind of Blue* did not come from nowhere. Like the scientist Erez Lieberman Aiden, Miles Davis laid the foundations for his creative leaps by repeatedly moving between playing styles. He had trained at the Juilliard School, recorded European classical music, and played many types of jazz with various groups.

Just over a year before *Kind of Blue* was recorded, Miles went to Paris to visit the actress Juliette Gréco, an old flame. She introduced him to a young director, Louis Malle, and Malle seized the opportunity to persuade the trumpeter to write and perform the soundtrack to Malle's first film, *Ascenseur pour l'échafaud* (*Elevator to the Gallows*). Miles rounded up an unfamiliar band of musicians and, in an overnight session, they watched the film while he led the group in improvised accompaniment.

Just as the unplayable piano was a productive obstacle for Keith Jarrett, accompanying *Ascenseur* may have been the challenge that allowed Miles Davis to make a stylistic leap. It's a noir movie about two lovers who conspire in a murder. Miles had been working in the bebop style, fast and technically demanding and useless for providing the sonic background to stark, spare, dreamy scenes. Because the film's scenes had their own timing and logic, Miles had to adapt, finding a fresh, sparse style in a session that lasted less than three hours. It was new territory for Miles Davis—and territory to which he would soon return in *Kind of Blue*.

asking why Miles preferred improvising to careful composition. To improvise is to lose control—with the consequence that the improviser may later shrug and write, "I just missed." So what do we gain in exchange for that loss of control, and when is the bargain worth accepting?

Some gains are obvious. Improvising a single performance is much faster and cheaper than scripting or composing one. *Kind of Blue* took less than nine hours to record.* In contrast, the Beatles' masterpiece *Sgt. Pepper's Lonely Hearts Club Band* took seven hundred.[17] Being quick and cheap isn't everything, but it isn't nothing, either.

Another clear gain is flexibility. When I wrote that "to improvise is to lose control" that wasn't quite right. We rarely have complete control, just a comforting illusion of control instead. The speaker without a script may bungle his lines—just ask Rick Perry or Ed Miliband—but he is also free to change course in response to a question, or to cut things short if the event is running late. Having a script makes that harder. The improviser has given up full control on her own terms; the person who relies on the script risks having control wrenched away on someone else's terms.

Speed, economy, and flexibility: these three advantages should already be enough to convince us that the messy process of improvising has its advantages over tidy, scripted alternatives. But there's something else that seems to happen during the process of improvisation, an almost magical creative spark that until recently has been elusive.

"It's magical, but it's not magic," says Charles Limb. "It's a product of the brain."[18]

Charles Limb is a neuroscientist and surgeon at the University of

*In 1956, Miles Davis signed with Columbia Records. To complete his contractual obligation to his previous record company, Prestige, he recorded four albums in two days: *Relaxin' with the Miles Davis Quintet*, *Steamin' with the Miles Davis Quintet*, *Workin' with the Miles Davis Quintet*, and *Cookin' with the Miles Davis Quintet*. The titles reveal the haste involved, but the music itself was and still is admired.

California, San Francisco. He is also a fanatical jazz saxophonist, and is convinced that jazz improvisation is one of the few creative acts that is currently feasible for neuroscientists to study. Unlike writing a novel, jazz improv is a fleeting process in which original material can be whipped up in a few seconds. The conditions under which the improvisation was produced can be repeated again and again, and the improvisation can also be compared to a control—for example, performing a memorized piece.

All this can be observed inside a brain scanner—a functional magnetic resonance imager, or fMRI. The scanner generates powerful magnetic fields that illuminate the contrast between oxygen-rich blood flowing to the brain and the oxygen-depleted blood flowing away again. An fMRI scanner is a challenging place to express your creativity, though. Imagine lying flat on your back as you're slid into a giant white plastic donut with the look of a vintage iPod. Your head is immobilized to allow the imaging to take place. You have a small plastic keyboard that sits across your knees. (Steel components would be unwise: the magnetic field would rip the keyboard apart and pull the shrapnel into the scanner with your head.) You can see your hands only through an array of mirrors, the keyboard speakers are in another room, and the sound has to be piped back so you can hear yourself play. Sound good? Now let yourself go and jam.

Despite the obvious limitations of this approach, Limb and other neuroscientists[19] have been discovering some intriguing hints about what goes on in an improvising brain. When they recruited six professional jazz pianists to improvise short passages of music, comparing them with scales and memorized tunes, Limb and Allen Braun consistently found an intriguing pattern in the prefrontal cortex.[20] This is the part of the brain that is most distinctively human when comparing our brains with those of animals. "It's where the apparent seat of consciousness resides," says Limb. "Complex memory, sense of self, sense of morality, sense of humor. Higher-order cognitive processing is all implicated in the prefrontal cortex."[21]

No surprise, then, that the prefrontal cortex behaves unusually during musical improvisation. But the striking pattern is that rather than being fired up during improvisation, some fairly broad areas of the prefrontal cortex are being shut down. (These are the dorsolateral areas, on either side of the top of your forehead, and the lateral orbital areas, behind your eyes.) At the same time, the medial frontal area, behind the bridge of your nose, becomes more active. Not only was this pattern robust in the work on jazz improv, it also emerges from a separate study of freestyle rappers by Braun and others.[22]

What does this all mean? It suggests that improvisers are suppressing their conscious control and letting go. Most of us go through our days censoring our own brains. We respect standards and norms. We try to be polite. We don't usually swear at people, or punch them. All this requires a degree of self-control—after all, sometimes we *really want* to punch people. So that filtering is a good thing. But you can have too much of a good thing, says Charles Limb; too much filtering. "Taken to the extreme maybe it squashes creativity. So rather than suppressing all these ideas the improvising brain lets them go."[23]

Improvising musicians shut down their inner critics. Improvisers stop filtering their ideas quite so assiduously, and allow the mess of new ideas to flow out. The improvising brain is a little like the tipsy brain, although alcohol is much cruder, making us clumsy as well as disinhibited. It is no wonder that at its best, improvisation can produce flashes of pure brilliance. No wonder, either, that with the internal censor asleep, it sometimes feels like a messy, reckless thing to risk. And that is where we will leave the likes of Miles Davis, and turn to what happens when ordinary people improvise.

• • •

On July 11, 2012, one of the UK's largest phone companies, O_2, suffered a dramatic outage. The trouble began in London and rolled out from there, for more than twenty-four hours. Hundreds of thousands of people were affected, with cell phones, landlines, and broadband Internet all at risk from the glitch. Many customers, naturally enough, took to Twitter to vent their frustration, posting pithy complaints—or sometimes foul abuse—in a way that both O_2 and anyone else could see.

The flow of incoming tweets and Facebook complaints was overwhelming. "We were faced with twenty times our weekly volume in one day," says Nicola Green, O_2's head of communication at the time. "We were having thousands and thousands of tweets coming in."[24]

O_2's social media team began by following the standard practice: apologizing and linking to a website with the latest information about the network problem. The safe, tidy option would be a quick cut-and-paste to each complaint: "We're sorry about the interruption to your service. For the latest service status update visit: http://status.o2.co.uk/." As for abusive complaints, the standard advice is to ignore them.

But one of the O_2 team—an introvert by the name of Chris—decided he'd try something different. Here are a few of the exchanges that resulted:

CUSTOMER: not gonna lie cannot wait to leave @o2—

O_2: but we still love you!

CUSTOMER: F*** YOU! SUCK D*** IN HELL.

O_2: Maybe later, got tweets to send right now.

CUSTOMER: Oh @O2 have said sorry. Nice. So when I don't pay my bill for another month will a sorry do? How about a***-f***ng your mothers you t***s?

O_2: She says no thanks.

These responses are risky. Imagine Chris's situation: he and a dozen colleagues were watching a waterfall of angry tweets scroll across their screens. Their boss, Nicola Green, was running a press office swamped with media inquiries, and talking to the chief executive himself to figure out a collective O_2 response. It would have been a lot safer for Chris and his colleagues to wait quietly for a tidy corporate line to be agreed upon by the higher-ups, and then push it out like a production line of human autoresponders. By responding to customer complaints with cheeky affection or the equivalent of a jokey wink, Chris was potentially giving himself a lot of explaining to do. Any one of the responses might have backfired. But Chris realized instinctively that the alternative, a hastily cloned response to thousands of dissatisfied customers, simply wasn't good enough.

Chris's tweets quickly attracted an audience, and his colleagues rallied around and copied his example. Tens of thousands of people started following O_2 to watch the show, and tweeting in their own suggestions and faux complaints. One alleged that his O_2 phone had grown arms and legs, and hurled his mother down the stairs, demanding that O_2 "get it sorted, please!" O_2 sympathized, then asked, "Was the phone running Angry Birds at the time?"

One wag tweeted a photograph of a pigeon, with the slogan "Carrier Pigeon Can Carry." O_2's deadpan response: "How much for the bird?"

When one customer helpfully chipped in, "I haven't had any problems," O_2 shot back, "I've had 99." Another opined, "Whoever is running the O2 twitter feed today is handling the abuse well. Go you! :-)"; O_2 replied, "I need a hug."

What all the responses had in common was that they were

undeniably human. Suddenly O_2 wasn't just a faceless brand letting down its customers. It was a collection of human beings trying to deal with difficult circumstances. The angriest customers didn't seem like O_2's victims anymore. They seemed more like bullies. Chris and his colleagues were standing up to those bullies with a sense of humor. Here was a large multinational company failing to meet its obligations to paying customers—and yet it was hard not to sympathize with it.

O_2's improvised defense was reported across the world and almost universally admired. But because a single misfiring joke might have undone all the good work, Nicola Green—who was far too busy at the time to police the tweets—describes the approach as treading "a very, very fine line."

What's the lesson here? It's not simply that whenever a company has a meltdown, it should respond with self-deprecating jokes. Green says that subsequent efforts to meet a customer complaint with humor have sometimes fallen flat. After some of the customers involved in the most-retweeted exchanges with O_2 found themselves on TV talk shows, people would fire off abuse at O_2 in the hope of triggering a witty response and winning fifteen minutes of fame. The company dialed back, adopting a blander tone for a while. What worked in one situation will not work forever.

Rather than try to specify what tone to use when, O_2's approach to social media is to recruit and retain a social media team with wit, courage, and, above all, good judgment. It's to establish, through training and management feedback, that an informal tone is acceptable. Tweets aren't micromanaged; instead there's a review every couple of weeks to discuss whether O_2's social media team is on the right track. This allows them room to improvise and adapt to circumstances. "The guys are tweeting at the moment, and I don't know what they're tweeting," Nicola Green told me. "It's wrong to be prescriptive: we have to trust people's judgment."

Another example of trusting employees' judgment comes from a well-respected—and expensive—Manhattan restaurant. Kate Krader, a restaurant critic, was reminiscing with a college friend about "Beerios," the popular student combo of beer and cereal. A waiter overheard, someone quietly slipped down the block to pick up some cereal, and within minutes Krader and her friend were presented with two bowls of Beerios. The beer was good, too: "Chocolate porter, it was amazing."[25] Of course, such service is a luxury, but when compared with the other ways in which high-end restaurants pamper their customers, the simple act of listening and improvising is both cheap and delightful.

Perhaps the company most famous for giving its staff freedom to improvise customer service is the online shoe retailer Zappos. One woman ordered boots for her husband and then wanted to return them after he died in a car accident; the Zappos rep who took the call immediately sent her flowers. A best man faced giving a wedding speech without proper footwear because the Zappos courier, UPS, had screwed up; on hearing his tale, a Zappos rep rushed him free shoes by express delivery. Another Zappos rep took a call from a customer who was staying in Las Vegas, not far from Zappos HQ. The customer was trying to get a pair of shoes that Zappos no longer stocked; the Zappos rep found them in stock at a rival retailer at a nearby shopping mall, left the call center, bought the shoes, and delivered them to the customer by hand.[26]

Zappos would soon be out of business if every customer received such treatment. But in each of these cases the customer was in an unusual situation: I'm returning my husband's shoes *because he just died*; my shoes haven't arrived *and I am best man at a wedding tomorrow*; I can't get the shoes I want *and I'm just a couple of miles from your office right now.* That means that in each case the Zappos rep had to have a genuine unscripted conversation to figure out what that unusual situation was. Yes, the reps went to extraordinary lengths, but before any of the spectacular customer service stunts came a very simple act: listening.

Miles Davis once explained his approach to jazz improv as creating "freedom and space to hear things."[27] The phrase is fascinating: not freedom and space to play things, but to *hear* things—what the other instruments were doing, even the sound of your own playing, and to respond. Any of us can have that freedom and space if we're willing to listen. Whether we're giving a speech, waiting on tables, or sitting in a corporate call center, the messier, improvised response is the one that takes in the entire context: the ambient noise, a customer's tone of voice, the reaction of an audience, even the weather. Sometimes it's only when a speaker delivers a line and sees the body language, hears the laughter, or senses the sharp intake of breath that she instinctively understands what she must do next.

Trained theater improvisers learn something called "the habit of yes." The idea is to keep opening up new conversational possibilities rather than shut them down. Always add to what has been said so far. Never say "no"; always say "yes, and . . ."; another way this is sometimes phrased is "Enter their world."

The idea of "yes" has applications far beyond customer service and stagecraft. Here's one student of improv describing how it has affected her parenting:

> Friday, my eight-year-old, Samantha, burst into the kitchen with a gleam in her eyes. "Mommy, Mommy, there's a monster in the closet!" she shrieked. Normally, I would have thought my best reply to be a reality check for her. I would have said something like: "No, dear, there is no monster in the closet. It's just your imagination, sweetie." Instead, considering the rule of yes, I turned from the dishes I was washing and said: "There is? Wow, let's go see!" I accompanied her to the closet, where we had a

dynamic encounter with the monster, capturing it and squealing with delight as we tickled it into disappearing. It was a magical shared adventure. I would never have thought of joining Samantha's fantasy before considering the rule of yes! Thanks, improv.[28]

Here's another example of two improvisers at work. Their names are Virginia and Mondy. Virginia points at Gus, a dog, who is rooting around for a bone in the garden.

Virginia: He's digging for his life.

Mondy: Oh yeah. Gus is busy working on his caverns. He's starting a coal mine. So he's going to get it started and you're going to finish it up, right?

Virginia: [*laughs*] I am—

Mondy: The coal mine.

Virginia: The coal mine? I never worked in a coal mine.

Mondy: I know . . .

But Mondy wants that to change. Virginia needs to go down the mine. There are bills to pay; Mondy needs the money. Virginia's laughing but she says no.

Mondy: Oh well, we'll have to shut down the whole operation then. All right, Gus. No, she doesn't want to go in, man . . . stop digging.[29]

While it's not the funniest dialogue in the world, this isn't a fully professional cast. Mondy is an actor with plenty of improv experience; Virginia, on the other hand, is his mother-in-law.

She has dementia.

By using his improv skills and his willingness to say yes and enter Virginia's bewildered world, Mondy keeps her joyful in the face of a terrible affliction. There is a name for this sort of approach: "validation therapy," and while we don't have a great deal of evidence on how well it works, what evidence we do have hints that it might help people with dementia feel less depressed and less likely to be agitated or aggressive.[30] What is the alternative? It is to continually remind dementia sufferers that it is Tuesday, that they live in a nursing home, that this is their name and these are pictures of their family. That provokes anger and frustration, and no wonder. To the sufferer, these constant admonitions are a long stream of "no." It is much more fun to hear "yes."

There is a cost to this, as the journalist Chana Joffe-Walt discovered while recording Virginia, Mondy, and the woman who brought them together—Karen Stobbe, another improv actor. She's Mondy's wife and Virginia's daughter. For Karen, validation therapy isn't quite such a blast. It's hard work, psychologically. Mondy has a blank slate and Virginia has a blank slate. But Karen has a lifetime of memories with Virginia, her mother—memories that Virginia doesn't have. Saying "yes, and . . ." isn't hard for Mondy; for Karen, it also means denying all her childhood memories. Still, in an awful situation, it is the least painful strategy. Karen now teaches improv skills for dementia caregivers.

Listening is easy, in principle. In practice it can be terribly hard—especially when, like Karen, you have so much to lose. A really good conversation is mentally demanding. Listening and responding is messy, exhausting—and exhilarating. A great conversation is a rare joy because it is full of surprises and thus requires constant improvisation. As the philosopher Gilbert Ryle wrote, "To a partly novel situation the response is necessarily partly novel, else it is not a response."[31]

• • •

From the accidental birth of *Kind of Blue* to a mother and daughter tickling a monster together, improvisation is fast, exciting, and very human. But improvisation can be dangerous, too. It is hard to forget the sad figure of Gerald Ratner—the man who had created a mighty jewelry empire, only to find himself ejected after going off script in search of a good joke. He bounced back in some ways, setting up a chain of health clubs, but no matter what he achieved nobody ever forgot his gaffe. He endured severe depression, and almost a quarter of a century later still bitterly regrets his mistake. "People ask me if I'm glad I said what I said. They're ridiculous. How could I be grateful? I lost everything."[32]

No wonder we hesitate to improvise. No wonder we fear letting go. Yes, improvising can be cheap and fast, flexible and responsive to the situation, authentic and conversational and breathtakingly creative. But it is truly risky.

But then, not improvising is risky, too.

Because the truth about Gerald Ratner's off-the-cuff remark about his products being "total crap" is this: it wasn't off-the-cuff at all. It was chosen with care. Ratner had told the joke in speeches before, without running into problems. And as he prepared to deliver the speech on a larger stage, he sought advice. Several people advised caution; others encouraged him to tell even more daring jokes. They thought Ratner would sound self-deprecating and that his audience would love the jokes—which on the night, they did. But when written up in the newspapers the next morning, in the depths of a recession, Ratner simply sounded like a millionaire mocking his struggling customers.

Ratner's downfall was caused not by a lack of preparation, but by a lack of judgment. Ratner did exactly what he planned to do—he had simply failed to foresee the consequences. Improvisation was not to blame.

What about Ed Miliband and Rick Perry, two politicians humiliated by their forgetfulness on a public stage? Again, improvisation didn't cause their downfall. Ed Miliband put his remarks down in black and white, distributed them to the media, and then promptly forgot what he was intending to say. That isn't improvisation—it's amnesia. Rick Perry, similarly, could have avoided embarrassing himself if he'd stuck to vaguer principles such as "small government." His failure was being unable to finish a list of three things; his mistake was to start listing them in the first place.

Improvising does expose us to new and different risks—but even careful preparation cannot remove risks entirely.

Sometimes it is wise not to improvise. If you never speak in public but must say something at a wedding, and your highest ambition is not to embarrass yourself, then the risk-reward calculation is likely to point to writing a script. But if you are delivering a talk that should be informal and interactive, yet you are reading out a backdrop of bullet-point slides, you've cast a vote of no confidence in yourself—just as a telemarketing script is the micromanagers' vote of no confidence in their junior staff.

So what does it take to successfully improvise? The first element, paradoxically, is practice. Comedians and musicians must also practice their craft until much of what they do is entirely unconscious. "Reflection and attention are of scarcely any service in the matter," wrote the pianist and teacher Carl Czerny, back in 1839. "We must leave nearly everything to the fingers and to chance."[33] But the most common form of improvisation is human conversation, and that is something all of us have been practicing all our lives.

The second element is a willingness to cope with messy situations. Miles Davis's drummer on *Kind of Blue* was Jimmy Cobb. Here's how he was recruited in 1958, as an emergency replacement for a drummer with a serious drug habit who had quit abruptly.

> When I first got the call from Miles it was like six-thirty in the evening and he said, "We're working tonight." I said, "Great, where?" He said, "In Boston." I was in New York and we hit at nine!

With full drum kit, Cobb dashed to Boston. When he arrived at the venue, the band was in full flight without drums. He set up his drum kit onstage behind them, and by the time they hit the interlude of "Round Midnight":

> The horn line says Bah-bah-bah-bah-bah. That's where I started. I played that lick and from then on I was with the band.[34]

If you can cope with that sort of mess, you can cope with a lot. The "habit of yes" helps.

The third crucial element is the ability to truly listen, whether you're a jazz trumpeter, a corporate tweeter, on a date, or working as a customer service rep at Zappos.

But perhaps the most important element in successful improvising is simply this: being willing to take risks and to let go. That is much easier when you have little to lose, but even when there is a lot on the line, improvising can be the best way forward. Consider the situation faced by Marco Rubio, seeking to consolidate his momentum as the Republican establishment's favored candidate going into the last debate before the New Hampshire U.S. presidential primary in February 2016. He needed only to avoid mistakes, and relying on memorized chunks of speech rather than thinking on his feet must have seemed like a safety-first strategy—until a rival mocked him for it, and Rubio responded disastrously. He blinked, he began to sweat, and he reached for another memorized chunk of speech; unfortunately, the line that came out was the same, word for word, as the one that had just prompted the mockery. A little later he said it all again. And again. The media were full of jokes about the "RuBot," a Twitter account called "Rubio Glitch" appeared (it repeats itself), and Rubio's campaign was over not long after.

A script can seem protective, like a bulletproof vest; sometimes it is more like a straitjacket. Improvising unleashes creativity, it feels fresh and honest and personal. Above all, it turns a monologue into a conversation.

In December 1955, Rosa Parks was arrested after refusing to give up her seat on a bus in Montgomery, Alabama, to a white man.[35] As a local church leader and already an orator of some renown, Martin Luther King was asked to organize a boycott of Montgomery's busses. He hesitated. He was exhausted; his newborn baby daughter, Yoki, wouldn't stop crying in the night. He wanted time to think. But an influential local activist, E. D. Nixon, would have none of that: "You ain't got much time to think, 'cause you in the chair from now on," he told King.

So it was that King found himself in an unfamiliar situation: he had to prepare his inaugural speech as president of the newly formed Montgomery Improvement Association, but he was in a hurry. He arrived home from the meeting with Nixon and the activists at half past six; he had to head to the venue, Holt Street Church, at ten to seven. He told his wife, Coretta, he would skip supper, although he had not eaten since breakfast. King retreated into his study and closed the door. He was terrified, "possessed by fear . . . obsessed by a feeling of inadequacy," he later wrote. Newspapermen would be there, perhaps even television crews. Yet just as the stakes were highest, the tidy habits of careful preparation that served him so well all his life were useless to him now: he couldn't research, draft, redraft, and memorize. He had no time.

King looked at his watch—already five minutes had ticked away while he fretted. Every Sunday he delivered a sermon based on fifteen hours of hard work. Now he was about to deliver the most important speech of his life, and he had just fifteen minutes. He sketched a couple of thoughts with his hand shaking. He stopped, reversed, turned the problem around in his head. He mentally sketched out the balance he had to strike in his comments, and the themes that he had to touch on. He prayed. That was all the preparation he could spare before driving to the Holt Street Church.[36]

Ten thousand people stood outside, unable to cram themselves in, listening to the proceedings via loudspeaker. The Montgomery police were there in force. So were the television cameras, pointing at the pulpit as King stepped up and began to speak.

"We're here this evening for serious business," he began. And then, without notes, without a careful script lovingly prepared and committed to memory, his words began to trickle out, and then to pour forth freely. He had had no time to prepare, but he had found something more valuable: in Miles Davis's phrase, "the freedom and space to hear things." As he spoke, King listened to the crowd, feeling out their response, speaking in the moment. His early sentences were experiments, grasping for a theme, exploring how each sounded and how the crowd responded. Each phrase shaped the phrase that followed. His speech was not a solo; it was a duet with his audience.

After a cautious opening, King talked of Rosa Parks, of her character and "the depth of her Christian commitment," and of how "just because she refused to get up, she was arrested." The crowd murmured their assent. And after a pause for breath, King changed direction.

"There comes a time when people get tired of being trampled over by the iron feet of oppression."

"Yes! Yes!" replied individuals in the crowd, and suddenly those individual voices turned into something more, a roar of approval, of shared anger, of joy, too, at the sense of community. King had crested a rhetorical hill to find that behind it was a mountain of emotion and noise. That noise climbed and climbed. It was inexorable. And just when it seemed that the volume had reached a summit, an even higher peak emerged and those inside the church became aware of the voices of the thousands outside. The cheering continued. The sound was everywhere. And then, as at last it began to fade, King's voice rose again, to repeat the theme that he and the crowd had selected together.

"There comes a time when people get tired of getting pushed out of the glittering sunlight of life's July, and left standing amidst the piercing chill of an Alpine November. There . . ." The roar of the crowd became too loud again. Amid the sound of feet thundering on the church's wooden floorboards, King was forced to pause.[37]

As with any extemporaneous performance, King's was imperfect. His conclusion was limp. Some lines fell flat: "I think I speak with—with legal authority—not that I have any legal authority—but I think I speak with legal authority behind me—that the law—the ordinance—the city ordinance has never been totally clarified."

He had never in his life delivered a sermon with such flaws. Fifteen hours of preparation always ironed out every wrinkle. And yet despite those wrinkles, this improvisation, this free-for-all, was easily the finest speech that King had yet given.

"That was the great awakening," said one witness. "It was astonishing, the man spoke with so much force."

"Nobody dreamed of Martin Luther King being that sort of man under these conditions," said another.

King himself, one suspects, had not truly understood what he could unleash once he let himself go. He didn't want to improvise the speech. He preferred the tidy approach, not the messy one. But when the situation gave him no alternative, he came to understand what older preachers had told him: "Open your mouth and God will speak for you."

The days of meticulous preparation were behind him: as the civil rights campaign took shape with King at its head, he would travel from church to church, from speech to speech, and rarely have the time to prepare speeches of tidy perfection. But seven and a half years later, in 1963, he found himself faced with speaking to a quarter of a million people who had marched on Washington, D.C., and live on every national television network. This speech demanded the preparation of old. It was too important to be left to chance.

Dr. King and his aides had prepared a typewritten script, unpromisingly titled "Normalcy, Never Again." King's team was trying to navigate complex waters with the text of this address. King needed to reach out to white allies, to rebut the hard-line approach of Malcolm X and others, and to respond to President Kennedy's civil rights bill. Was it to be criticized as inadequate, or welcomed as progress? There was much politicking behind the scenes.[38] And each speaker had been given just seven minutes; there was no exception for Martin Luther King. All these constraints called for tidy, precise drafting.

"Normalcy, Never Again" was over-formal and flawed. Parts of it read like poetry; others were clumsy legalese. As King read out the speech, it did not stir the soul. But then, toward the end, came a biblical flourish: "We will not be satisfied until justice runs down like waters and righteousness like a mighty stream." Approving cheers rippled up and down the Mall as King delivered the line, the crowd responding to its emotive imagery.

Then King looked down at his script. The next line was pretentious and limp: "And so today, let us go back to our communities as members of the international association for the advancement of creative dissatisfaction." He couldn't bring himself to say the words, and so instead, he started to improvise: "Go back to Mississippi. Go back to Alabama . . ."[39]

Behind him stood his friends and colleagues. They knew that King had stepped away from his script, and at the moment of maximum danger and maximum opportunity, the climax of his speech, he was looking for something to say—something that would touch the people there at the Mall, and people watching across the country.

"Tell 'em about the dream, Martin," yelled the singer Mahalia Jackson. It was a reference to something Dr. King had been talking about over the previous months as he preached to church congregations—a dream of a brighter future, in which whites and blacks lived in harmony. And so, facing the television cameras and the expectant crowd, responding perfectly to the situation, Martin Luther King began to create on the fly one of the most famous speeches of the century. He spoke of his dream that "one day on the red hills of Georgia, the sons of former slaves and the sons of former slave owners will be able to sit down together at the table of brotherhood . . . that my four little children will one day live in a nation where they will not be judged by the color of their skin but by the content of their character."

"Normalcy, Never Again" was forgotten. King's impromptu words provided the conclusion to a speech that shook the twentieth century. That speech would forever be known as "I Have a Dream."

5

Winning

"What else matters but beating him?"

Bezos, Rommel, Trump: How to Use Mess as a Weapon in Business, Politics, and War

The trenches of the First World War were not famous for rapid maneuvers, but one night late in January 1915, near Binarville in northeast France, was an exception. The Germans planned an attack, to be led by the thousand men of 3rd Battalion. The assault began well, and the flanking 9th Company, consisting of just two hundred men, were invited to take a break from a dank, frozen, four-foot dugout to join in. Their young glory-seeking commander accepted the invitation hungrily. His name was Lieutenant Erwin Rommel.[1]

Rommel quickly led his men forward toward the French trenches. For a moment they were pinned down on the frozen ground by heavy but aimless gunfire; Rommel decided a rapid advance would be safer than staying put. The French, panicking, fled; the Germans saw flashes of blue jackets and red trousers as their opponents ran. Rommel's men pressed ahead through a French defensive line, then a second, and then a third, pausing occasionally to shoot at the retreating French. Rommel crawled through a tangle of barbed wire several hundred feet deep. At one point, he realized that nobody was following him, but he scouted around and found a safe passage through. Then he crawled back and told his second-in-command, "Obey my orders instantly or I shoot you."

Duly encouraged, Rommel's company penetrated deep into the French position, seizing buildings and fortifications that the French had abandoned. Rommel sent a message back to his battalion commander requesting support. From a position of relative safety, he harried an entire battalion of French soldiers on his right flank as they tried to withdraw through their own barbed wire. But he was vastly outnumbered and the French re-formed and began to close in, recapturing one of the buildings to his right. Rommel knew that he was vulnerable unless reinforcements arrived to support him. Then a message was shouted across from the German lines: 3rd Battalion had abandoned its attack. Ninth Company was surrounded.

Rommel had two obvious options: hold his fortified position until his soldiers' ammunition ran out, then surrender; or retreat across a daunting set of obstacles under fire from all sides. He chose neither. Instead he threw his men into a fresh attack, routing the French from the building they'd just occupied. The French were astonished; their assault faltered while they tried to understand what was happening, and Rommel seized his opportunity to lead his company in single file back through the wire and across the trenches. By the time the French had gathered themselves, Rommel's company was three hundred yards away and out of danger. He suffered no fatalities and left no injured men behind.

Rommel became a master of the messy craft of war, with this early engagement at Binarville setting the tone. He believed that opportunities arose from confusion on the battlefield, and tried to generate more opportunities by creating more confusion. His rapid movement and bold independent action created a feedback loop: the enemy would be confused; that would produce unpredictable openings; Rommel would seize those openings, creating more chaos and further opportunities.

This was a messy approach because the rapid, relentless, and unpredictable movements that so baffled the enemy would also confuse his own side. As a result, Rommel often found himself outnumbered, his forces scattered and out of touch with one another, low on fuel or physically exhausted, and with supply lines in disarray. And yet he kept winning. His men might be tired and confused, but his enemies were utterly bewildered.

Rommel triumphed repeatedly by creating a chaotic situation that nobody understood—and trusting, usually correctly, that he could improvise his way through the mess before his enemies did. It is a strategy with applications far beyond the battlefield.

In a competitive situation, you win by beating your opponent. Sometimes the opponent is relevant only as a benchmark; a 100-meter sprinter can tune out his rivals and focus on the finish line. But many competitors—a chess player, a boxer, a military commander, a business leader, a politician—cannot ignore the opposition. And one way to win is to encourage your opponent to lose.

In the film *Rocky II*, the plucky left-handed—"southpaw"—challenger Rocky Balboa adopts an orthodox right-handed stance to fight the champ, Apollo Creed. For most of the bout he's a human punching bag, but in the final round Rocky switches to his preferred southpaw stance and knocks out the bewildered Apollo. Switching from southpaw to orthodox and back must have been a handicap for Rocky, but it was outweighed by the trouble it caused for Apollo Creed.

If this seems like something that could happen only in Hollywood, tell that to Wladimir Klitschko. One of boxing's great heavyweight champions, the Ukrainian boasted a record total of twenty-eight title fights and was on a run of eleven years and eighteen successive defenses. Then, late in 2015, Klitschko fought Tyson Fury, an underdog from Manchester noted mainly for strange stunts such as showing up at a press conference in an ill-fitting Batman costume. Few people gave Fury much chance—but in the middle of the fight he emulated Rocky, switching to southpaw and outboxing an unsettled Klitschko to take his world title belt away.

"I know how good Wladimir is and Wladimir did not show how good he is. I know his strengths but I couldn't see any of it," said Klitschko's own brother, Vitali, himself a former world champion. Boxing pundit Steve Bunce was one of many to conclude that Klitschko hadn't been able to cope with the sheer awkwardness of his unfancied foe: "Wladimir looked bad tonight because Tyson Fury made him look bad."

There's even a theory—the Faurie-Raymond hypothesis[2]—that left-handed people have continued to survive in a right-handed world, despite numerous disadvantages and indignities, because right-handed people aren't used to fighting them.* Whatever the truth of that, the lesson is that success in a competitive situation isn't just about what you do—it's about the effect your actions have on your opponent.[3]

For another example, look at chess. There's little doubt about the world's best player: it's the twenty-five-year-old world champion Magnus Carlsen, a dashing young Norwegian who when just thirteen beat the great Anatoly Karpov. Carlsen was the youngest player to be rated

*Dioula speakers of Burkina Faso enjoy a peaceful existence, and only one person in thirty is left-handed. In contrast, for the Yanomami in South America, combat is a way of life: the homicide rate is sixty times that of New York and three hundred times that of the Dioula; left-handers make up almost a quarter of the Yanomami population. It's not that left-handed people are more violent—it's just that they have an edge in a violent world full of right-handers.

number one in the world, and he has won both of his world championships with comfort. He's the highest-rated player in history and his endgames are particularly admired, with Carlsen conjuring victories seemingly out of nothing. But the curious thing about Carlsen is this: For all his brilliance, his *moves* just aren't that good.

How do we know this? Who would dare to second-guess the greatest player to grace the board? Computers, of course. The top computer programs are vastly better than any human, and can be used to evaluate human moves relative to the computer's best.

Ken Regan, a professor of computer science at the University at Buffalo, and a former chess professional, has been using chess software to evaluate human players. He finds that Carlsen's moves are good, of course, but others also play good moves—Vladimir Kramnik, for example, plays superbly, rarely falling far short of the move that the computer would recommend. Why, then, isn't Kramnik still the world champion? The answer isn't in the moves that Carlsen plays, but in what those moves do to his opponents. Put simply, other humans don't play to the best of their ability against Carlsen. And this doesn't seem to be just because of fear (although other players do fear him) or exhaustion (although he is fit and sometimes grinds out victories in very long games). It is that the specific moves he chooses somehow pose problems for his opponents.[4]

Another chess-and-computing analyst, Guy Haworth, notes that one of Carlsen's tactics is to complicate the game just as the players are pushed for time. In professional games this is usually as move 40 draws near. Guy Haworth tracks the average error of human players; in games involving Magnus Carlsen, that error explodes just before move 40.[5] Carlsen seems to relish dragging both players into a fiendish puzzle of a position at the very moment that time is running out. After all, Carlsen doesn't need to play perfectly to win; he just needs to ensure that his opponent plays worse.

• • •

As Rommel rose through the ranks, from commanding a handful of men at the start of the First World War to becoming one of the most feared and admired generals of the Second, he developed a distinctive philosophy, founded on the observation that fleeting opportunities often emerge in the confusion of war.

Those ideas could clearly be seen when Rommel was a company commander in 1917, in charge of a detachment of around eight hundred men in mountainous terrain north of Venice. Rommel's men were to support an ambitious German offensive against seasoned Italian troops manning three fortified defensive lines.[6]

He began with a rapid scouting expedition, which discovered a concealed path through the hills and captured several Italians and a defensive fortification without trouble. A rainstorm was lashing the battlefield—difficult conditions for most commanders, but for Rommel the storm provided ideal cover for rapid movement. Far ahead of the agreed schedule, he led his entire detachment along the secret path, nearly a mile ahead of his own lines. The next day, he attacked the Italians from an unexpected angle, taking many prisoners and seizing their defensive positions.

Rommel was now a victim of his own success: deep behind enemy lines, he was outnumbered and surrounded just as he had been at Binarville. And as at Binarville, Rommel counterpunched with speed just when the enemy was massing for an attack. Despite his limited firepower, the surprise unmanned the Italians. Rommel's prisoner count was now up to 1,500. And so it continued, surprise attack after surprise attack through the moonlit night, while Rommel's detachment rolled behind and parallel to the Italian front line. Thousands more prisoners were captured.

At dawn, Rommel faced heavy fire from fortified positions, and he abruptly changed tactics, charging uphill across exposed ground, overrunning the Italians through sheer speed.

Finally, Rommel's elated and exhausted troops faced a possible catastrophe: so many prisoners were now pouring back from the battle that Rommel's commanding officer presumed that the battle was won and gave the order to retreat and regroup. Some troops obeyed, others did not. In the confusion, Rommel found himself exposed and outnumbered yet again. Most commanders would have taken that moment to pause, gather their forces, and coordinate with their superiors. Rommel reckoned that the situation, however messy, was still in his favor despite the fact that he was outnumbered ten to one. Any delay would allow his disoriented and demoralized enemy to regroup. He was proved correct: the Italians were reeling, and so Rommel seized a strategically vital summit, Mount Matajur, by improvising another sudden attack.

Rommel had created a messy situation and triumphed by navigating that mess better than anyone else on the field of battle. In two and a half days of almost continuous fighting, Erwin Rommel's detachment of a few hundred men had taken nine thousand prisoners for the loss of six soldiers.

Rommel believed that opportunities were often fleeting, and that the chaos created in the scramble to seize them was a price worth paying—especially since chaos could give an edge to the side best able to cope. Rommel's strategy holds lessons for any competitive situation, and it can work just as well in business and politics as it does in war.

At the start of 1994, the World Wide Web was a niche pursuit. Microsoft, the most powerful software company in history, didn't have a website, let alone provide a Web browser. But Web traffic was over two thousand times busier than it had been a year earlier. That explosive growth meant a brief window of opportunity, the kind of opportunity that Erwin Rommel would have lunged for had he been a businessman rather than a general. Instead, it fell to a young computer scientist working on Wall Street to seize the moment. His name was Jeff Bezos.

"When a company comes up with an idea, it's a messy process," Bezos told Brad Stone, the author of the definitive biography both of Bezos and of the company he created: Amazon.[7] From the outside, that is a puzzling claim. To the consumer, Amazon is a byword for tidy efficiency: you want a product, you search Amazon, you find the product, you buy the product, the product arrives. To competitors, fighting Amazon is like fighting a machine: every move is calculated, every strategy quantified. It's a killer robot that feels no pain. And there is a kind of truth in both these caricatures of Amazon, but it's a partial truth. The story of Amazon is a long series of crazy goals, brutal fights, and squandered billions—an utter mess.

Bezos combined a grandiose vision with the sketchiest understanding of how that vision would be achieved. The name "Amazon" is inspired by the fact that the River Amazon "blows all other rivers away";[8] he wanted his company to be the "everything store," the largest retailer on the planet, capable of swiftly supplying any consumer with any product they could imagine. And yet despite these big dreams, when the company opened for business selling books in 1995—by which time Microsoft still hadn't launched its Internet Explorer browser—Bezos was utterly unprepared for the demand.

In the first week, Amazon sold $12,000 worth of books but shipped only $846. In week two, it shipped $7,000, still behind on the first week, while sales were up to $14,000. Right from the start, Bezos was behind and desperately scrambling to catch up. The company overdraft kept maxing out because the business was growing faster than the checks could be cashed; the management team was working late into the night to send out the books that had been ordered. (They sat on the floor: nobody had gotten around to buying tables.)

Bezos was making big claims to his customers—that there were a million books available; that there was a no-quibble thirty-day return policy—but he didn't know how those promises were going to be kept. He trusted that they would figure something out.[9]

One might have thought that these early weeks were a good time to pause and regroup, to concentrate on making sure that Amazon was able to deliver on its early promises. But like Rommel, Bezos believed in seizing opportunities rather than pausing for breath. In Amazon's second week of business, he received an e-mail from David Filo and Jerry Yang, the founders of one of the early Web's most popular sites, Yahoo! Filo and Yang wanted to list Amazon on the Yahoo! home page—would that be okay? Bezos's computer guru warned him that it would be like trying to sip from a fire hose. Bezos ignored him and accepted the offer from Yahoo!

Now they were even more of a success, and under even more pressure. The workload was inhuman. Bezos, his desk a cluttered mess, nearly poisoned himself after distractedly gulping down a rancid week-old cappuccino. When journalist Stone later tried to interview employees about that time in Amazon's history, they didn't remember much: they were getting so little sleep that their memories simply couldn't function.

Accepting the Yahoo! offer within a fortnight of launch was characteristic of Bezos. To launch Amazon he'd given up a well-paid job on Wall Street, against the advice of his family to keep working at least until he picked up his hefty annual bonus. Bezos decided that the opportunity would not wait.[10]

In 1999, Bezos decided to start stocking kitchen equipment. In Amazon warehouses that had been designed to store, sort, and dispatch books, naked carving knives were suddenly scything down the chutes and into the sorting machines. Meanwhile the company's database would be asking whether the knife was a hardback or a paperback.[11]

Amazon started stocking toys in the same year. The company held a press event in New York that was intended to show off its stock with tables piled high with merchandise—but when Bezos saw the modestly sized display he was livid at its lack of shock-and-awe scale. "Do you want to hand the business to our competitors?" he screamed. "This is pathetic!" And so some of Amazon's top executives fanned out across Manhattan, stretching their personal credit cards to the limit as they scrambled to buy whatever they could find in the local Toys"R"Us stores.[12]

When Christmas came, the desperate scrabble for toys was repeated on a colossal scale, as Amazon employees across the United States bought Costco and Toys"R"Us inventory in bulk and drove it to the Amazon warehouses. Amazon also bought the entire Pokémon stock from the new—and evidently naïve—ToysRUs.com site.[13]

The scramble was too much for Amazon's systems. The company's warehouses began to choke on pallets of Pokémon Jigglypuffs and Walk 'N Wag dogs from Mattel. Products lost somewhere in the vast distribution centers would send Amazon's databases haywire. Unshipped orders would clog the chutes in the sorting facility, each blockage spawning half a dozen further delays. Internally, the company was on its knees: it launched a "Save Santa" campaign and Amazon staff members were booked into hotels near the warehouses (two to a room) and didn't go home for a fortnight. As Christmas passed, 40 percent of the toy inventory was unsold and probably unsellable. ("If I have to, I will drive it to the landfill myself!" Bezos had declared when he'd placed a vast order with a toy manufacturer.) The losses on the toys Amazon had bought at retail from its rivals, then resold at a discount to consumers, must have been appalling. But the company survived and customers were happy.

In the summer of 2000 came the dot-com bust. Amazon, as one of the oldest and best-established businesses on the Web, should have easily weathered the downdraft, but it was a closer call than it might have been because Amazon was running substantial losses in pursuit of further growth. Top analysts were telling the world that Amazon was running out of cash. Bezos's aggressive discounts gave his finance team nightmares as they tried to borrow money from a suddenly skeptical financial market. *Barron's*, a prominent financial magazine, ran the headline "Amazon.Bomb." Suppliers started wanting to be paid in advance in case Amazon went bust.

There was a real possibility that Amazon wouldn't see Christmas 2001. Yet Bezos refused to slow down. Amazon was saved by a clever finance director, who had arranged a cash flow cushion, and some cobbled-together joint ventures. It had been close. As Brad Stone writes, "Amazon survived through a combination of conviction, improvisation, and luck."[14]

Most companies would have retrenched at that point. Instead, over the next few years, Amazon launched products as disparate as the Kindle (which immediately and repeatedly sold out, as Amazon struggled to manufacture it), Mechanical Turk (an unsettlingly named global clearinghouse for labor, which pioneered crowdsourcing but was criticized as being a sweatshop), the Fire Phone (widely reviewed as ugly, weird, and disappointing), Marketplace (where competitors to Amazon would use Amazon's own product listings to advertise their own cheaper alternatives), and Amazon Web Services. AWS in particular was a bold stroke—a move into cloud computing in 2006, four years ahead of Microsoft's Azure and six years ahead of Google Compute.

As Bezos liked to say during the crunches of 1998 and 1999, "If you are planning more than twenty minutes ahead in this environment, you are wasting your time."[15] He was a man in a hurry. No wonder he created such an almighty mess.

• • •

Come the Second World War, the Italians were the Germans' allies, but they seemed as prone as ever to losing battles. At the end of 1940 and beginning of 1941, a small British army under General Richard O'Connor had destroyed a vastly larger Italian force in North Africa, taking 130,000 prisoners and pushing the Italians back from the borders of Egypt to the middle of Libya. It seemed likely that the British would soon advance to Tripoli itself, driving the Italians out of Africa entirely. Faced with this alarming prospect, the Italians accepted Hitler's offer of assistance—a small, defensive detachment, just one division of tanks and one division of mechanized infantry. It was led by General Rommel.[16]

Rommel was flushed with success after the *Blitzkrieg** invasion of France, when his panzer tanks had surged far ahead of their own troops, roaming freely behind French lines and taking 97,000 prisoners. Nobody knew what was going on: French peasants often assumed Rommel's men were British troops; the French army called them "The Ghost Division"; not even German High Command knew where Rommel was or what he would do next.

But when Rommel arrived in Tripoli in February 1941, he faced a situation that seemed desperate. His men had no experience of desert warfare, and shipments of his panzers were trickling too slowly across the Mediterranean. He feared that the British would seize their opportunity to attack before he was ready to mount a defense.

**Blitzkrieg*, or "lightning war," turns out itself to be a messy piece of improvisation from the German army. Karl-Heinz Frieser, a German military historian, notes in *The Blitzkrieg Legend*: "The campaign in the west . . . was not a planned campaign of conquest. Instead, it was an operational act of despair to get out of a desperate strategic situation" (Frieser with John T. Greenwood, *The Blitzkrieg Legend: The 1940 Campaign in the West* [Annapolis, MD: Naval Institute Press, 2013]). After *Blitzkrieg* tactics were developed by Rommel and his fellow officers, and proved surprisingly successful, they were then embraced as a more official doctrine.

"If the British advance on Tripoli immediately without regard for casualties, our general situation will be very grave indeed," he warned Berlin. Improvising, he drove his panzers in a big continuous loop through Tripoli, so that his meager force looked much larger to the locals; he also commissioned hundreds of dummy tanks, hoping to deceive British air reconnaissance. As with the piles of toys that Bezos's team had scrabbled together from the toy stores of Manhattan, this was a bluff—a display of strength that didn't exist, designed to slow down a more cautious opponent. To his wife Lucy, Rommel wrote, "The next two or three weeks are going to be crucial. After that things will even up."[17]

Rommel was lucky: the British did waver, conserving strength and diverting some forces to Greece instead. Rommel sensed his enemy's hesitancy and began jabbing forward along the North African coast, searching for weakness. At each point he found that the British were withdrawing. A few weeks after Rommel's arrival, the British were digging in at Mersa El Brega, a defensive position protecting Cyrenaica, a land mass that bulged out from the desert into the Mediterranean. Cyrenaica was a prize: its coast was adorned by the fortified port of Tobruk, where vast quantities of petrol and ammunition were stored; there were numerous airfields there; and there was plenty of water, essential for fighting a desert campaign.

Rommel's immediate superior, the fat, white-mustached general Italo Gariboldi, wanted him to stay on the defensive—a demand that Rommel simply ignored, provoking furious shouting matches. More worryingly for Rommel, German High Command had also ordered him to wait before mounting any major counterattack against the British. But why? What Rommel did not know was that the awful slaughter of Operation Barbarossa, Hitler's war with Stalin, was about to be unleashed. As he had done before, he decided to finesse his orders and attack anyway; with the British fortifying Mersa El Brega, he felt that he had to act immediately if he was to act at all.*

After outflanking a stout defense at Mersa El Brega and capturing many British vehicles, Rommel saw yet another opportunity. The British were retreating in a long, slow curve around the bulging coast of Cyrenaica. Rommel pressed them with his left wing, and sent his right wing directly across the interior.

To call this daring was an understatement. It seemed insane. He'd been told that the route was impassable. (He personally explored it and concluded that it wasn't.) He was then informed that his thrusting force was running out of gasoline and needed four days to allow replenishment vehicles to shuttle back and forth from their supply dumps with more fuel. His response was a remarkable piece of risky improvisation: he ordered the division to unload every truck and car and send them all back across the desert for fuel, leaving the men and their panzers stranded and vulnerable for twenty-four hours. Rommel's calculation was simple: the British were in full retreat; they wouldn't be looking for helpless German soldiers in the middle of the desert, and even if British scouts did find the Germans they wouldn't be able to organize to attack the Germans quickly enough. He was correct.[18]

Rommel's counterstrike was shambolic. Cyrenaica was a land of fine red sandstorms, land mines, and soft, soft sand. The Germans kept getting lost and bogged down. Rommel would fly over the battlefield trying to find everyone's bearings. At one stage his scout plane buzzed his own troops at shoulder height and a piece of paper fluttered down, bearing a note: "If you don't move off again at once, I'll come down!—Rommel." So great was the confusion that he almost landed in the middle of a column of men that turned out to be British.[19] Later,

---

*Rommel was lucky here. He never realized that Ultra, the brilliant British code-breaking operation, was intercepting and deciphering his communications with German High Command. When he disobeyed orders, he astonished not only his own superiors, but also the British generals who had been given a sneak peek at the very same instructions.

Rommel's subordinates complained about the disarray and constant changes of plan. Back in Berlin, a German general mournfully noted in his diary in late April 1941, "Rommel has not sent us a single clear-cut report all these days, and I have a feeling that things are in a mess."

That assessment was right: Things were in a mess. But while the Germans were in chaos, the British were in a worse state: bewildered, outflanked, and desperately trying to withdraw around a congested coastal road. Many men were captured—including the British General Richard O'Connor—and the remainder of the British forces barely scrambled away. Six days after Rommel began his absurd and disorganized campaign to take the strategic prize of Cyrenaica, he had succeeded.

Over the course of a year and a half, Rommel's small expeditionary force rolled over a thousand miles of North African desert, from Tripoli in the west almost to Alexandria in the east, prompting the British fleet to flee to the safety of the Suez Canal and the British High Command to prepare a list of assets to be demolished if they were forced to surrender. As news of Rommel's victories reached Britain, Winston Churchill almost lost his job as prime minister, and paced the corridors of power, muttering: "Rommel, Rommel, Rommel! What else matters but beating him?"[20]

The idea that Donald Trump could mount a serious challenge to be the 2016 Republican nominee for president was initially regarded as a joke. A real estate developer, reality TV star, notorious blowhard, and political dilettante, Trump would be taking on far more experienced rivals—notably former Florida governor Jeb Bush, the brother and son of presidents.

Confounding all expectations, by the autumn of 2015, Trump had become a front-running phenomenon while Jeb Bush languished in the polls. The same pattern played out time and again: Trump would broadcast some inflammatory comment—about immigrants, for example—playing to the basest instincts of the Republican electorate. His rivals for the nomination would tiptoe in, trying to show that they empathized with the concerns of Trump-admiring voters without saying anything offensive, and often tying themselves in knots in the process; at one point Jeb Bush, in trying not to echo Trump's criticism of Mexicans, ended up seeming to smear Asians. Then, seemingly before the interview was even finished, Trump would pop up on Twitter, mock his rival, and do something else outrageous—such as take a misogynistic swipe at a female interviewer. After Trump performed a crude schoolboy impersonation of a disabled *New York Times* reporter, provoking predictable outrage, he took to Twitter again to change the subject, criticizing the "dopes" at *The New York Times* for overpaying to buy *The Boston Globe*.[21]

Trump's career-politician opponents were tidy-minded, surrounded by complicated messaging operations that crafted press releases and briefed them for interviews, trying to protect their image and prevent gaffes. But no matter how carefully his opponents worded their speeches and statements, a quick tweet from Trump would seize the headlines and keep his poll ratings high.

One day in 2015, I received a message from a friend, containing a link and a single line of commentary on Trump: "He's in their OODA loop."

The OODA loop is military jargon. It was coined by a retired U.S. Air Force colonel named John Boyd, who, two decades after his death, continues to be a cult figure among military thinkers. Boyd's theory helps explain everything from Rommel to Bezos to Trump. The theory was set out in a much-photocopied document known as "Patterns of Conflict," a mess of typed and retyped paper, hand-annotated and 196 pages long.

As a young man, Boyd had a reputation as the best pilot in the Air

Force. He was a thinker: he outthought his enemies in the air, and soon he was working on a toolkit of aerial maneuvers for his fellow pilots, explaining how each move could be used to confuse and outflank an opponent. It became a bible of air combat around the world. In the 1960s, Boyd developed a carefully quantified theory of why some fighter planes seemed much more effective than others, despite looking unpromising on paper. In the Korean War, American F-86 Sabre pilots beat the Soviet MiG-15 pilots time after time—the kill ratio was around ten to one. This was a puzzle: the MiG-15 flew higher, turned more tightly, and accelerated faster than the F-86. All of that didn't matter. Boyd showed that the U.S. planes could brake and maneuver in ways that confused their adversaries, and they had better visibility so avoided confusion themselves. The Soviet and North Korean pilots felt like they were fighting ghosts. Boyd's analysis shattered the received wisdom in the U.S. Air Force and led to the introduction of totally new types of aircraft.

Then, in 1975, Boyd quit the Air Force. He had bigger things to think about. In his youth, he'd been called "Forty Second Boyd," because that's how long it took him to beat any other fighter ace. After he'd perfected "Patterns of Conflict," he became associated with a somewhat longer time period: six hours. Delighting in his freedom from authority, Boyd went around in slippers, frayed shirts, and polyester trousers, and steadfastly refused to compromise on the length of the "Patterns" briefing, no matter how senior the person who expressed an interest in hearing it. "Since your boss is so pressed for time," he once bellowed down the phone at the assistant to the Chief of Naval Operations at the Pentagon, "here's an idea that will save him a lot of time: how about no brief?" Then Boyd hung up.[22]

Despite Boyd's truculence, "Patterns" was a hit. First the briefings were small, but by the end of the 1970s, word was spreading across Washington, D.C.: *You've got to hear Boyd*. Congressional staffers crowded into his briefings; so did reporters. James Fallows of *The Atlantic Monthly* became a fan. So did the management guru Tom Peters. So did a future defense secretary and vice president, Dick Cheney.

So what does "Patterns" say? Essentially, Boyd took the lessons he learned thinking about those fighter planes—that the F-86 pilots beat the MiG pilots because they could change tactics more quickly—and extended them to combat across history. His presentation ranged across wildly different circumstances: from the Battle of Cannae in 216 BC, in which Hannibal's Carthaginian army surrounded and annihilated a vastly superior force of Roman soldiers; to the Entebbe raid in the summer of 1976, in which Israeli special forces landed in hostile territory and freed more than a hundred people being held hostage by Palestinian militants. The unifying thread between these and countless other victories against the odds: the way that the successful commanders kept changing the situation faster than their adversaries could figure out what was going on. Chaos wasn't just something that happened on the battlefield—it could and should be deliberately deployed as a weapon.[23]

Boyd invented the OODA acronym to describe this process of decision making. OODA stands for "Observe-Orient-Decide-Act"—or, in plain English, working out what's happening, then responding. Boyd's six-hour briefings drove home the idea that this OODA loop of information gathering and decision making was crucial in any competitive struggle. If you could make quick decisions, that was good. If you had a strong sense of what was going on around you, that was good, too. But more profoundly, if you could disorient your opponent, forcing him to stop and figure out what was going on, you gained an advantage. And if you could do this relentlessly, your opponent would be almost paralyzed with confusion. Just as he was about to act, something new would happen and he would have to stop and think again. You would have more than an edge—you would have him at your mercy.

The friend who thought of OODA loops when he saw Trump in action had learned about them in his job at Greenpeace, where Boyd's theories are used to teach activists how to keep oil companies off balance. In the description of political commentator Josh Marshall, comparing "Jeb's painful and drawn-out efforts . . . with Trump jumping from one attack to another on Twitter, entirely at his own pace and on his own terms," is a perfect illustration of what it means to get inside your opponent's OODA loop.[24]

Trump's image took plenty of knocks over the course of the campaign, but he minimized the damage through an ability to change the conversation whenever he wanted. He chose his battlefields, even skipping a televised debate on the eve of the vital Iowa caucuses, and dominating the headlines as a result. Trump made sure both the media and his opponents reacted on his terms. He wasn't always perfectly prepared, but his preference for speed over perfection ensured that opponents were always scrambling to figure out a response.

In contrast to Trump's agility, the presidential campaigns of rivals such as Jeb Bush could be encapsulated by a word the German High Command used in conversation with Rommel in 1941 to describe the leadership qualities of the British Army. The German word was *schwerfällig*—ponderous. The historian David Fraser elaborates: "There was demonstrated, in British actions, rigidity of mind and reluctance to change positions as swiftly and readily as situations demanded . . . great fussiness and over-elaboration of detail in orders."[25]

In other words, the British were Rommel in reverse: rather than quick, deft, heedless of detail, and happy to make things up on the fly, they were slow, clumsy, tidy-minded, and unwilling to improvise.*

*The British did have a leader with Rommel's qualities: Richard O'Connor, the man who had routed the Italians. But thanks to Rommel's daring, chaotic thrust across Cyrenaica, General O'Connor was a prisoner of war.

If you're trying to win by creating a mess and betting on yourself to figure it out more quickly than your opponent, then it helps if your opponent is *schwerfällig.* That was Jeff Bezos's calculation, as he explained at the beginning of 1997 when invited to speak at Harvard Business School about his new dot-com business. At the time Amazon was no mighty river, but a mere trickle. Most people had never heard of it and, of those who had, few felt comfortable sending a credit card number into the confusing, anarchic World Wide Web. The savvy business thinkers of Harvard Business School heard Bezos's explanation of what he was trying to do, and they were skeptical. It wasn't that e-commerce itself looked infeasible—smart people could see that it might well be big. It was that Bezos had a competitor capable of swatting him on a whim.

Bezos had chatted with this terrible adversary a few months earlier. He and a colleague had a steak dinner at the Dahlia Lounge in Seattle with the Riggio brothers, Len and Stephen. Len Riggio, a tough-minded son of a boxer, had turned Barnes & Noble from a troubled company with a single Manhattan shop into a bookselling behemoth. Barnes & Noble had pots of money: $2 billion in sales in 1996, more than a hundred times larger than Amazon's $16 million. It had serious clout with publishers, who knew that Barnes & Noble could make or break any book. It enjoyed a prominent place in malls across North America and in the awareness of book lovers. It was used to crushing the life out of competitors—independent bookstores had lost almost half their market share in the five years running up to 1997. And of course, Barnes & Noble understood books.[26]

Len Riggio amiably told Bezos that Amazon should agree to some sort of joint venture, and soon, because Barnes & Noble was planning to sell books online itself. A Bezos lieutenant recalls the message thus: "You're doing a fantastic job, but, of course, we're going to kill you when we launch."[27]

It turns out that the students and faculty of Harvard Business School were thinking along the same lines as Len Riggio. They could see the potential of online bookselling but they could also see that Barnes & Noble was in a far stronger position than Amazon. When Barnes & Noble moved into the tiny online market, Amazon would be history.

"You seem like a really nice guy, so don't take this the wrong way," one MBA student advised Bezos, "But you really need to sell to Barnes & Noble and get out now."[28]

Bezos acknowledged the risk, but he wasn't afraid. He was convinced that as long as he kept moving, kept improvising, kept being willing to make a mess, his competitors would hesitate. This was true not just of Barnes & Noble, but the giants he planned to confront next: Toys"R"Us, Target, and even Walmart.

"I think you might be underestimating the degree to which established brick-and-mortar business, or any company that might be used to doing things a certain way, will find it hard to be nimble or to focus attention on a new channel," he told the class at Harvard. "I guess we'll see."[29]

Bezos, it turned out, had judged Len Riggio's perspective perfectly. Barnes & Noble was making good money in its bookstores and didn't want to spoil the corporate balance sheet by running a loss-making website; its distribution systems were large and well-established and designed to send large shipments to large stores, rather than one book at a time to individual customers. And Riggio didn't want his best people to be distracted by a website, so Barnes & Noble's e-commerce operation received too little management attention for too long. Barnes & Noble had developed excellent systems for running retail bookstores. But it hesitated to engage with the chaos of the new world of e-commerce. Amazon thrived on it. To use John Boyd's jargon, Amazon was inside Barnes & Noble's OODA loop, and Barnes & Noble's response was *schwerfällig*—ponderous.[30]

Toys"R"Us also found itself made to look ponderous. Bezos's chaotic and costly foray into the toy business looked insane during the Christmas season of 1999, as Amazon tangled up its own warehouses, exhausted its staff, and bled money. Viewed from the Toys"R"Us position, though, Amazon had achieved something enviable: it had happy customers and had established itself as a great place to shop online for toys.

ToysRUs.com, meanwhile, had been cleared out of the best toys by Amazon's own buyers. A couple of days before Christmas, the media carried headlines such as "Toys'R'Us Falling Short on Christmas Deliveries"; the next summer, the Federal Trade Commission fined Toys"R"Us $350,000 for not keeping shoppers informed about shipping delays over Christmas. Several other companies were fined for similar reasons. Amazon wasn't among them. It had lost far more money in its pre-Christmas scramble for stock than Toys"R"Us had been fined, but it had gained something much more valuable: consumers who remembered that while Toys"R"Us had let them down at Christmas, Amazon had delivered the goods.[31]

These slow or clumsy responses from Amazon's competitors weren't simply a matter of underestimating a new entrant: they continued after Amazon became an established player. When Amazon was rumored to be launching its Kindle e-reader in 2007, Len Riggio's brother Stephen was the CEO of Barnes & Noble. Scarred by an earlier costly experiment with primitive e-reader technology, he was in no hurry: "Certainly there's an opportunity to get back into the business, but we think it's small at this moment and probably will be small for the next couple of years. When the market is there, we'll be there."[32]

Schwerfällig.

Publishers also realized that they had blundered: in their negotiations over e-book rights with Amazon, they had failed to specify a minimum price at which Kindle e-books would be offered for sale.

Amazon announced a loss-making price of $9.99, far cheaper than a $30 hardback. At that price, people were clamoring for Kindles.[33] Yet again Amazon created chaos that threatened to overwhelm it, selling out of Kindles in hours, before discovering that it was impossible to manufacture fresh stock because of a problem with a supplier.

Viewed in isolation, Amazon looked laughable and amateurish—as did Rommel's thrust across Cyrenaica. But step back and consider the entire marketplace and it becomes clear that, however messily, Amazon had outflanked its rivals. By Christmas 2009, Amazon had a market share in e-books of around 90 percent.[34]

One can tell almost exactly the same story about Amazon's initially baffling venture into cloud computing: a crazy rush, a series of early technical problems, a loss-making price. Then within a few years, Amazon, a mere bookseller, was the dominant player in cloud computing, and analysts were pronouncing that Amazon Web Services was a more valuable business than Amazon's online retailing operation. The opportunity had been there to take, but the titans of the industry, IBM, Google, Apple, and Microsoft, had all hesitated at the prospect of a costly battle with the upstart.[35]

Again and again, we see Amazon moving quickly, losing money, struggling to cope with the demand it created, and in the end, dominating a market. Yet because of Amazon's decisiveness and its tolerance for creating and then navigating an almighty mess, it left *schwerfällig* competitors outmaneuvered and gasping to catch up.

From Rommel's half-formed expeditionary force against the might of the British Empire, to Bezos taking on Barnes & Noble, to Donald Trump targeting the Bush dynasty—the messy strategy has been embraced by the underdog. This is no coincidence. Maintaining momentum is exhausting; constantly improvising at speed is terribly risky. There is nothing in Boyd's theory that says a strong force cannot act swiftly and confusingly, getting inside an enemy's OODA loop. Yet it rarely seems to happen that way: few people are willing to take the messy path if a tidier approach of organizing, preparing, and coordinating looks like it might deliver victory.

Messy improvisation doesn't guarantee success. It does, however, guarantee that there will be mistakes, recriminations, and stress along the way. Erwin Rommel's swashbuckling style was a catastrophic failure when he tried to storm the heavily fortified port of Tobruk and was thrown back by 27,000 veteran Australian defenders. Careful planning might have broken through, but Rommel relied, as he usually did, on speed and energy, throwing his men into hopeless situations until his own generals refused to obey him. Again, these failures are intimately tangled up with the way Rommel conjured his successes. His tactics were designed to rout his enemies through sheer dynamism; they often succeeded brilliantly, but proved costly on the few occasions that they failed.

Jeff Bezos's fast-and-messy strategy causes him constant headaches. Consider the time, in the spring of 2013, that a third party on Amazon's UK website started offering T-shirts with slogans such as KEEP CALM AND RAPE A LOT, the result of recklessly designed software churning out hypothetical T-shirts and listing them on Amazon to see what would sell. Amazon's website has also offered spam books, full of nonsense or plagiarized wholesale from existing works.[36] In January 2015, police raided Amazon offices in Japan, investigating the alleged sale of child pornography by third-party retailers on the Amazon website. And in the summer of 2015, Amazon discovered that it was selling a magazine produced by and promoting the murderous group Daesh, better known to Westerners as ISIS.[37]

Embarrassing episodes are an almost unavoidable by-product of the messy way in which Amazon lets third parties hawk their goods on the Amazon website. As the designer Tim Maly comments, "Amazon isn't a store, not really. Not in any sense that we can regularly think about stores. It's a strange pulsing network of potential goods, global supply chains, and alien associative algorithms with the skin of a store stretched over it, so we don't lose our minds."[38]

Amazon's experiments with third-party sellers began with Amazon auctions—"That didn't work out very well," admits Bezos[39]—and then Z-shops, and finally Marketplace. Marketplace drove Amazon's own category managers crazy because they found themselves undercut *on their own website* by third-party sellers; meanwhile it leads to the never-ending risk that a third-party seller will do something embarrassing—such as sell pro-rape T-shirts—on the Amazon site, right beneath the Amazon logo.

Bezos has been willing to keep experimenting and keep taking chances, no matter how much hassle those experiments might cause within Amazon, or how ugly they might sometimes seem outside. And so far, his messy strategy seems to be working. Amazon Marketplace accounted for almost half the items sold on Amazon in 2014, and analysts speculate that it may be a fundamentally more profitable business than Amazon's regular retail operation.[40] Although Amazon's relentless tempo has kept profits slim, the company is a triumph from a financial point of view. When the *Harvard Business Review* conducted a statistical review of the most successful living chief executives in America, few of the top CEOs were household names. (John Martin of Gilead Sciences? David Pyott of Allergan?) Howard Schultz of Starbucks was down in fifty-fourth place. Steve Jobs was dead. But Jeff Bezos? Bezos was number one.[41]

So if you're in some kind of contest, and you feel the potential benefits of the messy approach outweigh the risks and costs, then what does it take to get inside your opponent's OODA loop—to make him seem *schwerfällig*?

For a lesson, let's turn to a man who played Rommel at his own game in 1941–1942, giving him some of his biggest headaches in North Africa—a man who struck almost at will at Rommel's supply lines, and so mysteriously that he took on a mythical persona: the Germans named him "The Phantom Major."

The Phantom Major's real name was David Stirling. He dreamed up the idea for a tiny, hand-picked force while in a hospital bed, having nearly broken his back in a parachute drop gone wrong. On discharge, he immediately set about attempting to get his idea approved.

In Cairo, Stirling limped up to the Middle East Headquarters of the British Army, a gangling, six-foot-five giant of a man on a pair of crutches. Lacking a security pass, he amiably tried to bluff his way past the sentry. After failing, he hobbled over to rest against a nearby tree and, when the sentry was distracted, slipped through a gap in the fence and lurched in a hobbling sprint across the forecourt. By the time the sentry noticed, Stirling was slipping through the front door.

Inside, Stirling barged into offices at random and pitched his idea to the first officer he found. Stirling argued that a small group of talented men could be dropped by parachute behind the German and Italian front lines, and they could destroy Rommel's air support in a surprise attack.[42] Unfortunately, the first officer he met knew and disliked the easily recognizable giant: Stirling had fallen asleep during one of his lectures. Not only did the officer dismiss Stirling's idea, he promised to crush it. But then, another opportunity—the sentry post phoned to report the security breach, and as the officer picked up the phone, Stirling vanished.

The next man Stirling found was a senior officer, General Sir Neil Ritchie, who was far more impressed with Stirling and his ideas.

Stirling's detachment was soon assembled and training for its first parachute drop. Its name: Special Air Service, or SAS.[43]

Stirling's audacious raid on his own headquarters* demonstrates some of the principles of messy tactics. First, get yourself into a position of opportunity: Stirling didn't know which officers he might meet if he broke into British headquarters, but he knew he'd meet somebody. Jeff Bezos felt much the same way about the early Web: it was impossible to predict how it might evolve, but clearly something exciting would be possible.

Second, improvise your way around obstacles. The sentry didn't buy his excuses, so Stirling sneaked past him instead. The first officer he met despised Stirling and his plan, so Stirling quickly found someone else to persuade.

Third: speed counts for a great deal. Both Stirling's break-in and his successful briefing to General Ritchie were possible because he moved faster than the people who were trying to stop him.

An unexpected corollary of this third principle is that while your team should understand their broad goals, they shouldn't waste time trying to coordinate with one another. Stirling was happy to split his forces and let them operate independently. So was Rommel. Perhaps surprisingly, so too was Jeff Bezos, who notoriously once told his management team to spend less time communicating.[44] Bezos's point was that small teams should get on with achieving things rather than

---

*This wasn't the only time Stirling penetrated the defenses of his own military during the North Africa campaign. Once, starved for equipment, Stirling's men burgled what they needed from some well-equipped New Zealanders who seemed to have ready access to replacements; when challenged as to why they were loading up truckloads of equipment in the middle of the night, the soldiers bluffed their way out of the situation. And when Stirling's plan to destroy German planes in a surprise attack was criticized by an air force captain, he bet the critic ten pounds he could sneak undetected into the British airfield at Heliopolis, near Cairo, and plant pictures of bombs on all the planes. Although the sentries at Heliopolis had been warned what was planned, David Stirling won his bet and was rewarded with a cordial letter and a check for his winnings. He later rehearsed a naval attack by planting fake bombs on British ships at Suez. See Virginia Cowles, *The Phantom Major: The Story of David Stirling and the SAS Regiment* (1958; Barnsley, England: Pen and Sword Books, 2010), pp. 35–36, 123; Gavin Mortimer, *The SAS in World War II* (Oxford: Osprey, 2011), p. 16.

constantly checking with one another. For much the same reason, John Boyd opposed "synchronization," once a big idea in the U.S. military. Boyd argues that synchronization was for watches, not for people: trying to synchronize activities wasted time and left everyone marching at the pace of the slowest.[45]

The early SAS missions follow all three principles. The first operation, a parachute drop in the teeth of "the most spectacular thunderstorm in local memory," was a disaster in which more than half his men were killed or captured.[46] Stirling simply changed tactics, abandoning the parachute idea and deciding instead to raid through the deep desert with experienced navigators in trucks.

In the first truck-borne attack, the convoy was spotted on the way to the target by Italian planes. Rather than call off the mission, Stirling split his forces to attack two separate airfields. One attack failed because the planes had flown off, but the other—led by his second-in-command, Paddy Mayne—was a big success. Mayne's men had machined-gunned the officer's mess, and then while the firefight raged had planted incendiary bombs that destroyed almost every plane on the airfield.[47]

Stirling and Mayne decided that they would have been even more successful if they had spent less time scouting around. Such scouting improved their knowledge of the target, but in both cases it had let their enemy prepare and respond. On future missions they resolved to move in quickly and silently, even without full knowledge of the target, because that would achieve total surprise. Speed and shock were more important than careful preparation.[48]

Sneak attacks behind enemy lines were an accepted part of warfare long before Stirling's SAS was formed, and didn't always work well—the British Army Commandos, formed over a year before the SAS, were launching daring raids along the coast of France and Norway. But these raids operated on a different principle: hundreds or thousands of brave men were involved in each raid, and they were synchronized and planned to run like a machine. While there were some notable successes, there were many failures and casualty rates were enormously high. The commando attacks couldn't follow the messy approach of surprise and improvisation. They were too big. By trying to bulk up their fighting strength, they reduced their flexibility and stealth. Their enemy gained more from the commando's efforts to strike in force than the commandos themselves did.

In contrast, Stirling's men continued to adapt and improvise even after their tactics had been well honed. Consider an assault on the port of Bouerat, far behind enemy lines in North Africa, in the spring of 1942. Stirling planned to transport a canoe to the coast just outside the port, then paddle through the defenses in the dark, planting limpet mines on the gasoline tankers and other ships. After weeks of preparation and travel, Stirling's plans were shredded when his truck hit a pothole and the impact broke the canoe. All hope of attacking Bouerat's shipping had gone.

"We'll have to reorganize a little," he told his twenty men in a confident tone. "There are plenty of targets waiting for us at Bouerat. If we can't get the ships, we'll get the harbor installations instead."[49] In fact, he reassured the men, he'd been itching to attack land-based targets but just didn't have the time to do both jobs.

The way Stirling was telling the story to his men, losing the canoe was a blessing. And he was proved right. Over the course of the next few hours, his men spread out, planted bombs on pumping equipment, wrecked vast stores of food, destroyed a dozen supply trucks—and best of all, blew up nearly twenty fully loaded gasoline tanker trucks. This was a real blow against Rommel, perhaps even better than destroying tanker ships. In any case, the SAS also discovered that there had been no tankers docked at Bouerat that night. Had the canoe been intact, it would still have been useless.[50]

In a later attack, the SAS planted their incendiary bombs on a group of forty German planes.* Normally the bombs were reliable, but on this occasion they had been prepared incorrectly. Only half of them exploded, and the German ground crew were able to put out many of the fires.[51]

As they sat in the darkness within sight of the smoldering airfield, Mayne and Stirling hatched a plan to turn this setback into another opportunity. The SAS patrol had a jeep armed with anti-aircraft guns, and the targets were sitting around not far away. Why not just drive to the airfield and shoot the planes into splinters? They did exactly that, destroying twelve more German planes.

The improvised attack worked so well that in the future the SAS repeated it: eighteen to twenty jeeps armed with sixty-eight anti-aircraft guns drove in formation onto a German airfield and destroyed every plane they could see. All this was under the light of the full moon, poor conditions for the usual bomb-planting but perfect for close-formation jeep maneuvers.[52]

Much like Rommel, Bezos, and Trump, David Stirling followed a messy road in pursuit of victory. If the opportunity was there, he would seize it and figure out the details later. When he hit an obstacle, he would abandon his plan and start improvising a way around it. And he pursued speed and surprise. A coordinated, well-researched move might look good on paper, but it would be useless if it meant giving the enemy time to react.

David Stirling was eventually undone by the tidy-mindedness of his superiors. When the British High Command saw how well he was doing, they recalled him to Cairo and told him he was to

*The bombs themselves were an improvised mixture of plastic explosive, thermite, and lubricant oil. They were cooked up by Jock Lewes, an SAS man with a science degree from Cambridge. Lewes and Stirling had been assured by British Army explosives experts that the lightweight high-explosive incendiary bomb he wanted simply couldn't be made.

participate in something much grander and more coordinated: there would be far more men in the raid, and many more targets. All this would support a grand new assault against the Germans. Stirling tried his best to dissuade them, but it was hopeless. With so many people involved there was too much loose talk and the advance was conspicuous; the Germans saw the raids coming well in advance and the mission was a disaster.

Rommel's most famous defeat, at the battle of El Alamein, was also sealed by a rare piece of tidy-mindedness. Perhaps defeat was inevitable anyway: Rommel was on sick leave in Germany when the battle began, and his deputy was killed almost immediately; Rommel's British adversary, Montgomery, had much shorter supply lines, excellent air support, four times as many good tanks, and seven times as many men. But Rommel's undoing was a rare emphasis on careful logistical planning. Dreadfully short of fuel, Rommel insisted on knowing to the hour when and where tanker ships from Italy would be docking to supply his forces. He didn't know about Ultra and Bletchley Park, the top-secret codebreaking center; he never realized that every single one of those "unbreakable" coded messages was being decoded. Supplied with that tidy German schedule, the British air force destroyed most of the gasoline tankers, and Rommel's dynamic panzers were stranded. It's hard to get inside your enemy's OODA loop when he's reading your mail.

In 1943, Stirling was captured and sent to a German prisoner-of-war camp. He escaped, but it wasn't easy for the giraffe-limbed colonel to travel inconspicuously as an escapee, and he was recaptured. He escaped again, and was recaptured again. That happened at least four times, before he sat out the remainder of the war in Colditz. He was knighted in 1990, shortly before his death at the age of seventy-four.

Rommel met a more ironic end. In the last days of the Third Reich, two of Hitler's generals visited Rommel's home to inform him he had been implicated in a plot to assassinate the Führer.* They presented him with the offer of a cyanide capsule and a hero's funeral, as an alternative to public exposure and a show trial. Rommel briefly weighed his options, before realizing that for once, there was no opportunity for counterattack. He could not have known, as he swallowed the poison, that the order of service for his state funeral had already been prepared. The wreath for his coffin had been delivered and stood ready at the local army barracks, waiting only for the final element: Field Marshal Rommel's corpse. Sometimes the forces of careful forward planning cannot be defeated.[53]

*From a modern perspective, it would be comforting to believe that Rommel had a hand in the attempt on Hitler's life. There is little evidence for this, although from a Nazi viewpoint Rommel was still a traitor: he was hoping to meet with his old foe Montgomery and negotiate terms for peace.

6

Incentives

"You wouldn't need a large army. You'd need a small SWAT team."

The Prime Minister and the Paramedic: The Pitfalls of Imposing Tidy Targets on a Messy World

In his decade as British prime minister, Tony Blair was eager to improve the performance of the National Health Service. The NHS is a vast government-funded health care organization that British voters adore in principle for providing free health care to all, but fret about in practice, because treatment is sometimes patchy and slow to materialize. Mr. Blair made the NHS a political priority and introduced a system of targets to hold NHS providers accountable. One of those targets was that when patients called their NHS doctor, they would be given an appointment within forty-eight hours.

The target was soon to rebound upon the prime minister. During the election campaign of 2005, the smooth-talking Blair found himself floundering when confronted by an ordinary voter in a televised discussion. Diana Church's complaint was simple: Her doctor refused to book a follow-up appointment in a week's time. "You have to sit on the phone for three hours in the morning trying to get an appointment because you are not allowed to ask for the appointment before that," she protested, as the prime minister looked confused. She then explained why.

Mrs. Church and her doctor had both seen the flaw that Blair had overlooked. A doctor could maximize her chances of hitting the forty-eight-hour waiting target by keeping her appointment book clear. Every advance booking was a potential obstacle to an urgent case, so advance bookings were simply prohibited. Instead, each patient had to call the clinic, wait on hold, and hope to get through on a day-by-day basis. Those who succeeded would almost certainly get an appointment within forty-eight hours. Those who did not would not be recorded by the system because their request would never have been noted. The target became far more achievable for the doctors, even though the quality of service was falling apart.

When Blair suggested that Mrs. Church's experience might be atypical, the TV program's host turned to the audience to ask who else had experienced similar problems. A third of them raised their hands.

Blair, flustered, observed that "obviously it shouldn't work like that."[1]

Obviously.

In 1763, in what is now Germany, a man named Johann Gottlieb Beckmann assembled a team of workers. He equipped them with special utility belts: each belt had five leather pouches, and each pouch contained a known number of nails of a different color. The men formed a line and walked slowly through some wild forest, keeping abreast of one another as they surveyed their surroundings as though looking for a lost set of keys or the body of a murder victim.

The men were trying to count and assess every tree they passed. Each tree was assigned a size of one to five. Into each tree was hammered a colored nail representing that size. When the men had finished their carefully calibrated march across the densely wooded terrain, they emptied the contents of their pouches and counted the nails that remained. Simple arithmetic revealed how many trees, and of what size, the tangled forest contained.[2]

Forests are messy. If your interest in a forest is to stroll through it, that mess seems charming. Differences in the soil, the slope, where the sun and shadows fall, and the scars of old fires mean that ancient woodlands are a patchwork of different trees of different sizes, some gnarled and weatherworn, others hemmed in by undergrowth, yet others slim and sparse and painted with sunlight. However, if your interest in a forest is to sell the timber from it—or to levy taxes on what the timber is worth—the mess obscures what matters. It's difficult to count trees, or compare one tree with another as a potential source of wood, in a messy forest. Johann Gottlieb Beckmann was on a mission to tidy up.

Governments continue to be motivated by the idea that the better they comprehend the world, the better they will be able to control and exploit it. They have been joined by large corporations, which also see the value in quantifying and classifying our world. From high-resolution drone and satellite images, to geographically tagged photos and tweets, mobile phones that constantly ping their location to colossal databases, and the "Internet of things"—the idea that most of the objects around us will soon be capable of communicating their whereabouts and status—one way or another, we continue to wander through the world, size it up, and digitally hammer colored nails into it.

The trouble is that when we start quantifying and measuring the world, we soon begin to change the world to fit the way we measure it.

At first, the eighteenth-century scientific foresters limited themselves to trying to measure the forests, deploying integral calculus and experiments with woodpiles to estimate the volume of wood in a

Normalbaum, or "standard tree." The volume of wood, above all, was the metric of interest. Before long, though, it wasn't just the forest maps and tables of timber yields that looked tidy. The mess of the old forests began to be tidied up, too. The confusing patchwork of trees of various ages and species was replaced with stands of a particular species—the Norway spruce was popular—and of a particular age. The foresters lined up the rows to make the forests easier to survey, to police, and in due course to harvest. Dead trees were felled, rotting hulks dragged away, underbrush cleared. The *Normalbaum*, once a statistically convenient idealization of a tree, took physical form. The forests eventually came to resemble the neat abstractions of the map itself.

The project was influential and profitable. How could it not be? The forests had been both physically and intellectually a tangled, incomprehensible mess. Now both the forests and the statistical tables describing them were set out neatly in organized, legible rows and columns. But the local peasants lost out—they were no longer able to access fallen trees for firewood, saps for glues, medicines and firelighters, acorns to feed pigs, and many other resources too messy and trivial to register on the official surveys of the forest. And since these resources had never been registered in the first place, whatever the peasants lost did not officially count.

Official measures and targets can never measure the messy reality of the world perfectly, but they have enough power to change it. Since the measurement isn't perfect, the change may well be for the worse.

Tony Blair's plan for the NHS target was a top-down affair, and Beckmann's scientific forestry had the power of the state and of large landowners behind it. Sometimes, however, simply having a way to count things can be enough to trigger an arms race.

Consider the Apgar score. A minute or so after a baby is born in hospitals around the world, a nurse or obstetrician can, at a glance, give it marks out of ten for whether it seems to be thriving. The Apgar score includes two points for being pink, two points for crying, two points for a brisk pulse, and so on. The score was devised in the early 1950s by Virginia Apgar, an American anesthesiologist, and it's by no means absurd: it's quick and convenient, and a baby with a low Apgar score is more likely to suffer problems.[3]

But because the Apgar score allowed for tidy quantification, it had unintended consequences. As Atul Gawande explains in *The New Yorker*, the Apgar score "turned an intangible and impressionistic clinical concept—the condition of a newly born baby—into a number that people could collect and compare."

Doctors, a competitive bunch, wanted to improve their scores. Hospital administrators started taking an interest, too. "When chiefs of obstetrics services began poring over the Apgar results of their doctors and midwives, they started to think like a bread factory manager taking stock of how many loaves the bakers burned," writes Gawande. "They both want solutions that will lift the results of every employee, from the novice to the most experienced. That means sometimes choosing reliability over the possibility of occasional perfection."

Demanding procedures such as the use of forceps gave way to the more predictable use of the cesarean section, in which the mother's abdomen is sliced open to retrieve the baby. Done well, the forceps delivery can spare the mother a major piece of surgery. But the C-section is simple, routine, and easily taught. It's a tidy, one-size-fits-all approach, because no matter why a baby is stubbornly stuck, the C-section will get it out. C-sections are now used in almost a third of all deliveries in the United States. This is the logic of the factory floor, and it emerges once a simple score becomes available to the factory managers. But C-sections are no joke for the mother, who does not have her own Apgar score as she recovers from having her lower abdomen sliced open. Nudging doctors into performing C-sections was surely not what Virginia Apgar had intended.[4]

Or ponder what happened in the early 1990s, when New York and Pennsylvania introduced a system of "report cards," publicly disclosing how patients were faring at the hands of particular doctors and hospitals. Unlike the Apgar score, which was supposed to be a handy diagnostic for medical professionals, the report cards were designed to inform patients about whether their doctors knew one end of a stethoscope from the other. The U.S. health care system is built on the assumption that patients will choose the physicians they prefer, and that means that patients need information so that they can make informed choices. By telling patients, insurance companies, and primary care physicians how well particular surgeons were doing, the report cards were supposed to reward the skilled, punish the incompetent, and give improved incentives to both to raise their game.

Alas, there are many ways to win a game, and not all of them involve respecting the spirit of the rules. Four economists, David Dranove, Daniel Kessler, Mark McClellan, and Mark Satterthwaite, looked at the impact of these report cards on elderly patients who had suffered heart attacks. They discovered that the report cards had a most unwelcome side effect. Doctors were avoiding operations on seriously ill patients, preferring to operate on patients who did not need surgery at all.

This makes sense within the logic of the report card system. After all, who wants to operate on a very sick patient who may die and spoil your rating as a competent heart surgeon? And conversely, who is more likely to thrive after surgery than a patient who was in decent shape before the surgery began?[5]

Dranove and his colleagues concluded that, overall, the report card system was pushing doctors into performing more expensive treatments, but patients were sicker as a result. As Tony Blair might have said, obviously it shouldn't work like that.

Tony Blair's waiting-time target nudged family doctors into refusing routine appointments. Scientific forestry reduced biodiversity and hurt the welfare of local peasants. Virginia Apgar's newborn score tempted obstetricians to perform C-sections. Report cards encouraged cardiac surgeons to perform heart bypasses on patients who didn't need them. In each case, trying to measure performance—and sometimes making it an explicit target—had surprising and unwelcome side effects.

Three of these examples are from health care, which is no coincidence: health care is usually heavily regulated, and offers apparently clear outcomes (How long must I wait? Will I die?) floating on a thick swamp of unmeasurable complexity. Yet similar problems pop up in many other places.

For example, each year the *U.S. News & World Report* website ranks the best colleges in America. A popular element in such rankings is how selective a college is—after all, if a college turns down lots of applicants, it's reasonable to guess that it is popular and has high standards. But since every college administration wants to rise up the rankings, once the selectiveness of the college becomes part of those rankings, it can and will be gamed.

Northeastern University in Boston, for example, was reported in 2012 to be sending out 200,000 personalized letters to high school seniors, then following up those letters with six to eight e-mails, all to increase the number of applications it receives. It could then reject tens of thousands of applicants, boost its selectivity, and therefore rise in the USNWR rankings.[6]

An even simpler technique is to embrace a national standardized application form, the Common App, which allows students to apply to many colleges at once by filling out one form for electronic distribution to multiple colleges. Some colleges, including the University of Chicago, held out against such applications for a while, but found their selectivity rates suffered. When the University of Chicago began to accept standardized applications in 2007, thousands of students who had no hope of being accepted were able to apply to Chicago with the click of a mouse. Its acceptance rate fell and the university's selectivity score soared, helping to boost its ranking.[7]

In the UK, universities found a different target to game: the Research Excellence Framework, which is designed to measure the quality of academic research done and hand out public money to the top performers. A loophole quickly became apparent: a university department could get credit for research conducted by an academic on a part-time contract that demanded only 20 percent of full-time hours. Getting a full-time research credit for 20 percent of a full-time salary is a good deal—and universities promptly embraced it. An investigation by *Times Higher Education* revealed that in just two years, UK universities had increased their recruitment of staff on 20 percent hours by nearly two-thirds. For example, the University of Birmingham was recently rated as producing the best research in philosophy in the UK; skeptics pointed out that several of their staff were superstar academics who spent much of their time at Harvard and New York University.[8]

Moving from academia to international development, the Millennium Development Goals were a broad set of aspirations adopted by members of the United Nations in the year 2000. They were originally intended as an inspirational target to fight poverty in the world's poorest countries, but they quickly became used as a guide to which countries should receive development aid, and distortions swiftly emerged.[9] The most famous of the goals was to halve the extreme poverty rate in every country around the world. This turns out to be easier in a middle-income country such as Bulgaria or Mexico, where the extreme poverty rate might be just 2 percent, than in a destitute country where the extreme poverty rate is 20 percent. Just as Brian Eno confessed to scanning a list of strategies and choosing whatever looked easiest, the Millennium Development Goals presented a list of easy and difficult targets—and gave donors an incentive to funnel money away from the countries with the most serious problems. (Wiser donors resisted the temptation, but it is a shame that the temptation existed at all.)

What explains all these problems with reasonable-seeming measures? The fundamental problem was pithily summarized in 1975 by the title of an article in the *Academy of Management Journal*: "On the Folly of Rewarding A, While Hoping for B."[10] Apparently it's easy to make the mistake of setting the wrong target. Why is it so easy to make this mistake, though? Why not simply set the *right* target?

In 1995, Peter Smith, an economist at the University of York, attempted to provide an exhaustive list of all the ways in which targets might have unintended consequences. It's a sobering array of potential calamities.[11]

One cluster of headaches reflects the fact that targets tend to be simple, while the world is complicated. Anything specific enough to be quantifiable is probably too specific to reflect a messy situation. The Apgar score is an example of this: a newborn baby's Apgar score is not the only thing that matters, but because it is easy to measure, it looms large. It is easier to count trees in a forest than it is to measure biodiversity.

Or consider a bus driver who is rewarded for sticking to the timetable, and who keeps on time by driving past lines of passengers without stopping. These cases are all examples of tunnel vision, resulting from a target or measure that is too narrow.

In extreme cases, the target may not be just too narrow, but also downright misleading. David Dranove's study of cardiac report cards in New York and Pennsylvania shows this starkly. The report cards were supposed to measure whether a surgeon was good at performing heart bypass operations, but they inevitably also reflected how ill patients were before the operation started. The report cards were easily misunderstood by patients, and surgeons were being pulled into fixating on what would make those report cards look good—namely, finding healthier patients rather than improving their medical skills. A further irony is that when two statisticians, Harvey Goldstein and David Spiegelhalter, looked at the report card data, they concluded that the main determinant of patient survival rates wasn't the surgeon's skill—they were all broadly similar—but pure luck. A surgeon might be one of the most dangerous doctors one year, and one of the safest the next.[12]

Such tunnel vision may be related to a time period. This results in short-termism, where long-term investment is sacrificed in order to hit a short-term target. For example, a manager can skimp on training or maintenance, or just squeeze pay. In the short term, profits will rise; in the long term, the company will suffer. A wise manager understands this, but she may wish to hit her targets anyway. Then there is the "silo effect," where one department hits its targets by taking short cuts that damage other departments. In each case, we assume that by measuring one thing, we're really measuring everything. That is delusional. We hit the target, but miss the point.

Sometimes a target reflects yesterday's problems, not today's. The world tends to change faster than bureaucracies can keep up, which causes problems for any organization that has lashed itself to an unbending framework of performance measures. Imagine a company with targets for resolving queries from customers who phone the call center, but no target for dealing with a problem using the Web. The target demands that resources should be funneled to the call center, when they might be better used on the website. Anyone who wants to improve will have to ignore the target.

There are also two ways to sidestep a target completely: lying and cheating. It's sometimes possible to lie—miss your target, but say you hit it—and that sounds bad enough. But cheating, or "gaming"—where you cynically distort your behavior to hit the target—may be worse. The family doctors who refused to take advance appointments were gaming Tony Blair's target; patients might have been better served if the doctors had been able simply to ignore the target and lie about it when challenged.

Connoisseurs of unintended consequences may appreciate a particular episode in the history of the British National Health Service, where a clumsy target managed to trigger almost every single unintended consequence on Peter Smith's list.

The target was first set in the 1990s, then given much more political emphasis in the early twenty-first century. It was designed to improve how ambulance services responded to emergency calls. When an emergency call was made from an urban area, and the case was judged to be "immediately life-threatening," the target became active: the ambulance service had eight minutes to get to the scene.

The unintended consequences soon began to emerge.

The most obvious was the outright lie. This lie becomes obvious if one plots the data for reported response times on a graph. The graph rumbles gently along, showing an even distribution of response times.[13] And then something curious. The graph starts to rise sharply at 7 minutes and 50 seconds, reaching implausibly high levels at 7 minutes and 59 seconds, and soaring further at 8 minutes exactly.

Yet by an astonishing coincidence, hardly any calls were recorded as having taken 8 minutes and 1 second. After the fact, who can gainsay the call handler who says the ambulance hit the target rather than missing it by a second or two?

Such lies probably don't matter too much: they will not be the difference between life and death, because they don't affect what ambulance crews actually do. But other responses to the target were not so benign—these were the ones that involved "gaming," changing the behavior of the ambulance service in ways that made the target easier to hit but may well have harmed patients.

One problem was that "within eight minutes" turns out to be a poor substitute for "as soon as possible." Imagine an ambulance on route to a patient as the clock ticks away. Six minutes pass; then seven. Then eight minutes pass and the case has missed the target—"breached," as hard-bitten professionals would put it. Now what is to be done? The logic of the target dictates that the ambulance should now be rerouted to a patient who has not yet breached; the original patient no longer counts toward the target. He may find himself waiting indefinitely. The best defense against such grotesque abuse is the hope that professional ambulance crews would ignore the target—but that does not say much for the target's merits.

Another serious piece of gaming involved the definition of "life-threatening" cases. The definition varied widely across regional ambulance services and could easily be manipulated. The target gave ambulance services an incentive to say that a call wasn't urgent—because at that point they were spared from hitting the goal.

Ambulance services even changed their vehicles to flatter the target. Two paramedics in a single ambulance could be split and put onto motorbikes or even bicycles. That makes it more likely that a paramedic will arrive within eight minutes, but if the patient needs to be taken to the hospital, then a bicycle will not do the job.

There were also accusations of short-termism. Ambulance crews complained that rather than being based at the hospital, they were being sent out in their vehicles to face an uncomfortable wait through the night at strategic positions from where they might be able to reach an emergency more quickly. Patient care in the short term may have improved, but the crews' morale suffered.

Finally, an allegation that was widely suspected but never proved was that managers relocated ambulances to urban areas, where the targets were tough to hit, from rural areas, where the targets operated differently. The target wasn't designed to favor the cities over the countryside, but it may have had that effect.

The target, then, encouraged ambulance services to lie about the stopwatch, to reclassify urgent cases, to put ambulance crews in vehicles that weren't ambulances, to pull staff out of rural areas, to risk the health and morale of their paramedics, and to celebrate all of this as having hit their target.

For one simple, tidy target, that is quite a result.

What's the solution to the problem of the tidy-minded target? One possible approach is to make the targets more sophisticated, covering more measures with more attention to detail. An instructive example of this approach is the way that financial regulations have developed over the past three decades.

The first international agreement about how banks should be regulated to prevent financial crises was the Basel Accord of 1988, often known as Basel I.[14] It established standards for every internationally active bank in the world, setting a minimum threshold for how much capital the bank should have. Capital is what stands between a bank and bankruptcy: a bank with lots of capital can take large losses before becoming insolvent, whereas a bank that funds its activities by borrowing rather than using capital is far more vulnerable.* The Basel Accord was simply an international agreement that banks wouldn't borrow too much—or wouldn't become too highly "leveraged."†

While Basel I was celebrated as a first step toward financial stability, it was a crude rule because it did not do justice to the fact that different banks take very different risks. For example, a bank that lends $100 million to a Silicon Valley start-up is taking much more risk than a bank that lends $100 million to the U.S. government. It seems rash to have capital rules that are designed to safeguard against risks but which ignore what the risks might be.

Basel I did allow for five different categories of risk, and the capital requirement varied according to how much business the bank was doing in each of these five areas. But regulators soon concluded that five categories of risk weren't enough; their rules had been too simplistic and had too many loose ends. While banks were using cutting-edge computerized risk models based on oceans of digitized data, the Basel I capital requirements were so simple that they could be calculated with pen and paper. Banks were trying to push up against

---

*Roughly speaking, capital is money that the bank has from previous profits, or from shareholders. Capital is special because the bank isn't obliged to pay this money to anyone, unlike the deposits it has from customers, which those customers can withdraw at will, or money that the bank has borrowed from other banks or companies, which has to be paid back with interest on an agreed date. Shareholders aren't owed any specific amount at any particular time—just a slice of whatever the bank can spare, whenever it chooses to spare it. This matters if a bank loses money. Because a bank must repay its debts on schedule, a bank that relies on a lot of borrowing as a source of funds is always at risk of going bankrupt. A bank that relies more on capital has a bigger margin for error in tough times. Its shareholders will lose money but the bank itself will stay in business.

Imagine two banks, RiskyBank and SafeBank. Both banks have lent out $100 million, and in both cases, some of those loans have gone bad, so they are repaid only $98 million. That same $2 million loss bankrupts RiskyBank but not SafeBank. Why? The difference between the two banks is that RiskyBank borrowed $99 million of the $100 million it lent out, supplemented with just $1 million of capital, while SafeBank borrowed $90 million of the $100 million it lent out, supplemented with $10 million of capital. Both raised $100 million, both lent out that $100 million, and both lost $2 million. But RiskyBank is now out of business, because it cannot repay its debts. SafeBank, by contrast, can repay its debts by dipping into its capital. Its shareholders may be annoyed, but SafeBank is still up and running.

The quick way to describe this difference is to say that RiskyBank was highly "leveraged" at 99 times its capital; SafeBank was leveraged at only 9 times its capital. Leverage calls to mind the way a lever can turn small forces into big ones; a leveraged bank turns small profits into big gains for shareholders, but also turns small losses into a wipeout for shareholders, and bankruptcy.

†Arguably, how much capital a bank has is none of the regulator's business. In principle we might expect market forces to keep banks in line, because nobody will want to lend money to a highly leveraged bank. In practice, we have not seen this idea put to the test, because regulators have taken the view that banking is too important to leave to pure market forces.

the regulatory limits, maximizing their leverage and looking for wiggle room within the rules.* Given the gap in sophistication between banks' commercial-risk models and the simple Basel rules, that wiggle room was easy to find. Banks would seek out investments that the rules defined as boring and safe, but which banks themselves knew were exciting, risky, and therefore potentially very profitable.

And so a series of regulatory upgrades were published in 2004, embracing a far more sophisticated definition of risk. While Basel I had been just 30 pages long, Basel II was 347 pages long and piggybacked on the banks' own risk models, with literally millions of different data-driven, market-tested risk parameters.

The loose ends had been tidied up, but in retrospect Basel II was not a success. The most complicated financial stability agreement in history was promptly followed by the most complicated financial crisis in history. Why? It would be absurd to identify a single cause, but it is clear that the now familiar problems that bedeviled health care system targets also corrupted Basel II.

Because Basel II orbited around the concept of risk-weighting, banks could take on more leverage if they could find assets with a very low risk-weighting. The lowest possible risk-weighting was zero: if a bank could find an investment with a risk-weighting of zero, yet a decent return, Basel II encouraged the bank to borrow vast sums to sink into that investment. But what kind of asset had zero risk on paper, yet paid a fat return to investors? The answer: Greek government bonds. Basel rules were set by rich governments, and so—naturally enough—they shaped them to suit themselves. European Union banks were allowed to lend money to European Union governments with a zero risk-weighting.[15]

---

*Leverage is risky, so why were banks so keen to minimize the amount of capital they held? The cynical answer is that senior bankers made more money when the bank took more risks. A simpler answer is that senior bankers were overconfident, not realizing how much risk they were taking. Both answers are likely to be true.

So, catastrophically, banks could borrow huge sums and lend that money to Greece, which was risk-free on paper but (curiously) paid a hefty return. While the rules said that Greece was risk-free, the high return on Greek debt showed that the market thought otherwise. This was typical of the perversity of the Basel rules: they rewarded banks for making investments that had low risk on paper but high market return, which implied that the true risk was high. The Basel rules encouraged banks to seek out all the places where the rules seemed to be wrong—and to pour as much money as possible into those blind spots.

This demand for safe-on-paper assets encouraged complex financial engineering, producing theoretically safe investments on the back of highly risky subprime mortgage lending. These investments had "black swan" properties—perhaps by accident or perhaps by design, they squeezed risk into the worst cases, meaning that the assets were usually safe, and had a track record of looking very stable, but had a modest chance of blowing up catastrophically.

A final grim consequence of Basel was that the perverse incentives were the same for everybody. Rather than competing in a natural way, investing in real projects all over the world, banks tended to try to squeeze through the same loopholes—lending money to Greece, buying subprime derivatives—and so all found themselves in distress at the same time for the same reason.

Has follow-up legislation solved the problem? Perhaps; the post-crisis Basel III agreement is more conservative than Basel II. But it is also more complex. Basel III is twice as long as Basel II, and domestic legislation such as the Dodd-Frank Act in the United States is even longer—tens of thousands of pages. The lesson of Basel II seems to be that making targets more complex doesn't stop their being gamed—it merely leads to their being gamed in more complex and unpredictable ways.

• • •

A few years after the crisis had broken, one of central banking's most imaginative figures asked a daring question. His name is Andy Haldane; he is chief economist of the Bank of England. His question was this: What if these ever more refined attempts to quantify risk were useless—or worse?[16]

Haldane reviewed what was known about banks that had gone bankrupt in the crisis, and how safe they had looked earlier according to the various sophisticated criteria laid out in Basel II and Basel III. He compared those numbers with the crudest possible measure of risk: Had the bank borrowed a lot of money?

At an annual convocation of central bankers at Jackson Hole, Wyoming, Haldane presented his conclusions: every single way you sliced the data, the highly rational, hyper-quantified risk management methods were less effective than a crude rule of thumb: "Beware indebted banks." Perhaps Basel I hadn't been too crude in dividing leverage into only five categories; perhaps instead, it had been too clever in dividing it up at all.

Rules of thumb like Haldane's have proved surprisingly effective in a variety of environments: the psychologist Gerd Gigerenzer has assembled a large library of simple heuristics that rival or even outperform complex decision rules that are widely thought to be theoretically optimal. Here are just three examples: avalanches, heart attacks, and investment portfolios.

Avalanches are difficult to forecast; they emerge from subtle and complex interactions among snowfall, temperature, slope shape, and other factors. The avalanches that do the most damage are rare and thus hard to predict, putting wilderness skiers at risk. Yet it turns out that a solution exists. A simple method called the "obvious clues" checklist, easily memorized by skiers, has been shown to be a surprisingly good safeguard. For example: Have avalanches been reported in the area in the past forty-eight hours? Does the surface of the snow show signs of melting? Has there been a new snowfall or rain shower in the past forty-eight hours? If several of these "obvious clues" are present, skiers should avoid the slope in question. When researchers reviewed a database of 751 avalanche accidents in the United States, they concluded that in most cases, several clear risk factors were present, and the "obvious clues" method would have prevented tragedy.[17]

The parallel with the banking crisis seems clear. Andy Haldane's analysis found a single "obvious clue" that a bank was vulnerable—how much it relied on borrowed money rather than its own capital.

If simple rules can predict avalanches, perhaps they can also predict heart attacks? Consider the decision that a doctor has to make when a patient shows up at the emergency room with severe chest pains. If patients are in the early stages of a heart attack, they need to go straight to a specialist coronary care unit. But that is expensive, possibly dangerous—since hospitals are a breeding ground for drug-resistant infections—and also inconvenient for any patient who really just needs an indigestion tablet and a rest. There are many tests that could be done, many different possible ways in which the diagnosis could be made.[18]

Researchers at the University of Michigan, led by Lee Green, looked at doctors' decision making in these situations.[19] They found that doctors tend to err on the side of caution—so much so, they were just as likely to refer patients who weren't having heart attacks as those who were. They might as well have been rolling dice.

The researchers responded by putting together a complex diagnostic guide: a table of probabilities, packaged with a handy pocket calculator. The guide required doctors to run some tests, consult the table, tap the numbers into the calculator, and thus produce an estimate of the probability that the patient needed urgent coronary care. This guide had some success: it enabled doctors to cut back dramatically on their mistaken referrals, while only slightly increasing the number of heart attack sufferers who were wrongly passed over. That is a painful trade-off, of course, but medicine is full of them. The bigger problem was that the guide was too complex to appeal to doctors.

So Lee Green and his colleagues developed a simple decision tree, throwing away most of the detail in the diagnostic table and focusing on a few obvious clues. The decision tree asks three yes/no questions: First, does the patient display a particular anomaly on a heart monitor? If so, straight to the coronary care unit. Otherwise, question two: Is the patient's main complaint about chest pain? If not, then there is no need for coronary care. But if so, then a third question tells the doctor to look for one of five obvious clues—any one of them is enough to send the patient to coronary care.

The decision tree can be written on a postcard. Unlike the sophisticated algorithm, it requires no calculator. But it works. In fact it seems to work better than either the doctors *or* the complex diagnostic tool, referring almost every single patient with a heart attack—even more than the defensively minded doctors—yet generating fewer false positives than the diagnostic. More important, it saves time and effort in an urgent situation—which means that unlike the complex diagnostic, it gets used.*

A similar story can be told about the very different problem of choosing an optimal blend of investments—for example, when we set aside money for a pension. In 1952, a young finance professor, Harry Markowitz, worked out a sophisticated method for selecting the optimal financial portfolio, either minimizing risk for any given expected

*The fact that the simple decision tree outperformed the diagnostic tool shows that the diagnostic algorithm could have been better designed. However, Gigerenzer's research does suggest that in many cases, even the best complex algorithms will have only a modest advantage over a well-chosen rule of thumb.

return or maximizing expected return for any given risk. The basic idea is simple: If you buy shares in an umbrella company and a maker of sunglasses, you will be fine in all weathers. The details, of course, are cleverer—clever enough to win Markowitz a Nobel Memorial Prize in Economics.

There's a funny story about Markowitz, though: Shortly after publishing his theory, he started a job with a retirement savings plan, and he had to decide on the optimal blend of investments for his own retirement. This was the perfect opportunity to put his brilliant new theory to use. He passed up that opportunity, and instead, put half of his money in stocks and half in bonds. People often find this tale a perfect illustration of the idea that economic theory is far too sophisticated for humans to understand—even the human who developed it.

Yet the Markowitz story contains an irony within an irony. Markowitz the small investor was right all along; it was Markowitz the Nobel Prize–winning theorist who was wrong. The reason for this is that the Markowitz theory is perfect when fed infinite amounts of data, but it may fall far short in practice, with more limited information.

For example, consider stocks in two oil companies. The Markowitz theory assumes we understand how those stock prices tend to fluctuate relative to each other, and will then recommend an efficient blend of the two. But how *do* those stocks fluctuate relative to each other? Looking back, we see periods when the stocks move together: the oil price rises, the share prices rise; the oil price falls, the share prices fall. But at other times—perhaps a major oil spill such as the Deepwater Horizon disaster in 2010—the company involved with the spill may see shares crash, while its rivals do fine. And while history is some guide, it's not perfect—especially not when estimating the likelihood of rare events. (By definition, history will offer few examples of rare events—perhaps no examples at all.)

Recent research shows that when limited data are available,

Markowitz's rule of thumb—divide assets equally between categories such as stocks, bonds, and property—outperforms Markowitz's Nobel-worthy theory. What do we mean by "limited" data? Remarkably, anything less than five hundred years' worth is probably limited enough to tip the balance in favor of the simple rule of thumb.[20]

Again, there's a parallel here with the Basel II rules. Like Markowitz's Nobel-winning theory, they required a lot of data to be robust. Those data weren't available. The risk models that banks were using in the early 2000s—that Basel II encouraged them to use—were able to draw on only a few years' worth of data yet involved hundreds of thousands of parameters. These were enormously complex statistical structures built on the shallowest of foundations.

The problem here is known as "overfitting"—what happens when a detailed statistical analysis slavishly follows historical data. Imagine a scatterplot graph with a line or a smooth curve drawn through a cloud of dots to pick out the trend. An overfitted line looks more like a dot-to-dot puzzle, trying to pick out a pattern in the incidence of heart attacks or avalanches that isn't really there. When new data arrive—new dots—they are unlikely to be anywhere near the wriggling curve. The complex rules are like the overfitted line: designed with too much hindsight, but poor foresight. A cruder rule—draw a straight line or a smooth curve—doesn't fit the old data so well but will often do better when fresh data arrive.

Making the targets more complex can't be the right answer. A complex measure is just as likely to be gamed, and a simple rule of thumb is often an accurate guide to what is happening.

The problem, then, comes back to gaming. Avalanches and heart attacks can't game a system to recognize them—they may be dangerous, but they aren't dishonest. But what would happen if Basel's regulators simply concluded from Andy Haldane's analysis that they should rip up hundreds of pages of rules and replace them with one about limiting the amount a bank could borrow relative to its capital? We'd be back to Tony Blair's doctor appointments. Somehow or other, banks would find a way to subvert the simple leverage rule.

Just as "How much has a bank borrowed?" is a good rule of thumb only when the banks aren't trying to meet this target, "How many patients can get an appointment in forty-eight hours?" is probably a good rule of thumb for judging the overall quality of doctor surgeries that don't know they're being judged on it. "How many ambulances arrive within eight minutes?" is likely an excellent proxy for how well ambulance services are being run, provided they aren't actually trying to meet that target. But as soon as we formalize a rule of thumb into a target, it becomes a source of distortion.

Fortunately, there is an old solution to this problem—and it's familiar to every student.

Think about how examinations work. You study for months, or years, knowing that only a tiny fraction of the knowledge you're accumulating will come in handy when you sit for your final exam. As the philosopher Jeremy Bentham put it in 1830, when pondering civil service exams, the deliberate ambiguity as to what might be asked had the effect of "impossibilizing the knowledge" of how to game the examination. The only response to having one's knowledge of the test "impossibilized": work hard and try to be good at everything.[21]

The answer is neither the weighty rule book of Basel nor one simple rule of thumb. Instead, we should be defining many rules of thumb, and deliberately leaving it ambiguous as to which will be used in any given situation. With ambulances, for example, you might keep "percentage of calls answered in 8 minutes" as one possible metric to check, and add some more: percentage of calls answered in 12 minutes, or 20 minutes, or 6 minutes, 37 seconds; proportion of patients who die having not been classified as "immediately life-threatening"; consistency of service across rural and urban areas; and so on. You could define hundreds of rules of thumb like this. It would be impossible to game them all, because gaming any one would reduce performance on others. But an ambulance service that was generally well run should be doing well on most of them.

It would be foolish to try to check every one of these rules of thumb, because a regulator's inspection would end up being both impossibly bureaucratic and absurdly superficial. There's another risk: if ambulance services knew how all the many targets were weighted to produce an overall score, they would find a way to game that, too. Instead, for each assessment, the regulator would choose a few measures at random and examine them in depth.

Banks are already subject to a tough examination called a "stress test." Stress tests are disaster scenarios in which a bank calculates what would happen in certain gloomy situations—for example, if interest rates rose sharply, or if there was a sudden currency devaluation or a collapse in the housing market. These tests are too predictable, however, like an exam paper with the questions announced in advance. Regulators in the United States have started to notice that banks have made some specific, narrow bets—for example, that mortgage-related debt will do very badly—that look unprofitable, but which pay off gloriously in specific stress-test scenarios.[22]

Applying the Jeremy Bentham solution—the solution favored by examiners all over the world—simply means that the stress test has to be unpredictable. Andy Haldane, chief economist of the Bank of England, thinks that's quite possible.

"You would turn up unannounced, in other words not on an annual schedule, to a financial firm and you would say, 'Could you show us your stress tests for'"—Haldane pauses, reaching for an example—"'for your leveraged loan portfolio?'"

Rather than give the bank months to cook up a response, the regulator would insist on results within hours. If the bank produced a good answer promptly, "Thumbs-up, see you in six months' time for your next spot check. It might not be six months, by the way. It might be tomorrow, or might be a year from now."

And if the timing of the test is deliberately vague, so is the punishment. "If they give a bad answer, that's a black mark. I'm not sure what a black mark means but, you know, why not three strikes and you're out? It might be okay not to know your leveraged loans today, but if you don't know your emerging market portfolio tomorrow, or your sovereign government exposure the day after tomorrow, are you really the right person to be chief executive of this company?"[23]

Andy Haldane isn't the only person to argue for randomness in targets. A senior health care regulator under Tony Blair, Gwyn Bevan, has made much the same case for ambiguous or unpredictable targets in the UK's National Health Service. So has David Spiegelhalter, one of the UK's leading medical statisticians. And so has Andrew Dilnot, the head of the UK Statistics Authority.[24]

U.S. bank regulators have dipped their toes in the water of ambiguity, requesting information from banks without telling them how that information will be assessed. That's good. But in general, financial regulators are not rushing toward the idea of randomness and ambiguity in their rules. Says Haldane, "I think we're moving away from it."

So why don't regulators embrace the constructive ambiguity of randomly timed tests of arbitrarily chosen areas, which is likely to be much more effective than tidy, predictable checklists?

One possible concern is that ambiguous regulation could give too much discretionary power to the regulator. But that's not necessarily true. After all, any exam system has safeguards: a syllabus that lists the kind of topics that will be tested; a consistent history of previous exam papers to establish context; independent external examiners who provide a reality check; an appeals process. A similar system can work for regulating areas such as health care and finance. If the regulators set out their priorities clearly, outline the sorts of questions that might be asked, and have to justify their actions in the case of an appeal, then the scope for abuse—either by the regulator, or the companies they regulate—is greatly reduced.

A more cynical explanation is that regulators themselves often have a conflict of interest that gives them the perverse incentive to create a system that can be gamed. Government departments that are responsible for testing how well schools or hospitals are doing also tend to be responsible for making sure they do well; financial regulators are tasked not only with finding out how safe banks are, but also with keeping the banking system safe. When Tony Blair introduced the waiting time target for family doctors, he must have hoped that he would generate statistics that would impress the voters. Naturally, such regulators will be attracted to approaches that can produce a neat series of data showing an improvement with the least amount of effort and risk. The answer here is to split, as far as possible, the role of testing the system from the role of making the system better.

Perhaps the simplest reason, though, is our general fear of messy ambiguity. We humans are attracted by the tidiness of both the regulator and the regulated knowing exactly the procedures that must be followed and the boxes that must be ticked off.

"It's a rather messier approach to supervision," admits Andy Haldane of his alternative vision. "But it can be done on an administrative shoestring. You wouldn't need a large army. You'd need a small SWAT team."

The mobility and unpredictability of the SWAT team is what many regulators desperately need.

• • •

In September 2015, Volkswagen, one of the largest car manufacturers in the world, was caught cheating on U.S. emissions tests. Public opinion was shocked. Shares in the German car giant plunged; the boss, Martin Winterkorn, resigned; and Germans worried that the reputation of every manufacturer in the nation might be tarnished by association with VW.[25]

How was such cheating possible? Manufacturers must submit to a program of laboratory tests designed to ensure that the engines emit low levels of nitrogen oxides, gasses that can cause a variety of local pollution problems—acid rain, smog, and soot, damaging agricultural crops and causing breathing difficulties in elderly people and children, sometimes with fatal results. The tests are tough and the standards are high. But the tests are also absurdly predictable—a series of predetermined maneuvers on a treadmill.

As a result, VW was able to cheat. The company's cars—tricked out with computers and sensors as all modern engines are—would recognize the distinctive choreography of a laboratory test. They would switch to a special testing mode, one where a nitrogen oxide trap in the exhaust system would filter out the pollutants, but at the cost of a sluggish, fuel-hungry engine. Outside the laboratory, the engine would be zippier and more efficient, but would spout vastly more nitrogen oxides, perhaps twenty or thirty times more.

What VW did is strikingly similar to what regulators observed in banking, with banks buying unprofitable assets with the specific aim of performing well on Federal Reserve stress tests. The banks had a "special mode" to do well on those tests just as VW had a special mode that flattered its emissions. The difference is that what is illegal in a car is apparently legal in a bank.

But the real scandal is not that VW found a way to cheat a predictable test. It is that the regulators kept the test so predictable when they were perfectly well aware of the problem. In 1998, the U.S. Environmental Protection Agency found evidence that truck manufacturers were using special modes to fool emissions tests. The EPA successfully acted against seven truck manufacturers, including Volvo, Renault, Caterpillar, and Mack—manufacturers that collectively produced almost every diesel truck engine in the United States. Not much seems to have changed. (Smug Europeans may wish to note that EU regulations are widely regarded as being even slacker.)

VW was not caught because the EPA introduced yet more predictable rules. They were exposed when a nonprofit group, the International Council on Clean Transportation, looked into the emissions of VW cars. The ICCT wasn't a hostile prosecutor; it fully expected to find a clean car. But it did something simple and unexpected: it strapped emissions monitors to some VW cars and drove them from San Diego to Seattle. That was enough to reveal the scam.

The world's toughest exam isn't so tough if everyone is carrying a cheat sheet. A simple question from an unexpected direction can prove far more searching.

7

Automation

"But what's happening?"

Flight 447 and the Jennifer Unit: When Human Messiness Protects Us from Computerized Disaster

When a sleepy Marc Dubois walked into the cockpit of his own airplane, he was confronted with a scene of confusion. The plane was shaking so violently that it was hard to read the instruments. An alarm was alternating between a chirruping trill and an automated voice: *STALL STALL STALL.* His junior copilots were at the controls. In a calm tone, Captain Dubois asked, "What's happening?"[1]

Copilot David Robert's answer was less calm. "We completely lost control of the airplane, and we don't understand anything! We tried everything!"

Two of those statements were wrong. The crew were in control of the airplane. One simple course of action could have ended the crisis they were facing, and they had not tried it. But David Robert was certainly right on one count: he didn't understand what was happening.

Air France Flight 447 had begun straightforwardly enough—an on-time takeoff from Rio de Janeiro at 7:29 p.m. on May 31, 2009, bound for Paris. Hindsight suggests the three pilots had their vulnerabilities. Pierre-Cédric Bonin, thirty-two, was young and inexperienced. David Robert, thirty-seven, had more experience, but he had recently become an Air France manager and no longer flew full-time. Captain Marc Dubois, fifty-eight, had experience aplenty, but he'd been touring Rio with an off-duty flight attendant. It was later reported that he had had only an hour's sleep.

Fortunately, given these potential fragilities, the crew were in charge of one of the most advanced planes in the world, an Airbus 330, legendarily smooth and easy to fly. Like any other modern aircraft, the A330 has an autopilot to keep the plane flying on a programmed route, but it also has a much more sophisticated automation system called fly-by-wire. A traditional airplane gives the pilot direct control of the flaps, rudder, and elevators. This means that the pilot has plenty of latitude to make mistakes. Fly-by-wire is smoother and safer. It inserts itself between the pilot, with all his or her faults, and the plane's mechanics, its flaps and fins and ailerons. A tactful translator between human and machine, it observes the pilot tugging on the controls, figures out how the pilot wants the plane to move, and executes that maneuver perfectly. It will turn a clumsy movement into a graceful one.

This makes it very hard to crash an A330, and the plane had a superb safety record: there had been no crashes in commercial service in the first fifteen years after it was introduced in 1994. But, paradoxically, there is a risk to building a plane that protects pilots so assiduously from even the tiniest error. It means that when something challenging does occur, the pilots will have very little experience to draw on as they try to meet that challenge.

The challenge facing Flight 447 did not seem especially daunting: thunderstorms over the Atlantic Ocean just north of the equator. These were not a major problem, although perhaps Captain Dubois was too relaxed when, at 11:02 p.m. Rio time, he left the cockpit for a nap, with the inexperienced Bonin in charge of the controls.

Faced with the storm, Bonin seemed nervous. The slightest hint of trouble produced an outburst of swearing: *"Putain la vache. Putain!"*—the French equivalent of "Fucking hell. Fuck!" He wished he could fly over the storm. More than once he expressed a desire to fly at "three-six"—36,000 feet—and lamented the fact that Air France procedures recommended flying a little lower. This desire for altitude was to become important: while it is possible to avoid trouble by flying over a storm, there's a limit to how high the plane can go. The atmosphere becomes so thin that it can barely support the aircraft. Margins for error become tight. The aircraft will be at risk of stalling.

Unlike stalling a car, stalling an aircraft has nothing to do with the vehicle's engine. An aircraft stall occurs when the plane tries to climb too steeply. At this steep angle, the wings no longer function as wings and the aircraft no longer behaves like an aircraft. It loses airspeed and falls gracelessly in a nose-up position.

In the thin air of high altitudes a stall is more likely. Fortunately, a high altitude also provides plenty of time and space to correct the stall. This is a well-known maneuver, fundamental to learning how to fly a plane: the pilot pushes the nose of the plane down and into a dive. The diving plane regains airspeed and the wings once more work as wings. The pilot then gently pulls out of the dive and into level flight once more.

In any case, an Airbus A330 will not stall. The fly-by-wire system will not allow the pilot to climb so steeply in the first place. Or so Pierre-Cédric Bonin seemed to believe.

As the plane approached the storm, ice crystals began to form on the wings. Bonin and Robert switched on the anti-icing system to prevent too much ice from building up and slowing the plane down. Robert nudged Bonin a couple of times to pull left, avoiding the worst of the weather; Bonin seemed slightly distracted, perhaps put on edge by the fact that Robert could have plotted a route around the storms much earlier. A faint odor of electrical burning filled the cockpit, and the temperature rose—Robert assured Bonin that all this was the result of the electrical storm, not an equipment failure.

And then an alarm sounded. The autopilot had disconnected. An airspeed sensor on the plane had iced over and stopped functioning—not a major problem, but one that required the pilots to take control. But something else happened at the same time and for the same reason: the fly-by-wire system downgraded itself to a mode that gave the pilot less help and more latitude to control the plane. Lacking an airspeed sensor, the plane was unable to babysit Pierre-Cédric Bonin.

The first consequence was almost immediate: the plane was rocking right and left, and Bonin was overcorrecting this with sharp jerks on the stick. With the fly-by-wire in its normal mode, those clumsy tugs would have been translated into smooth instructions. In the alternate mode, the plane did not intervene and the rocking continued. Gone was fly-by-wire as smooth-tongued interpreter; replacing it was fly-by-wire as a literal-minded translator that would relay any instruction, no matter how foolish.

And then Bonin made a simple mistake: he pulled back on his control stick and the plane started to climb steeply.

It's not clear why Bonin was seeking altitude. Perhaps it felt safer up there. He had been muttering that it was "too bad" he couldn't fly a little higher, above the storm clouds. But in the thin air, a steep climb would cause the plane to stall. The A330 knew this perfectly well, and as the nose of the plane rose and it started to lose speed, an automated voice barked out in English: *STALL STALL STALL.* That word was to be repeated seventy-five times in the following four and a half minutes. At no point did any of the crew members mention it.

Despite the warning, Bonin kept pulling back on the stick, and in the black skies above the Atlantic the plane climbed at an astonishing rate of 7,000 feet a minute. But the plane's airspeed was evaporating; it would soon begin to slide down through the storm and toward the water, 37,500 feet below. Bonin's error was basic—every pilot is taught about stalling and about how to fix a stall: put the nose of the plane down and regain speed. Had either man realized what was happening, they could have fixed the problem, at least in its early stages. But they did not. Why?

Perhaps language was a barrier. The men were French and spoke French in the cockpit; the *STALL STALL STALL* was in English. Yet all pilots speak English so that they can communicate with air traffic control wherever they are in the world.

David Robert—still young, a little rusty—may not have realized what Bonin was doing. In some airplanes Bonin's yank back on his control stick would have been mirrored by the stick in Robert's hands, so the more experienced pilot would have received some visceral information about his colleague's error. But in the A330 the parallel controls are not directly linked. Nor did Robert have a direct indicator of the degree to which Bonin had stuck its nose in the air. And since the airspeed indicator had iced over, Robert may have lost confidence in what other indicators were telling him.

As for Bonin, he seems to have responded to the crisis by behaving as he should in the only challenging situation he was likely to have faced as a young pilot: aborting a landing. (At one stage he mentioned to Robert that he was in "TOGA"—Take Off, Go Around.) When aborting a landing, a pilot needs to fire up the engines and climb quickly away from the ground. The air is thicker at ground level, so the plane can climb much more steeply without stalling; and in any case, any aborted landing Bonin would have conducted would have been with the help of the fly-by-wire system that simply would not have allowed him to stall. Perhaps Bonin's instincts were telling him to climb out of danger, above the lightning and the turbulence. If so, his instincts were wrong. Far from climbing out of danger, his climb *was* the danger.

But the real source of the problem was the system that had done so much to keep A330s safe across fifteen years and millions of miles of flying: the fly-by-wire. Or more precisely, the problem was not the fly-by-wire system, but the fact that the pilots had grown to rely on that system. Bonin was suffering from a problem called *mode confusion*. Perhaps he did not realize that the plane had switched to the alternate mode that would provide him with far less assistance. Perhaps he knew the plane had switched modes but did not fully understand the implication: that his plane would now let him stall. That is the most plausible reason Bonin and Robert ignored the *STALL STALL STALL* alarm—they assumed that this was the plane's way of telling them that it was intervening to prevent a stall. In short, Bonin stalled the aircraft because in his gut he felt it was impossible to stall the aircraft. And he failed to pull out of the stall for exactly the same reason.

Aggravating this mode confusion was Bonin's lack of experience in flying a plane without computer assistance. While he had spent many hours in the cockpit of the A330, most were spent monitoring and adjusting the plane's computers rather than directly flying it. And of the tiny number of hours spent manually flying the plane, few if any would have been spent in the degraded fly-by-wire mode, and almost all would have been spent taking off or landing. No wonder Bonin instinctively moved the plane as if for an aborted landing. And no wonder he felt so helpless at the plane's controls.

The Air France pilots "were hideously incompetent," says William Langewiesche, a writer and professional pilot.[2] And Langewiesche thought he knew why. He argued persuasively in the pages of *Vanity*

Fair that the pilots simply weren't used to flying their own planes at altitude without the help of the computer. Even the experienced Captain Dubois was rusty: of the 346 hours he had been at the controls of a plane during the past six months, only four were in manual control rather than overseeing the autopilot, and even then he'd had the help of the full fly-by-wire system. All three pilots were denied the ability to practice their skills, because the plane was usually the one doing the flying.

This problem has a name: the paradox of automation. It applies to a wide variety of contexts, from the operators of a nuclear power station to the crew of a cruise ship to the simple fact that we can't remember phone numbers anymore because we have them all stored in our cell phones and that we struggle with mental arithmetic because we're surrounded by electronic calculators. The better the automatic systems, the more out-of-practice human operators will be, and the more unusual will be the situations they face.[3] The psychologist James Reason, author of *Human Error*, wrote: "Manual control is a highly skilled activity, and skills need to be practiced continuously in order to maintain them. Yet an automatic control system that fails only rarely denies operators the opportunity for practicing these basic control skills . . . when manual takeover is necessary something has usually gone wrong; this means that operators need to be more rather than less skilled in order to cope with these atypical conditions."*[4]

The paradox of automation, then, has three strands to it. First, automatic systems accommodate incompetence by being easy to operate and by automatically correcting mistakes. Because of this an inexpert operator can function for a long time before his lack of skill becomes apparent—his incompetence is a hidden weakness that can

*The Air France Flight 447 conditions were atypical, but they were not unique. In December 2014, AirAsia Flight 8501 flew into a thunderstorm near Borneo and the autopilot disengaged as a result of a minor mechanical glitch. The inexperienced junior pilot unwittingly put the plane into a stall; the captain spotted the problem but was unable to recover in time. The plane crashed and 162 people died.

persist almost indefinitely without being detected. Second, even if operators are expert, automatic systems erode their skills by removing the need for them to practice. Third, automatic systems tend to fail either in unusual situations or in ways that produce unusual situations, requiring a particularly skillful human response. For each of these three strands, a more capable and reliable automatic system makes the situation worse.

There are plenty of situations in which automation creates no such paradox. A customer service webpage may be able to handle routine complaints and requests, so that customer service staff are spared repetitive work and may do a better job for customers with more complex questions.

Not so with an airplane. Autopilots and the more subtle assistance of fly-by-wire do not free up the crew to concentrate on the interesting stuff. Instead, they free up the crew to fall asleep at the controls, figuratively or even literally. One notorious incident occurred late in 2009, when two pilots let their autopilot overshoot Minneapolis airport by over a hundred miles. They'd been looking at laptops and had become distracted.[5]

When something goes wrong, it is hard to snap to attention and deal with a situation that is very likely to be bewildering.

His nap abruptly interrupted, Captain Dubois arrived in the cockpit a mere 1 minute and 38 seconds after the airspeed indicator had failed. The plane was still above 35,000 feet, although it was falling at over 150 feet a second. The de-icers had done their job and the airspeed sensor was operating again, but the copilots no longer trusted any of their instruments. The plane—which was now in perfect working order—was telling them that they were barely moving forward at all, and were slicing through the air down toward the water, tens of thousands of feet below. But rather than realize the faulty instrument was fixed, they appear to have assumed that yet more of their instruments had broken. Dubois was silent for twenty-three seconds—a long time, if you care to count them off. Long enough for the plane to fall 4,000 feet.

It was still not too late to save the plane—if Dubois had been able to recognize what was happening to it. The plane's nose was now so high that the stall warning had stopped—it, like the pilots, simply rejected the information it was getting as anomalous. A couple of times, Bonin did push the nose of the plane down a little, and the stall warning started up again—*STALL STALL STALL*—which no doubt confused him further. At one stage Bonin tried to engage the speed brakes, worried that they were going too fast—the opposite of the truth. The plane was clawing its way forward through the air at less than 60 knots, about 70 miles per hour—far too slow. It was falling twice as fast. Utterly confused, the pilots argued briefly about whether the plane was climbing or descending.

Bewilderment reigned. Bonin and Robert were shouting at each other, each trying to control the plane. All three men were talking at cross-purposes. The plane was simultaneously climbing—nose up—while losing altitude rapidly.

Robert: "Your speed! You're climbing! Descend! Descend, descend, descend!"

Bonin: "I am descending!"

Dubois: "No, you're climbing."

Bonin: "I'm climbing? Okay, so we're going down."

Nobody said: "We're stalling. Put the nose down and dive out of the stall."

At 11:13 p.m. and 40 seconds, less than twelve minutes after Dubois first left the cockpit for a nap, and two minutes after the autopilot switched itself off, Robert yelled at Bonin, "Climb . . . climb . . .

climb . . . climb . . . ," the precise opposite of what needed to be done. Bonin replied that he'd had his stick back the entire time—the information that might have helped Dubois diagnose the stall, had he known.

Finally the penny seemed to drop for Dubois, who was standing behind the two copilots. "No, no, no . . . Don't climb . . . no, no."

Robert took the hint. He announced that he was taking control and pushed the nose of the plane down. The plane began to accelerate at last. But Robert was about one minute too late—that's 11,000 feet of altitude. There was not enough room between the plummeting plane and the black water of the Atlantic to regain speed and then pull out of the dive.

In any case, Bonin silently retook control of the plane and tried to climb again. It was an act of pure panic. Robert and Dubois had, perhaps, realized that the plane had stalled—but they never said so. They may not have realized that Bonin was the one in control of the plane. And Bonin never grasped what he had done. His last words were: "But what's happening?"

Four seconds later the aircraft hit the Atlantic Ocean at about 125 miles an hour. Everyone on board, 228 passengers and crew, died instantly.

Earl Wiener, a cult figure in aviation safety who died in 2013, coined what's known as "Wiener's Laws" of aviation and human error. One of them was "Digital devices tune out small errors while creating opportunities for large errors."[6]

We might rephrase it as: "Automation will routinely tidy up ordinary messes, but occasionally create an extraordinary mess." It's an insight that applies far beyond aviation.

A few years ago, the police department in San Leandro, California, near Oakland, took at least 112 photographs of two cars owned by a local resident, Michael Katz-Lacabe. This fact did not emerge in some scandalous court case demonstrating Katz-Lacabe to be a terrorist or a gangland kingpin—it emerged because he filed a public records request to see the photos. And Katz-Lacabe's cars weren't photographed because he was suspected of any offense. They were photographed because *everybody's* cars were photographed, the digital files scanned, license plates logged, and everything filed away with a date and a location. Mr. Katz-Lacabe's daughters were photographed, too, aged five and eight at the time. Why? Because they were near the car when the virtual shutter clicked.[7]

The photographs of Mr. Katz-Lacabe's cars—and children—were sent, with millions of others, to the Northern California Regional Intelligence Center, which is run by the U.S. federal government. A hundred million license plate photographs a second can be searched, thanks to software developed by Silicon Valley's Palantir Technologies. The crime-fighting potential of such a vast and easily analyzable dataset is obvious. So, too, is its potential to be used in less palatable ways: as Katz-Lacabe mused to Andy Greenberg of *Forbes* magazine, the government could wind back the clock through its database of photos to see if someone has been "parked at the house of someone other than their wife, a medical marijuana clinic, a Planned Parenthood center, a protest."

There's clearly a debate to be had about the advantages and the authoritarian risks of such powerful technology, and it has been well discussed in recent years. But there's another danger, a problem that gets far less attention but that Wiener's observation brings into focus: What do we do in the rare cases when the technology fails?

Consider the tale of Victor Hankins, an ordinary British citizen who received an unwelcome seasonal gift for Christmas: a parking fine. Rather than return to an illegally parked car to find a ticket tucked under the windshield wipers, the first Hankins knew of his punishment was when a letter from the local council dropped onto his doormat. At 14 seconds after 8:08 p.m. on December 20, 2013, his car had been blocking a bus stop in Bradford, Yorkshire, and had been photographed by a camera mounted in a traffic enforcement van driving past. A computer had identified the license plate, looked it up in a database, and found Mr. Hankins's address. An "evidence pack" was automatically generated, including video of the scene, a time stamp, and data to confirm the location. The letter from Bradford city council demanding that Mr. Hankins pay a fine or face court action was composed, printed, and mailed by an equally automatic process. There was just one problem: Mr. Hankins hadn't been illegally parked at all. He had been stuck in traffic.[8]

In principle, such technology should not fall victim to the paradox of automation. It should free up humans to do more interesting and varied work—checking the anomalous cases, such as the complaint Mr. Hankins immediately registered, which are likely to be more intriguing than simply writing down yet another license plate and issuing yet another ticket. But the tendency to assume that the technology knows what it's doing applies just as much to a bureaucracy as it does to pilots. Bradford's city council initially dismissed Mr. Hankins's complaint, apologetically admitting their error only when he threatened them with the inconvenience of a court case. We are reminded of an old joke: "To err is human, but to really foul things up takes a computer."

On the very same day that Victor Hankins's car was snapped, Google unveiled a neural network that could identify house numbers in photographs taken by the Google Street View cars. Give the network an hour, announced Google's research team, and it could read every house number in France with 96 percent accuracy.[9] That sounds impressive—but even a low error rate produces a vast number of mistakes. There are 25 million homes in France, so another way to describe Google's new neural network is that it can misidentify a million street numbers an hour.

Such a high error rate is actually a source of comfort, because it means the method won't be relied on. Companies such as UPS or FedEx would never accept as many as one in twenty-five of their parcels going to the wrong address; it would be a reputational disaster. Nor—one would hope—would the French armed police be happy to barge through a door being only 96 percent sure that it wasn't the home of a startled, law-abiding innocent. And if they did so routinely, complaints would be taken seriously: if the police ombudsman service knows that the police screw up one case out of twenty-five, they should be disposed to give you a hearing when you complain that you were one of the mistakes.

But what if Google improves its accuracy by a factor of a million? Now there will be only a single mistake out of France's 25 million homes. But a mistake is going to happen to someone, and nobody will believe them. The rarer the exception gets, as with fly-by-wire, the less gracefully we are likely to deal with it. We will assume that the computer is always right, and when someone says the computer made a mistake, we will assume they are wrong or lying. What happens when private security guards throw you out of your local shopping mall because a computer has mistaken your face for that of a known shoplifter? (The technology already exists, and it is being modified to allow retailers to single out their most pliable customers for special offers the moment they walk into the store.[10]) When you're on the "criminal" list, how easy would it be to get off it?

Automated systems can be wonderful—but if we put too much trust in them, people suffer. Consider the experience of Rahinah Ibrahim, a thirty-nine-year-old lecturer and architect who was studying for a doctorate at Stanford University. On January 2, 2005, she tried to fly from San Francisco to Hawaii to present her research at a conference.

That was an arduous enough journey given that Rahinah was wheelchair-bound while recovering from surgery, but it was about to become more arduous still: after trying to check in, she was arrested in front of her teenage daughter, handcuffed, and driven to a holding cell. After a few hours, she was told she was cleared to fly to Hawaii the next day.[11]

Two months later, having gone on to her home country, Malaysia, she learned at the airport that her U.S. student visa had been revoked without notice. Although the mother of a U.S. citizen, she would never be able to return to the United States.

While it had taken only the mention of court for Bradford Council to relent over Victor Hankins's parking ticket, it took Rahinah nine years, and $4 million worth of volunteered legal assistance—battling constant efforts by the U.S. government to derail the proceedings—before U.S. District Judge William Alsup delivered a damning conclusion. Rahinah had been put on a no-fly list by mistake—possibly the result of confusion between Jemaah Islamiyah, a terrorist group, which killed 202 people with a car bomb in Bali in 2002, and Jamaah Islah Malaysia, a professional association of Malaysians who have studied overseas. Rahinah was a member of the second group, not the first.

Once that error entered the database it acquired the iron authority of the computer. As the judge wrote, "Once derogatory information is posted to the TSDB [Terrorism Screening Database], it can propagate extensively through the government's interlocking complex of databases, like a bad credit report that will never go away." The initial mistake spread like a virus that no official had any interest in curing.

The world is a messy place. Is that digit a 1 or a 7, a lowercase *l* or an uppercase *I*? A car is motionless: Is it parked or stuck in traffic? Is that person a shoplifter or a shoplifter's twin brother? Is a group with an unfamiliar-sounding name a gang of killers or an association of internationally minded scholars? In a messy world, mistakes are inevitable.

Yet automatic systems want to be tidy. Once an algorithm or a database has placed you in a particular category, the black-and-white definitions of the data discourage argument and uncertainty. You are a shoplifter. You were parked at a bus stop. You are on the no-fly list. The computer says so—with the authority that leads a government to defend itself doggedly for years, rather than acknowledge that sometimes mistakes are made.

We are now on more lists than ever before: lists of criminals; lists of free-spending shoppers; lists of people who often drive around San Leandro, California; even lists of rape survivors.[12] Computers have turned such lists from inert filing cabinets full of paper to instantly searchable, instantly actionable data. Increasingly, the computers are filling these databases with no need for humans to get involved, or even to understand what is happening. And the computers are often unaccountable: an algorithm that rates teachers and schools, Uber drivers, or businesses on Google's search will typically be commercially confidential. Whatever errors or preconceptions have been programmed into the algorithm from the start, it is safe from scrutiny: those errors and preconceptions will be hard to challenge.[13]

Yet for all the power and the genuine usefulness of such data, perhaps we have not yet acknowledged how imperfectly a tidy database maps onto a messy world. We fail to see that a computer that is a hundred times more accurate than a human and a million times faster will make ten thousand times as many mistakes. And—recalling Johann Gottlieb Beckmann's scientific forestry project—we fail to acknowledge the power of the database, not just to categorize the world, but to shape it.

This is not to say that we should call for death to the databases and algorithms. Even if we share the misgivings of Michael Katz-Lacabe, most of us will admit that there is at least some legitimate role for computerized attempts to investigate criminal suspects, keep traffic flowing, and prevent terrorists from getting on airplanes. But the database and the algorithm, like the autopilot, should be there to support human decision-making. If we rely on computers completely, disaster awaits.

Our learned helplessness in the hands of technology is sometimes more amusing than horrifying. In March 2012, three Japanese students visiting Australia decided to drive to North Stradbroke, guided by their GPS system. For some reason the GPS was not aware that their route was blocked by nine miles of the Pacific Ocean. These things happen, of course, but the reaction of the three tourists was extraordinary: in thrall to their technology, they drove their car down onto the beach and across the mudflats toward the ocean. As the water lapped around their Hyundai, they realized, to their embarrassment, that they were stuck. With astonished ferry passengers looking on, the students abandoned their car and waded to shore. The car was a write-off. "We want to come back to Australia again," said one of the men. "Everyone is very nice, even today."[14]

It's fun to laugh at incompetent tourists. But it is also worth asking how on earth three sentient beings can drive into the Pacific Ocean on the instructions of GPS gone haywire.* Automated systems tend to lull us into passivity. In other contexts, we have a well-known tendency to accept whatever defaults are being suggested to us—for example, in countries where people are signed up by default to an organ donor register unless they tick a box to opt out, almost everyone accepts this default. In countries where you have to tick a box to *opt in*,

*The incident is far from unique. People following GPS guidance have driven their cars into a lake in Washington state, straight on at a T-intersection and into a house in New Jersey, down a flight of stairs in Manhattan, along a rocky footpath to the brink of a cliff in Yorkshire, and into a large sand pit at a construction site in Hamburg. Tourist officials in the inland Italian town of Carpi were once confused by questions about sea caves from fat-fingered Swedes who turned out to believe they had driven to Capri, 400 miles and a boat ride away. Even more extraordinary is the tale of a woman hoping to pick up a friend from the local train station in Belgium who instead trustingly drove 800 miles to Zagreb, Croatia.

coverage is far less. Much the same is true for corporate pensions. If the default is different, we act differently—despite the fact that these are vital, life-changing decisions.[15]

This tendency to passively accept the default option turns out to apply to automated decisions, too; psychologists call it *automation bias*. The problem—in Bradford, on the U.S. no-fly list, everywhere—is that once a computer has made a recommendation, it is all too easy to accept that recommendation unthinkingly.

Driving your car into the sea is an extreme example of automation bias, but most GPS users will recognize the tendency in a milder form. The first time you use the GPS, you're wary. You check the map, perhaps print out some directions, familiarize yourself with the terrain, and manually estimate how long your journey will take. But after three or four successful outings, you're hooked: Why bother with all that paraphernalia when the GPS will find you a route more quickly and reliably?

The GPS won't let you down often, but when it does, it will let you down badly. The first time it happened to me, I was headed for a hotel in the center of York, a beautiful medieval city surrounded by city walls that constrain the flow of traffic. I arrived late at night to find my route blocked for overnight resurfacing works; the GPS hadn't gotten the memo and ordered me to plow on through the blockage. Fortunately I wasn't tempted to follow the GPS under the oncoming steam roller, but that was where my competence ended: I'd trusted the computer and had no backup plans. I didn't know where I was, or where my hotel was. I had no map—this was before smartphones—so I was reduced to driving around aimlessly in the hope that the machine might eventually form an alternative plan.

After a few more trouble-free trips, I soon started trusting the GPS again—and it performed faultlessly for years, until recently I set off in the general direction of a country wedding armed only with a zip code that the computer turned out not to recognize. Not knowing why the GPS failed me, I have no way of predicting when it might do so again.

Gary Klein, a psychologist who specializes in the study of expert and intuitive decision-making, summarizes the problem: "When the algorithms are making the decisions, people often stop working to get better. The algorithms can make it hard to diagnose reasons for failures. As people become more dependent on algorithms, their judgment may erode, making them depend even more on the algorithms. That process sets up a vicious cycle. People get passive and less vigilant when algorithms make the decisions."[16]

Decision experts such as Klein complain that many software engineers make the problem worse by deliberately designing systems to supplant human expertise by default; if we wish instead to use them to support human expertise, we need to wrestle with the system. GPS devices, for example, could provide all sorts of decision support, allowing a human driver to explore options, view maps, and alter a route. But all these functions tend to be buried deeper in the app. They take effort, whereas it is very easy to hit "Start Navigation" and trust the computer to do the rest.

Systems that supplant, not support, human decision-making are everywhere. We worry that the robots are taking our jobs, but just as common a problem is that the robots are taking our judgment. In the large warehouses so common behind the scenes of today's economy, human "pickers" hurry around grabbing products off shelves and moving them to where they can be packed and dispatched. In their ears are headpieces: the voice of "Jennifer," a piece of software, tells them where to go and what to do, controlling the smallest details of their movements. Jennifer breaks down instructions into tiny chunks, to minimize error and maximize productivity—for example, rather than pick eighteen copies of a book off a shelf, the human worker would be politely instructed to pick five. Then another five. Then yet another five. Then three more. Working in such conditions reduces people to machines made of flesh. Rather than ask us to think or adapt, the Jennifer unit takes over the thought process and treats workers as an inexpensive source of some visual processing and a pair of opposable thumbs.[17]

You could even argue that the financial crisis of 2007–2008, which plunged the world into recession, was analogous to absentmindedly driving a car into the Pacific. One of the weaknesses that contributed to the crisis was the failure of financial products called collateralized debt obligations (CDOs)—hugely complex structures, whose value depended in an opaque way on the health of the U.S. mortgage market. A grizzled market participant might have looked at rapidly inflating house prices and mused that a house price crash was possible, even though the United States had not experienced a nationally synchronized crash before. And if that grizzled market participant had been able to talk to the computers, the computers would have been able to demonstrate the catastrophic impact of such a crash on the value of CDOs. Unfortunately, there was no meeting of minds: the computers didn't have the tacit knowledge of the experienced humans, so they didn't process the idea that a crash was plausible, while the experienced humans didn't understand what their intuition would imply for the value of CDOs.

It is possible to resist the siren call of the algorithms. Rebecca Pliske, a psychologist, found that veteran meteorologists would make weather forecasts first by looking at the data and forming an expert judgment; only then would they look at the computerized forecast to see if the computer had spotted anything that they had missed. (Typically, the answer was no.) By making their manual forecast first, these veterans kept their skills sharp, unlike the pilots on the Airbus 330. However, the younger generation of meteorologists are happier to trust the computers. Once the veterans retire, the human expertise to intuit when the computer has screwed up will be lost forever.[18]

• • •

We've seen the problems with GPS systems and with autopilot. Put the two ideas together, and you get the self-driving car.

Chris Urmson, who runs Google's self-driving car program, hopes that the cars will soon be so widely available that his sons will never need to have a driving license. (His oldest son will be sixteen in 2020—Urmson is in a hurry.) There's a revealing implication in that target: that unlike a plane's autopilot, a self-driving car will never need to cede control to a human being. True to form, Google's autonomous vehicles have no steering wheel, though one hopes there will be some way to jump out if they start heading for the ocean.[19]

Not everyone thinks it is plausible for cars to be completely autonomous—or, at least, not soon enough for Urmson junior. Raj Rajkumar, an autonomous-driving expert at Carnegie Mellon University, thinks completely autonomous vehicles are ten to twenty years away. Until then, we can look forward to a more gradual process of letting the car drive itself in easier conditions, while humans take over at more challenging moments.

"The number of scenarios that are automatable will increase over time, and one fine day, the vehicle is able to control itself completely, but that last step will be a minor, incremental step and one will barely notice this actually happened," Rajkumar told the *99% Invisible* podcast. Even then, he says, "there will always be some edge cases where things do go beyond anybody's control."

If this sounds ominous, perhaps it should. At first glance, it seems reasonable that the car will hand over to the human driver when things are difficult. But that raises two immediate problems. If we expect the car to know when to cede control, then we're expecting the car to know the limits of its own competence—to understand when it is capable and when it is not. That is a hard thing to ask even of a human, let alone a computer.

Alternatively, if we expect the human to leap in and take over, how will the human be able to react appropriately? Given what we know about the difficulty highly trained pilots can have figuring out an unusual situation when the autopilot switches off, surely we should be skeptical about humans' capacity to notice when the computer is about to make a mistake. "Human beings are not used to driving automated vehicles, so we really don't know how drivers are going to react when the driving is taken over by the car," says Anuj K. Pradhan of the University of Michigan.[20] It seems likely that we'll react by playing a computer game or chatting on a video phone, rather than watching like a hawk how the computer is driving—maybe not on our first trip in an autonomous car, but certainly on our hundredth.

And when the computer gives control back to the driver, it may well do so in the most extreme and challenging situations. The three Air France pilots had two or three minutes to work out what to do when their autopilot asked them to take over an A330; what chance would you or I have when the computer in our car says "Automatic Mode Disengaged" and we look up from our smartphone screen to see a bus careening toward us?

Anuj Prajan has floated the idea that humans should have to acquire several years of manual experience before they are allowed to supervise an autonomous car. But it is hard to see how this solves the problem. No matter how many years of experience a driver has, her skills will slowly erode if she lets the computer take over. Prajan's proposal gives us the worst of both worlds: we let teenage drivers loose in manual cars, when they are most likely to have accidents. And even when they've learned some road craft, it won't take long being a passenger in a usually reliable autonomous car before their skills begin to fade.

Recall that Earl Wiener said, "Digital devices tune out small errors while creating opportunities for large errors."[21] In the case of autopilots and autonomous vehicles, we might add that it's *because* digital devices tidily tune out small errors that they create the opportunities for large ones. Deprived of any awkward feedback, any modest challenges that might allow us to maintain our skills, when the crisis arrives we find ourselves lamentably unprepared.

Every application of Wiener's insight about large and small errors involves a trade-off. The GPS routinely saves me the minor hassle of planning before a trip, but at the cost of occasionally sending me scuttling apologetically into a rural church just ahead of the bridal procession. Is the odd frustration worth the cumulative time saved? Given that I have again slipped back into trusting the GPS, I must have concluded that it is.

When it comes to tidy databases, the trade-off is fraught. Automation makes it easier to punish parking infringements and keep potential terrorists off airplanes. (While there are valid debates to be had about ends and means, respectively, let us assume these are both good things.) But it creates unusual situations where individuals have to battle to get an unlikely-sounding story accepted: "I wasn't parked illegally, I was stuck in traffic"; or "That's not a terrorist group, it's an alumni association." Does more efficient service in the majority of cases justify trapping a small number of individuals in Kafkaesque battles against bureaucracy? That is a question with no easy answer. But it does tell us we should strive to listen to people who say they have fallen victim to a rare and unusual error and set up mechanisms to sort out these errors quickly.

With fly-by-wire, it's much easier to assess whether the trade-off is worthwhile. Until the late 1970s, one could reliably expect at least twenty-five fatal commercial plane crashes a year. In 2009, Air France 447 was one of just eight crashes, a safety record. The cost-benefit analysis seems clear: freakish accidents like Flight 447 are a price worth paying, as the steady silicon hand of the computer has prevented many others.

Still, one cannot help but wonder if there is a way to combine the adaptability, judgment, and tacit knowledge of humans with the reliability of computers, reducing the accident rate even further. One priority could be to make semi-automated systems give feedback in a way that humans feel more viscerally. The crew of Air France 447 were told seventy-five times that they were stalling—*STALL STALL STALL*—but they didn't feel it instinctively. If the cockpit had displayed a large image of the plane with its nose in the air, that might have conveyed the danger. Similarly, the control sticks weren't physically mimicking each other, so the more senior copilot didn't realize that young Bonin was overriding what he was doing. Again, a verbal warning announced that the pilots were giving the plane contradictory instructions, but the verbal warning was easily ignored—a more physical connection might have produced a more attentive response.

Some senior pilots urge their juniors to turn off the autopilots from time to time to maintain their skills. That sounds like good advice. But if the junior pilots turn off the autopilot only when it is absolutely safe to do so, they aren't practicing their skills in a challenging situation. And if they turn off the autopilot in a challenging situation, they may provoke the very accident they are practicing to avoid.

An alternative solution is to reverse the role of computer and human. Rather than let the computer fly the plane with the human poised to take over when the computer cannot cope, perhaps it would be better to have the human fly the plane with the computer monitoring the situation, ready to intervene. Computers, after all, are tireless, patient, and do not need practice. Why, then, do we ask the people to monitor the machines and not the other way around? That is the way the best meteorologists acted when studied by psychologist Rebecca Pliske: the human made the forecast and then asked the machine for a second opinion. Such a solution will not work everywhere, but it is worth exploring.

If we are stuck with the problem of asking humans to monitor computers, it is vital to keep those humans interested, and there may be safe ways to add a little dose of mess. Airplanes are only one type of largely automated system that humans are tasked with keeping an eye on—others include high-speed trains, U.S. military drones, and warehouses full of robot forklifts. Supervising a drone sounds like an exciting job, but it can be dreadfully boring for much of the time. The drone might be circling over Afghanistan while the operator is snacking on M&M's at Creech Air Force Base in Indian Springs, Nevada, keeping half an eye on the screen and idly daydreaming—then they suddenly need to snap to attention and decide whether or not to kill a potential target.

Enter Mary "Missy" Cummings, one of the U.S. Navy's first female fighter pilots and now an expert in the field of humans supervising semi-autonomous machines. Missy Cummings and her team ran an experiment during which drone pilots were given a long, often boring simulated mission, punctuated with occasional life-or-death decisions. As they gazed at grainy images coming in from four different drones, tapped navigation instructions into the computer, and waited for something to happen, the pilots often became distracted. They'd sit with a book or a laptop in front of them, glancing back and forth between the mission and something more interesting. (These distractions were neither forbidden nor encouraged by researchers, who wanted to see what people would do.)

Unsurprisingly, the scientists showed that reaction times and other measures of performance dramatically deteriorated as the hours ticked by. But they also observed that many of the more successful pilots adopted an interesting tactic. Rather than attend to their task through sheer willpower, or divide their attention, trying to do both their job and their e-mail at the same time, they distracted themselves in brief bursts. A few minutes with their back to the drone monitors, doing something completely different, would refresh them as they returned to the task.

Such behavior suggests that when humans are asked to babysit computers, the computers themselves should be programmed to serve up occasional brief diversions. Even better might be an automated system that demanded more input, more often, from the human—even when that input wasn't strictly needed.[22] If you occasionally need human skill at short notice to navigate a hugely messy situation, it may make sense to artificially create smaller messes, just to keep people on their toes.

In the mid-1980s, a Dutch traffic engineer named Hans Monderman was sent to the village of Oudehaske. Two children had been killed by cars, and Monderman's radar gun showed right away that drivers were going too fast through the village. Monderman pondered the traditional solutions—traffic lights, speed bumps, additional signs pestering drivers to slow down. They were expensive and, Monderman knew, often ineffective. Control measures such as traffic lights and speed bumps frustrated drivers, who would often speed dangerously between one measure and another.

And so Monderman tried something revolutionary. He suggested that the road through Oudehaske be made to look more like what it already was: a road through a village. First, the existing traffic signs were removed. (Signs always irritated Monderman: driving through his home country of the Netherlands with the writer Tom Vanderbilt,

Monderman railed against their patronizing redundancy. "Do you really think that no one would perceive there is a bridge over there?" he would ask, waving at a sign that stood next to a bridge, notifying people of the bridge.[23]) The signs might ostensibly be asking drivers to slow down. However, argued Monderman, because signs are the universal language of roads everywhere, on a deeper level the effect of their presence is simply to reassure drivers that they were on a road—a road like any other, where cars rule. Monderman wanted to remind them that they were also in a village, where kids might play.

So, next, he replaced the tarmac with red-brick paving, and the raised curb with a flush sidewalk and gently curved guttering. Cars could stray off the road and onto the verge if they wished. They tended not to.

Where once drivers had, figuratively speaking, sped through the village on autopilot—not really attending to what they were doing—now they were faced with a messy situation and had to engage their brains. It was hard to know quite what to do, or where to drive—or which space belonged to the cars and which to the village children. As Tom Vanderbilt describes Monderman's strategy, "Rather than clarity and segregation, he had created confusion and ambiguity."[24]

A confusing situation always grabs the attention, as Brian Eno has argued. Perplexed, drivers took the cautious way forward: they drove so slowly through Oudehaske that Monderman could no longer capture their speed on his radar gun. Earl Wiener would have recognized the logic: by forcing drivers to confront the possibility of small errors, the chance of their making larger ones was greatly reduced.

Monderman was the most famous of a small group of traffic planners around the world who have been pushing against the trend toward an ever tidier strategy for making traffic flow smoothly and safely. The usual approach is to give drivers the clearest possible guidance as to what they should do and where they should go: traffic lights, bus lanes, cycle lanes, left- and right-filtering traffic signals, railings to confine pedestrians, and of course signs attached to every available surface, forbidding or permitting different maneuvers. Laweiplein in the Dutch town of Drachten was such a typical junction, and accidents were common. Frustrated by waiting in jams, drivers would sometimes try to beat the traffic lights by blasting across the junction at speed—or they would be impatiently watching the lights, rather than watching for other road users. (In urban environments, about half of all accidents happen at traffic lights.[25]) With a shopping center on one side of the junction and a theater on the other, pedestrians often got in the way, too.

Monderman wove his messy magic and created the "Squareabout." He threw away all the explicit efforts at control. In their place, he built a square with fountains, a small grassy roundabout* in one corner, pinch points where cyclists and pedestrians might try to cross the flow of traffic, and very little signposting of any kind. It looks much like a pedestrianization plan—except that the square has as many cars crossing it as ever, approaching from all four directions. Pedestrians and cyclists must cross the traffic as before, but now they have no traffic lights to protect them. It sounds dangerous—and surveys show that locals think it *is* dangerous. It is certainly unnerving to watch the Squareabout in operation—drivers, cyclists, and pedestrians weave in and out of one another in an apparently chaotic fashion.

Yet the Squareabout works. Traffic glides through slowly but rarely stops moving for long. The number of cars passing through the junction has risen, yet congestion has fallen. And the Squareabout is safer than the traffic-light crossroads that preceded it, with half as many accidents as before. It is precisely because the Squareabout feels so hazardous that it is safer. Drivers never quite know what is going on

*A roundabout is the European answer to a traffic circle, typically smaller and with no traffic lights.

or where the next cyclist is coming from, and as a result they drive slowly and with the constant expectation of trouble. And while the Squareabout feels risky, it does not feel threatening; at the gentle speeds that have become the custom, drivers, cyclists, and pedestrians have time to make eye contact and to read one another as human beings rather than threats or obstacles. When showing visiting journalists the Squareabout, Monderman's party trick was to close his eyes and walk backward into the traffic. The cars would just flow around him without so much as a honk on the horn.

In Monderman's artfully ambiguous Squareabout, drivers are never given the opportunity to glaze over and switch to the automatic driving mode that can be so familiar. The chaos of the square forces them to pay attention, work things out for themselves, and look out for one another. The square is a mess of confusion. That is why it works.

8

Resilience

"Everything had to be neat and orderly. No mess."

Broken Windows, Stomach Ulcers, and the Dangerous Belief That Cleanliness Is Next to Godliness

In 1968, Richard Plochman, a German forestry professor, called attention to forestry's ugly secret. Two centuries after Johann Gottlieb Beckmann had been tidying up messy ancient woodlands into neat rows of Norwegian spruce, the German forests were dying.

In *Forestry in the Federal Republic of Germany*, Plochman wrote that the "pure stands" of Norway spruce, so profitable in the early years after Beckmann's work, "grew excellently in the first generation but already showed an amazing retrogression in the second generation." Yields were down by a quarter and the decline was continuing. The trouble had started as early as the second generation of Norway spruce, but trees live long enough that it had taken a century to be certain that something was amiss.

The Germans gave the malaise the name *Waldsterben*, or "forest death" syndrome; in 1986, West Germany produced a set of commemorative stamps with the message "Save our forests in the eleventh hour."

What was happening? The single-minded focus of German foresters on timber was backfiring. According to the ecologist Chris Maser, merely removing fallen logs and dead trees would result in the loss of almost a third of non-bird wildlife species in a forest. These losses seemed irrelevant to scientific foresters, who targeted maximum "sustained yield" and, tellingly, "minimum diversity." Yet over time they altered the ecology of the forest and exposed the trees to fungi and other invasive species. The new, tidy forest, with each tree the same size and the same species, was easily exploited, not just by foresters but by parasites.

Yes, the Norway spruce had been profitable at first, but that profit concealed the fragility of the situation. The first generation of spruce trees had lived off the fertile humus laid down by the messier deciduous old-growth forest, and their roots had pushed down into the deep channels freed up as the old roots rotted. Over time, the spruce laid down their own acidic humus, which was far harder for the already weakened forest ecosystem to decompose. The soil gradually compacted, the nutrients leached away, and the second- and third-growth Norway spruce trees grew shallow roots in malnourishing soil.

None of this was anticipated by the foresters of yesteryear. They were sure their new forests were a simple, well-understood, and highly ordered system. Georg Hartig, one of the generation of scientific foresters to follow in Beckmann's footsteps, confidently produced tables forecasting the yield of the great Jagerthal forest for two centuries, through to 2019.

Such assured forecasting proved hubristic. The mess and diversity of the old German forests had to be painstakingly reconstructed, reintroducing dead logs—and leaving dead trees ("snags") standing—a more varied set of trees, woodpeckers, even certain species of spider. It is too early to tell whether this artificially created mess will prove a successful replacement for the original. Yet what is perfectly clear is that the attempt to map, quantify, and ultimately tidy the German forests not only transformed them but nearly killed them. It turns out that what you need to keep a forest alive cannot easily be quantified and mapped.

In nature, mess often indicates health—and not only in the forest.

In 1982, a trainee Australian doctor carried out the most famous piece of self-experimentation since Benjamin Franklin (perhaps) flew a kite in a thunderstorm. Barry Marshall was frustrated by treating stomach ulcers, which were thought to be caused by stress. Ulcers weren't curable, but managing their symptoms was a fantastically profitable business, producing the first blockbuster drugs, Tagamet and Zantac.[1]

Marshall and his colleague J. Robin Warren had a radically different view: ulcers weren't caused by stress at all, but by a corkscrew-shaped bacteria, *Helicobacter pylori*. They could be cured promptly and completely by a course of inexpensive antibiotics. Nobody else took this view seriously, and there was a lot of money riding on it being untrue.

Irritated and determined to prove his point, Barry Marshall drank a flask full of *H. pylori*. He swiftly became ill, with an inflamed stomach full of incipient ulcers—and just as swiftly cured himself with a course of antibiotics. Finally Marshall and Warren had the attention of the medical profession. Eventually they shared the Nobel Prize in Medicine in 2005.

We could end the tale there as a triumph for careful observation,

Aussie grit, and the wonders of antibiotics. There was even talk among gastroenterologists of trying to eradicate *H. pylori* entirely. But two years after Marshall and Warren's Nobel was awarded, Martin Blaser, a microbiologist at the New York University School of Medicine, discovered a twist in the story: *H. pylori* might be doing us some good.

Blaser found that Americans who had *H. pylori* in their guts were far less likely to suffer from asthma. A laboratory study of mice demonstrated that deliberately infecting them with *H. pylori* guaranteed that they would not develop asthmatic symptoms. Blaser and his colleagues also believe that *H. pylori* helps prevent obesity by regulating a stomach enzyme called ghrelin: again, this idea comes from observational studies of humans and controlled experiments in mice. When mice are dosed with antibiotics, *H. pylori* is scoured from the stomach system and the mice get fat. (The intensive farming industry has known for years that antibiotics help fatten up livestock, but not why.) It also turns out that if you transfer microbes from thin mice to the fat ones, the fat ones will lose weight.[2]

These discoveries hint at what might be possible as we begin to understand our microbiota (the microbes that live on and inside us) and their microbiome (their genes). The view used to be that the human body was under assault from bacteria, and that antibiotics were an unalloyed good, albeit one to be used with care lest bacteria evolve resistance. But recently medical researchers have realized that our relationship with bacteria is more complex than that. The average human is host to ten thousand bacterial species. These germs outnumber the cells of our own body, they weigh a total of about three pounds, and they play a crucial role in keeping our metabolism ticking. Some bacteria are dangerous, some are harmless passengers, and some are beneficial. Some, such as *H. pylori*, can be dangerous or beneficial depending on the situation.[3]

Martin Blaser has become one of the leading champions of the view that our bacterial guests are starting to become less diverse, and that this thinning of the microbiome is doing us harm.

Researchers at the University of Toronto found that it was easier to stay slim in the 1980s: looking at data about diet and exercise for tens of thousands of people since the early 1970s, they found that people today seem to be heavier than their forebears, even when they ate the same and were equally as active. One of the favored explanations for this is that young people today have denuded gut bacteria; a separate large study of European microbial genes has shown that a less diverse microbiome is correlated with a tendency to be obese.

Meanwhile a team at the University of California at San Francisco found that *Lactobacillus sakei*—another of the bacteria we have cluttering up our bodies—appears to prevent sinusitis, presumably by outcompeting the more harmful bacteria that might inflame our sinuses. A dose of antibiotics can wipe out the lactobacillus, and—paradoxically—invite a painful infection.[4]

The most disgusting example concerns the treatment of *Clostridium difficile* gut infections. Doctors have been facing an increasing struggle with this condition, which can cause severe and bloody diarrhea and crippling abdominal pain, and which kills almost thirty thousand Americans a year.[5] The affliction often results from prolonged treatment with antibiotics, which scour the gut's usual benign microbes and leave it open to an opportunistic takeover from the *C. difficile* bacteria. Perhaps unsurprisingly, given its origins, *C. difficile* itself is increasingly resistant to antibiotics.

But now a near-miraculous cure has been discovered—first there were anecdotes and occasional case reports, then a randomized trial that had to be abandoned because it was so dramatically effective that it would have been unethical to deny treatment to the control group. The treatment in question was fecal microbiota transplantation—which is a polite way to describe blending a healthy person's excrement with a little salty water, and injecting the mixture into the patient via the obvious orifice. Recovery is rapid, nearly ubiquitous, and often requires just a single enema of salted poo.[6]

Doctors and researchers are now wondering what else can be treated with fecal bacteria. For example, neurosurgeons have been discussing the possibility that *Enterobacter aerogenes*, a common bacteria in feces, can be used to treat glioblastoma, a kind of deadly brain tumor. The thinking is that, if surgeons smear the bacteria in the brain itself, the body's immune system will mount a ferocious response and attack the tumor. Doctors can then cure the infection. "A brain abscess can be treated, a glioblastoma cannot," one surgeon told *The New Yorker*.[7] It's a desperate gamble, and an enormously controversial one. But the basic idea—that some of our microbes can do us a great deal of good—is now widely accepted.

Why, then, are our microbes going missing? The most obvious culprit is the routine use of antibiotics. These powerful lifesaving drugs should be saved for serious bacterial infections but are often used to treat minor ones, wrongly prescribed for viral infections where they cannot work, or used simply to fatten up the animals that we eat. A second factor is that our surroundings have become more sterile thanks to the frequent use of detergents, antiseptic hand washes, and other attempts at purification. Some of these sterilizing processes take place without our realizing; for example, one research team found that hospital air-conditioning systems seemed to be filtering out many harmless microbes, and that dangerous pathogens had taken their place.[8]

A third explanation is the rise of the cesarean section, which is now how almost a third of American babies come into the world. Babies collect a rich broth of microbes from their mothers, but this transfer does not occur in the womb as one might expect. Instead, they are smeared with bacteria as they pass through the birth canal—*if* they pass through the birth canal. This may explain the otherwise puzzling fact that babies born by cesarean section suffer more from asthma and allergies. It also explains the mysterious behavior of Rob Knight, a microbial ecologist whose baby daughter was born by emergency cesarean section in 2012. Concerned that the baby had bypassed the microbes of the birth canal, Professor Knight waited until the doctors and nurses were out of the room, then rubbed his baby with a swab coated in her mother's vaginal fluids in an effort to colonize his daughter's skin with those maternal microbes. That was speculative—Wild West science in the tradition of Barry Marshall. But Professor Knight is now running a controlled study of much the same technique with babies born by cesarean section in Puerto Rico.[9]

Finally there is the simple fact that our microbiome is partially heritable, passed from mothers to daughters. It follows that if one generation thins out the messy diversity of their microbiome through antibiotics and antiseptics, the following generation will start from a less diverse foundation.[10]

It is worth acknowledging that these ideas have already become a fad—a great deal of nonsense is now being talked by quacks and purveyors of probiotic yogurt aiming to promote a "healthy microbiome." There is no such thing, or rather there is a vast range of healthy microbiomes. People can have very different microbiota, yet still be perfectly healthy; the biological makeup of the same person can also change rapidly, day by day. And of course, eating dirt can make you ill, and antibiotics save many lives. There is a balance to be struck here—a balance that we are still working hard to understand.[11]

Yet the early lessons of the new science of the microbiome chime strikingly with what we've already discovered: If you try to control a complex system, suppressing or tidying away the parts that seem unimportant, you are likely to discover that what seemed unimportant turns out to be very important indeed.

• • •

If we are increasingly understanding that mess makes natural systems more healthy and resilient, then could the same be true for artificial systems, such as the neighborhoods, cities, and countries where we live?

Jane Jacobs, the urban writer and campaigner, made the case for neighborhood diversity in *The Death and Life of Great American Cities*. She wrote of "the daily ballet of Hudson Street" in Greenwich Village, New York, where she lived.

"We may fancifully call it the art form of the city and liken it to the dance," she wrote. "Not to a simple-minded precision dance with everyone kicking up at the same time, twirling in unison and bowing off en masse, but to an intricate ballet in which the individual dancers and ensembles all have distinctive parts which miraculously reinforce each other."[12]

Jacobs explained that it was the diversity of this urban ballet that made it work. In the morning, shopkeepers opened their stores and children walked to school. Smartly dressed professionals emerged from their homes, hailing the taxis that had earlier brought the investment bankers south from Midtown, and riding them north. After the morning rush hour, the street was kept busy with mothers and housewives, and with local workers out for a coffee or lunch. In the late afternoon, children played safely on the sidewalk, and as dusk fell, people gathered in the pools of light around the pizza stand and the bars. Because the neighborhood had such a mixture of residents and such a mixture of attractions, it was always busy but never overwhelmed with people. The diversity of activities made Hudson Street pleasant and safe and engaging, and that very diversity was itself an attraction.

Diversity at street level was made possible by a mix of offices and homes, stores and workshops. It was also made possible, Jacobs argued, by a mix of old and new buildings. She would not have been surprised by the story of Building 20, the low-status structure in the middle of high-status MIT that was home to so many intriguing experiments. It sounds not unlike a building she describes in *The Death and Life of Great American Cities*:

> The floor of the building in which this book is being written is occupied also by a health club with a gym, a firm of ecclesiastical decorators, an insurgent Democratic party reform club, a Liberal party political club, a music society, an accordionists' association, a retired importer who sells maté [*sic*] by mail, a man who sells paper and who also takes care of shipping the maté, a dental laboratory, a studio for watercolor lessons, and a maker of costume jewelry. Among the tenants who were here and gone shortly before I came in, were a man who rented out tuxedos, a union local and a Haitian dance troupe. There is no place for the likes of us in new construction . . . what we need, and a lot of others need, is old construction in a lively district, which some among us can help make livelier.[13]

Diverse streets and neighborhoods work better than monotonous ones, and Jacobs argued that the same is true for diverse cities. It is preferable, she argued, to have an inefficient hodgepodge of different industries than to specialize in a single industry, however efficient that might seem in the short term. One of her favorite examples was the unromantic mess of Birmingham, the second-largest city in England. Birmingham is famous for making nothing in particular, yet over the years has been a hub for steam engines, pneumatic tires, pen nibs, toys, jewelry, cars, chocolate, buckles, buttons, tanks, planes, banking, and electrical engineering. Stumped for a marketing slogan to sell this hodgepodge to a skeptical world, Birmingham's elders have tended to go for "the city of a thousand trades." It hasn't really caught on.*[14]

When Jane Jacobs was admiring Birmingham in the early 1960s, her view seemed odd. Detroit, the quintessential one-industry town, was booming. The standard view was that cities could prosper by playing to their own strengths. But as deindustrialization ripped the life out of specialized cities from Detroit to Glasgow, it became clear that this view was shortsighted. Jacobs had been right that specialized cities were fragile. Diverse industries might seem untidy, and they might occasionally get in one another's way. But the diversity gave a city a chance to respond to shocks. And while nobody ever gets very excited about Birmingham, it has adapted and endured for hundreds of years.

In 1994, over three decades after Jane Jacobs set out this idea, AnnaLee Saxenian, an economist and political scientist, published a study comparing two famous technology clusters, Silicon Valley and Boston's Route 128. I say "famous," but Route 128, once regarded as the

---

*Specialized cities had also been widely thought to be hubs of innovation. The great economist Alfred Marshall had described the advantages of industrial clusters. "When an industry has thus chosen a locality for itself, it is likely to stay there long: so great are the advantages which people following the same skilled trade get from near neighborhood to one another," he wrote in *Principles of Economics* in 1890. "The mysteries of the trade become no mysteries; but are as it were in the air."

Jane Jacobs agreed with most of that analysis: ideas did spread, and they did so street by street. Cities were places where new ideas blossomed from a rich soil of old ideas. But Jacobs emphasized a process of cross-fertilization—a process that will be familiar to us from chapters 1 and 2. While Marshall wrote about people "following the same skilled trade," Jacobs pointed out that people could often learn more from others who were rather different from them. For example, the automotive giants in Detroit emerged from the city's shipbuilding industry. Lingerie makers learned from dressmakers. (Jacobs's favorite example was Ida Rosenthal, a New York dressmaker who developed the modern bra because it would look better under those dresses. Rosenthal made a fortune.)

In 1999, two economists, Maryann Feldman and David Audretsch, tried to resolve this debate with a detailed database of new product introductions as announced in specialist journals such as *Medical Product Manufacturing News*, the *Tea and Coffee Trade Journal*, and *Chemical & Engineering News*. Feldman and Audretsch found that specialized cities (Anaheim, a world leader in office machinery; St. Louis and Atlanta, agribusiness hubs) did not tend to be especially innovative overall. A much better recipe for success was a cluster of industries that drew on some common elements—for example, the same basic scientific research—but which were also diverse. Per person, San Francisco and Boston were comfortably the two most innovative places in the United States.

Feldman and Audretsch concluded that Jane Jacobs had been right that innovation emerged from diverse (but complementary) industries rather than specialized clusters. The great Alfred Marshall had missed this important point—while Jane Jacobs, a woman with no formal qualifications, dismissed as "a crazy dame" by establishment figures, had come at the subject from a different angle and discovered something important. That is, of course, exactly the kind of thing her own theory predicted.

leading technology hub in the world, was so comprehensively overshadowed by Silicon Valley that it is now just the name of a strip of tarmac around Boston.[15]

Saxenian found that the technology companies of Route 128—companies such as Wang, Raytheon, and Sun—kept themselves in tidy silos, specializing in narrow fields of excellence. The fledgling companies of Silicon Valley sprawled into one another, engineers constantly gossiping with each other or moving in informal networks that had little to do with the corporate structures that employed them. Initially, like Detroit or a German forest, the focused structure of Route 128 companies was hugely successful. But as technology continued to leap forward, the specialized Route 128 companies proved unable to adapt; many of them went out of business, or stagnated in the shadow of the Silicon Valley titans.

New data are adding further support to the view that economic diversity is integral to economic health. Cesar Hidalgo, a physicist at the MIT Media Lab, has produced innovative maps showing the underlying structure of different economies. (Unfortunately, city-level data aren't available in enough detail, so these maps describe national economies.) Hidalgo's structural maps look like fine cobwebs linking different types of product clusters and subclusters. They allow us to distinguish between products that require closely related capabilities (for example, handbags and shoes) and those that seem to require very different expertise (for example, clocks and medical devices).[16]

Hidalgo has discovered that there is a strong correlation between being a diversified economy, a complex economy, and a rich economy. It is unusual for a country that exports highly sophisticated products to do only that; they will also tend to export a wide variety of much simpler things. It is also unusual for a country to make lots of different kinds of simple products, yet no sophisticated products. And if a country exports only a small number of products, it's a safe bet that they will be simple, not complex. Variety and sophistication go hand in hand. For example: the Netherlands, a complex economy, exports almost everything that Argentina exports—94 percent of Argentine exports have equivalents that can be bought from the Netherlands, according to Hidalgo's latest data, from refined petroleum to engine parts and cut flowers. But the Netherlands also exports many products that Argentina does not, such as computers.

These highly diversified economies also tend to be rich. There are examples of rich yet specialized economies—the petro-states of the Middle East today, or, in the past, the agriculturally based prosperity of Uruguay and Argentina. But they are few. And Hidalgo finds that such prosperity is extremely fragile. Over time, rich but specialized economies usually lose ground to economies that enjoy more diversity.

Diverse economies, like diverse German forests, are more resilient. On first principles it is far from obvious that this should be true: forests are not cities and the organisms in a forest, like the organisms camping out in our bodies, have evolved together for thousands upon thousands of generations. While that long evolution is no guarantee of resilience, it is a process that is likely to have hidden depths. In contrast, an artificial system such as a city or a neighborhood will have developed over a time scale measured over years or decades rather than millennia. Perhaps we should not be surprised that classical economic theory has emphasized specialization, rather than following nature's lead and being wary of monoculture: cities or countries are advised to get very good at producing a few products, and then trade those products for everything else they need.

In recent decades, economists have started to realize that this theory doesn't capture what matters in reality. The old proverb "Jack of all trades, master of none" captures our intuition that we limit what we can achieve by targeting wide-ranging competence rather than choosing one domain in which to specialize. Perhaps that is true of an individual; it's not true of a city or a country. The economies that do lots of things tend to do most of those things very well. That is the road to prosperity—and in an unpredictable world, it is the road to resilience, too.

Jane Jacobs has deservedly attracted an army of admirers, and the intellectual battle in favor of diverse cities seems to have been won. But as Jacobs understood, two powerful forces stand in the way.

The first is hard to do anything about, as it seems deeply ingrained in human nature. It's a regrettable fact that neighborhoods have a tendency to segregate themselves, like oil and vinegar. If people prefer to live near similar people—perhaps people of the same race, class, ethnicity, or income—then even quite mild preferences can lead to marked social segregation.[17] (This is the same tendency we observed on university campuses: students seek out friendships with similar people.) The political implications of this tendency were parsed by Bill Bishop and Robert Cushing in their book *The Big Sort*, which showed that American neighborhoods were becoming more polarized. When Jimmy Carter won the U.S. presidency in 1976, just over a quarter of Americans lived in "landslide counties," where Carter had either won or lost by 20 percentage points. By the 2012 election, more than half of Americans lived in landslide counties.[18]

The second is more avoidable—a bureaucratic desire for tidy, segregated cities is expressed in zoning and planning laws that are designed to prevent different aspects of city life from getting tangled up with one another. The planner's vision, reasonable enough, is a world where smokestacks and brothels are kept far away from playgrounds and family homes. There is a question of balance here, but the problem is that what seems like the right balance on a planner's map will look very different at street level. Zoning restrictions seem pleasing in theory; in practice, they can produce dull city neighborhoods. Recall how Jane Jacobs's ballet of Hudson Street relied on the fact that the street was always active at any time of day, because so many different kinds of people used it. In contrast, thoroughly zoned neighborhoods are unbalanced. They are too busy at certain times, deathly quiet at others; they are unable to support local shops and businesses. They encourage a dependency on cars, because people tend to work far from where they live. They reinforce social divisions, too: Jonathan Rothwell of the Brookings Institution has shown that by preventing the development of new affordable housing, zoning restrictions often amplify existing racial and social inequalities.[19]

This, by now, should be a familiar story: the people who make the rules find themselves hypnotized by a tidy aesthetic that looks good on a map, graph, or screen—but which is a disaster for the people who have to live and work in a world defined by those tidy rules. Successful cities are a glorious mess of old and new, of houses and shops and workplaces, and where the richer residents and the poorer ones mingle together. And it is that diverse mess that makes them safe, innovative—and perhaps above all, resilient.

There are some forms of urban mess that nobody wants to live with. In the spring of 2010, cleaners at Utrecht railway station in the Netherlands went on strike. The station is a busy place, and in the absence of the cleaning staff it rapidly became the most appalling mess, the ground littered with newspapers, food cartons, and other trash. If this variety of mess has any positive effects on city living, then it's not clear what they are. But what's interesting in this context is how we instinctively seem to overestimate the benefits of tidying up.

Two Dutch psychologists, Diederik Stapel and Siegwart Lindenberg, decided to take advantage of the disruption to conduct a clever experiment. They asked commuters using the station to sit on a bench and fill in a questionnaire in exchange for a small reward. The questionnaire tested their tendency to stereotype others. The researchers also placed an actor on the bench: sometimes the actor was black, sometimes white. Would the experimental subjects sit near the stranger or far away? Stapel and Lindenberg repeated the experiment when the strike was over and the station was clean and tidy.

The experiment was a smash hit, reported around the world. Here's Diederik Stapel's recollection of the immediate response:

> I was in the paper—in fact I was in all the papers. I had published a study which showed that messy streets lead to greater intolerance. In a messy environment, people are more likely to resort to stereotypes of others because trash makes you want to clear it up, and the use of stereotypes lets you feel like you're clearing things up. Stereotypes bring clarity to a messy world. Women are emotional, men are aggressive, New Yorkers are in a hurry, Southerners are hospitable. Stereotypes make the world predictable, and we like that, especially if the world currently looks dirty and unkempt. The publication of this study caused a sensation. It was published in the most prestigious journal of them all, *Science*, and it made headlines around the world.[20]

Not only did people use more stereotypes when answering the questionnaire in the messy environment, they sat farther from the actor on the bench—but *only* if the actor was of a different race from their own. Stapel and Lindenberg theorized that stereotyping was an attempt to compensate for a messy environment: "a way to cope with chaos, a mental cleaning device." Mess invites us to impose our own oversimplified order on the universe: it makes us racists. And Stapel and Lindenberg had a clear policy recommendation:

> One way to fight unwanted stereotyping and discrimination is to diagnose environmental disorder early and to intervene immediately by cleaning up and creating physical order.[21]

What Stapel and Lindenberg had found seemed intriguing, surprising, yet strangely plausible. It seems to make sense that mess is bad for us, making us suspicious. We have a curious faith in the idea that if only we could live in a tidy world we'd be better people.

But within a few months of publication, social psychologists received some unsettling news: Diederik Stapel was a fraud. In paper after paper, he had fudged the data or even invented it completely, fooling the journals, his peers, and even his coauthors. (Stapel's colleague Siegwart Lindenberg was unaware of the deception.) Here, in Stapel's own words, is what really happened in Utrecht station:

> The empirical tests were completely imaginary. The lab research hadn't been carried out. The field studies never happened.[22]

The driving force, the bait that lured Stapel into a life of academic deceit, was simple: journal editors wanted to publish tidy results, too. And that is what Stapel kept providing for them. Stapel, it appears, was not only a fraud but something of a neat-freak himself.

> I'd been having trouble with my experiments for some time. Even with my various "gray" methods for improving the data, I wasn't able to get the results the way I wanted them. I couldn't resist the temptation to go a step further. I wanted it so badly . . . I was alone in my tastefully furnished office at the University of Groningen. I'd taken extra care when closing the door, and made my desk extra tidy. Everything had to be neat and orderly. No mess.[23]

Fortified by his scrupulously tidy environment, Diederik Stapel began to fabricate the data underpinning fifty-five research papers. And Stapel himself later told *The New York Times* that he was motivated by a desire for neatness, and by a desire to please the editors of academic journals who didn't like messy results any more than Stapel did.

Stapel, the newspaper reported, "had been frustrated by the messiness of experimental data, which rarely led to clear conclusions." His lifelong obsession with elegance and order, he said, led him to concoct sexy results that journals found attractive. "It was a quest for aesthetics, for beauty—instead of the truth."[24]

Diederik Stapel's fraud is a morality tale on two levels. His yearning for neatness led to his fraud. But more pertinent, it was our eagerness to believe what his fraudulent study was telling us—to overestimate the ill effects of mess, to imagine that tidying up would have profoundly transformative effects on our moral selves, rather than just make our morning commute more pleasant—that led to its generating so much publicity.

Not all messes have redeeming features: a train station that isn't strewn with litter is more pleasant than one that is. It's worth sweeping the platforms. But tidying up isn't going to turn us into better people.

The story of the "broken windows" theory of urban decay is another example of how we instinctively overestimate the benefits of tidying up certain kinds of urban mess. The theory was proposed in an influential article in *The Atlantic Monthly* in 1982 by criminologist George Kelling and political scientist James Q. Wilson. Kelling and Wilson argued that small signs of disorder led to the breakdown of community norms and, eventually, to serious criminality. Here's a taste of their argument:

A stable neighborhood of families who care for their homes, mind each other's children, and confidently frown on unwanted intruders can change, in a few years or even a few months, to an inhospitable and frightening jungle. A piece of property is abandoned, weeds grow up, a window is smashed. Adults stop scolding rowdy children; the children, emboldened, become more rowdy. Families move out, unattached adults move in. Teenagers gather in front of the corner store. The merchant asks them to move; they refuse. Fights occur. Litter accumulates. People start drinking in front of the grocery; in time, an inebriate slumps to the sidewalk and is allowed to sleep it off. Pedestrians are approached by panhandlers.

At this point it is not inevitable that serious crime will flourish or violent attacks on strangers will occur. But many residents will think that crime, especially violent crime, is on the rise, and they will modify their behavior accordingly. They will use the streets less often, and when on the streets will stay apart from their fellows, moving with averted eyes, silent lips, and hurried steps. "Don't get involved." . . . Such an area is vulnerable to criminal invasion. Though it is not inevitable, it is more likely that here, rather than in places where people are confident they can regulate public behavior by informal controls, drugs will change hands, prostitutes will solicit, and cars will be stripped. That the drunks will be robbed by boys who do it as a lark, and the prostitutes' customers will be robbed by men who do it purposefully and perhaps violently. That muggings will occur.[25]

This is a plausible idea, and its plausibility was greatly strengthened when it was embraced by New York City's police department, which began to focus on disorderly behavior in public spaces in the 1990s. Serious crime fell sharply.[26]

But just because the theory is plausible does not mean it is true. In Kelling and Wilson's breathless narrative, why exactly is a property abandoned in the first place? Properties are much more likely to be left derelict in poor areas than in prosperous ones. So did the abandoned property trigger the decline of this imagined neighborhood? Or was the neighborhood already in trouble when someone abandoned their property? The story that Kelling and Wilson spin tries to make cause and effect seem clear, but in reality they are hopelessly tangled.

Indeed, as one looks into the evidence base for the broken windows idea, it starts to look very thin. The psychologist Philip Zimbardo is mentioned by Kelling and Wilson:

> He arranged to have an automobile without license plates parked with its hood up on a street in the Bronx and a comparable automobile on a street in Palo Alto, California . . . The car in Palo Alto sat untouched for more than a week. Then Zimbardo smashed part of it with a sledgehammer. Soon, passersby were joining in. Within a few hours, the car had been turned upside down and utterly destroyed.[27]

Interesting, but it is a stretch to build a theory of urban decay on what happens after one psychologist takes one sledgehammer to one car in one California city.

The truth is that social science has not been able to muster much support for the broken windows theory of policing, nor for the idea that it deserves credit for breaking New York City's crime wave in the 1990s. There is no shortage of explanations for the decline in crime, and any plausible explanation must deal with the fact that crime fell across the United States, not just in New York. Steve Levitt, the economist now famous for the Freakonomics books, surveyed the evidence in 2004.

He began by looking at newspaper accounts of the trend, and found that broken windows policing usually got the credit for the fall in crime.

Levitt himself, armed with a rich set of data, disagreed with the newspapers. He concluded that four factors seemed to explain the timing, extent, and geographical pattern of the fall in crime: more police; a larger prison population (this may deter crime, and will also prevent crimes because would-be criminals are locked up); the waning of an epidemic of crack use; and the legalization of abortion in the 1970s, which reduced the number of unwanted children.* Levitt considered and dismissed several other explanations, including broken windows policing: "My reading of the limited data that are available leads me to the conclusion that the impact of policing strategies on New York City crime are exaggerated, and that the impact on national crime is likely to be minor."[28]

Levitt is not the only social scientist to be skeptical. Consider a fascinating debate in 2005 in the pages of *Legal Affairs* between two experts in the field, Bernard E. Harcourt and David Thacher. Each man cited the best available evidence based on various statistical studies. Harcourt was skeptical of broken windows policing. Thacher was supposed to be writing in support of a broken windows policing strategy. Yet even he was agnostic about the idea that disorder breeds serious crime. Instead, he made the much more defensible claim that police should deal with disorder because that's worth doing in its own right:

> Somehow the question of whether police should take order maintenance more seriously got equated with the question of whether doing that would reduce crime. I think that's an interesting and a little dispiriting comment on our culture . . . As if there were no reason for a cop walking by to do something about

*A fifth explanation has since been proposed: taking lead out of gasoline in the late 1970s seems to have improved children's cognitive development and thus (with a delay) reduced crime.

> a guy urinating in the middle of the street in a commercial district [unless this] would prevent a statistically-significant number of burglaries next month.[29]

Thacher is right—certain kinds of mess are worth tidying up for their own sake. But it's striking how easily we fall for the old-fashioned idea that "cleanliness is next to godliness"—that a mess is not just a mess, but the precursor to some dreadful evil.

There's another problem with piling too many hopes on broken windows policing. It turns out that when we perceive our neighborhoods as messy, we may not be quite as objective as we'd like to think. In 2004, two social psychologists, Robert Sampson of Harvard and Stephen Raudenbush of the University of Michigan, asked a basic but revealing question: When residents call their streets "disordered," what's really on their minds?[30]

Sampson and Raudenbush drove cars up and down the streets of Chicago, taking videos of over 23,000 segments of street frontage. Then they used a team of research assistants to rate the levels of disorder witnessed in those videos. They included physical disorder (graffiti, abandoned cars, litter, broken glass, beer bottles, discarded condoms), social disorder (loiterers, street prostitutes, drugs being sold, street drinking, gangs of teenagers), and structural disorder (vacant houses, boarded-up commercial buildings). The team members cross-checked one another's work to ensure consistency, leaving Sampson and Raudenbush with a neutral observer's rating of the visual level of disorder on each street.

Then Sampson and Raudenbush conducted a survey of thousands of Chicago residents, asking them about their own perceptions of disorder. How big a problem was graffiti in their neighborhood? What about litter? What about public drunkenness? Drug dealing? Teenagers causing a disturbance? Then they compared the subjective perceptions of the people who lived in these blocks with the objective observations of the external observers who had rated the street-level videos.

The answer is disturbing. There was, of course, a correlation between the perceptions of the residents and that of the external observers. But there was a stronger correlation: what really seemed to drive people's sense that they lived in a disordered neighborhood wasn't the visible manifestations of disorder on the street. It was whether the neighborhood was poor, and whether it was black. Neighborhoods with many poor families, or with a high proportion of African American residents, or both, were perceived as being more disordered by the people who lived there, relative to richer, whiter neighborhoods with the same levels of trash, graffiti, or panhandlers.

If we want to predict whether a city block's residents think that it's a mess, we would learn more from looking at data on race and poverty than we would learn from looking at videos of what the neighborhood actually looks like. People feel that richer white neighborhoods look neat and poorer black neighborhoods look disorderly, regardless of what is really happening on the street. So when people demand that police tidy up their neighborhood, to some extent they might actually be giving voice to a subconscious wish that they lived somewhere a little bit richer, and a little bit whiter.

A century ago, the greatest mathematician alive was the German David Hilbert. He was a man whose research program inspired a generation of younger mathematicians, and whose achievements include developing a more rigorous version of the theory of special relativity at around the time Einstein himself was discovering the idea. Hilbert was the beating heart of Göttingen University's stellar mathematics department.

Yet Hilbert had a long retirement, during which he saw many of his former colleagues forced out under Nazi rule, sometimes because of a single Jewish grandparent.[31] In 1934, Hilbert found himself sitting next to Bernhard Rust, Hitler's minister for education, at a banquet.

Rust asked Hilbert, "How is mathematics in Göttingen now that it has been freed of Jewish influence?"

Hilbert's reply: "Mathematics in Göttingen? There is really none any more."[32]

We all know the grotesque project of the extermination camps during the Second World War. But in the prewar buildup, the persecution was of a different kind: Jews were hounded and humiliated. Academics with Jewish ancestry found their careers in ruins. The best of them left, seeking less intolerant cultures in Britain and the United States. A torment for those that fled, this policy was also a self-inflicted wound. German science was crippled. Despite a formidable industrial base and engineering tradition, Germany was unable to keep pace with the innovations that emerged from Britain and the United States—often from the very people who had been driven out. Racial and ideological purity is not a recipe for scientific success.

The economist Fabian Waldinger has recently examined the impact of the purge and found something striking. Waldinger's research strategy was based on the fact that different subjects suffered very different rates of dismissal. At Hilbert's beloved Göttingen, for example, 60 percent of the mathematicians were forced to leave, but the chemistry department lost nobody. Using such random variations across Germany, Waldinger was able to show how serious the impact was of losing, say, 10 percent of the scientists at a department. Then he compared it with the impact of bombing raids on university departments during the war. He found the damage from losing Jewish or dissident scientists was far greater and longer-lasting than the damage to offices or laboratory facilities. Insisting on a racially pure scientific establishment inflicted permanent harm both to research output and to the productivity of young PhD students who lost some of their best mentors. Stripped of their diversity, the German universities could not bounce back.*[33]

Adolf Hitler's insouciant remark that "we'll have to do without science for a few years" was as self-destructive in his day as it would be in ours. Few people nowadays would publicly embrace the Nazi enthusiasm for racial purges from the intellectual professions, but in other ways fear of social diversity still runs deep. During the Republican primary campaign for the 2016 U.S. presidential election, for example, Donald Trump's artful courting of controversy to keep within his rivals' OODA loops often involved taking tough stances on immigration. He began his rise to frontrunner status by promising to build a wall along the U.S.–Mexico border, having linked Mexican immigrants with drugs, crime, and rape. It was when he later called for "a

*Of course, many of the Jewish scientists and mathematicians persecuted by the Nazis would not have regarded themselves as standard bearers for "diversity." They considered themselves just as German as the fellow in the next office; their religious heritage loomed large only from the perspective of a racist ideology. Fritz Haber, for example, was baptized as a Christian and was a patriot, yet because of his Jewish ancestry suffered anti-Semitism even before the Nazis took control in Germany. (Haber, a Nobel laureate in chemistry, was responsible for one of the most wonderful inventions in history—a process for synthesizing nitrogen-based fertilizers, helping to feed the world—and one of the most terrible, the use of chlorine gas as a weapon of war.)

In part because of such discrimination, scientists of the time with Jewish heritage arguably *were* different. Haber, for example, struggled to find a professorship. Looking for a source of income elsewhere, he turned to industry, signing a contract with the optical firm Zeiss and aggressively pursuing patents. As a result, when he did eventually secure a professorial appointment, he had different contacts and a more practical outlook. His work on fertilizers followed from that problem-focused perspective, and it was work that changed the world.

The historian of science David Bodanis argues that the outlook of Germany's Jewish scientists was also shaped by discrimination they had suffered elsewhere. Several of the mathematicians at Göttingen were originally Russian or Polish Jews who viewed the university as a safe harbor from persecution in their home countries. They had a distinctive training, and the contrast between the German, Polish, and Russian styles of mathematics was a great source of ideas.

It is possible, however, that the main effect Fabian Waldinger's research is detecting is not the expulsion of people who had a different perspective because they had been pushed out of Poland or Russia, or been forced to sidestep discrimination by dabbling in industry—but simply the expulsion of scientists who were outstanding because they had to be. Only the very best would be able to overcome the disadvantage of biased appointment committees. "A fine example is Emmy Noether," writes Bodanis (personal correspondence, February 2016). As a Jewish woman, Noether had to overcome a double dose of prejudice. "She really was stupendous . . . being 'averagely brilliant' would not have been enough." Emmy Noether laughed when the first students started coming to class wearing Nazi brown shirts, but she was one of the first of Göttingen's Jews to lose her job. With the help of Albert Einstein she secured a position at Bryn Mawr College near Philadelphia in 1933.

total and complete shutdown of Muslims entering the United States" that media commentators seemed confident he had finally overstepped the mark. Evidently not: his poll ratings climbed higher.[34]

Modern societies continue to flirt with subtler versions of the same desire for homogeneity that underpinned the Nazi purges, and which research shows is self-defeating. Consider the work of two economists, Gianmarco Ottaviano and Giovanni Peri, who asked what impact a stream of immigrants from across the world might have on American cities. In particular they wanted to look at cities with a large number of foreign-born residents, from a range of countries. One might expect that such melting pots might struggle with social cohesion, gangs, and classrooms overstretched by language barriers. Instead, Ottaviano and Peri found that cities that hosted a complex patchwork of nationalities prospered as a result. U.S.-born residents enjoyed higher wages and, if they were landlords, could charge higher rents. If they were tenants, they paid extra for the privilege of living in such vibrant, productive cities.[35]

To many modern ears, some of the stories in this chapter about how diversity builds resilience may not seem surprising. Most of us know that monoculture is a risky idea, and would scoff at the hubris of replacing an entire ecosystem with a single species and expecting everything to go well. We've all read about the importance of "good bacteria." But it seems hard for us to take these warnings to heart. When a doctor tells us we have a minor bacterial infection and prescribes antibiotics, few of us say that we'd really rather not take them unless absolutely necessary. Indeed, many patients demand to be prescribed antibiotics for viral infections, a situation where antibiotics are useless. We grumble at the city planners when they reject our application for a house extension, but few of us who live in leafy residential areas are clamoring to have more shops, restaurants, offices, and light industrial units intermingled with our homes.

And we still fear outsiders. Most of us living in rich countries seem content with immigration policies that exclude people from our own societies simply because of where they were born. The idea that immigration is excessive, out of control, and damaging is not just acceptable but the majority view in many countries. That view may be popular, but it is a mistake. Recall that Katherine Phillips and her colleagues found that small student groups disliked having a stranger in their midst, even as the stranger was helping them solve the murder-mystery problem they faced. We suffer the same problem at a societal level: we find it easy to overlook the contributions that immigrants make, and are acutely aware of our own discomfort. Somehow we must get over that: every society needs its outsiders to bring new attitudes, ideas, and perspectives.

These stories are not just about particular examples of diversity. They are about our reaction to diversity, again and again. In our organizations, politics, marketplaces, and personal lives, we continue to enjoy the apparent convenience, neatness, and short-term profits of imposing order, and fail to notice when it is sowing the seeds of fragility.

9

Life

"Appointments are always a no-no. Planning ahead is a no-no."

Franklin, Schwarzenegger, and the Genius Who Hacked OkCupid: Why We Should Value Mess in Our Inbox, Our Conversations, and Our Children's Play

While whiling away the long voyage from London to Philadelphia in 1726, a young printer named Benjamin Franklin conceived the notion of a notebook in which he would record systematically his efforts at self-improvement. Franklin aspired to thirteen virtues, including frugality, industry, sincerity, and cleanliness. His plan was to spend a week focusing on a particular virtue, in the hope of making it a habit, before moving to the next virtue, and the next, cycling through the virtues in an unending quest to become a better man. Each day he would reflect on his activities and every failure to live up to his own standards would be commemorated with a black mark in his notebook. The custom stuck with him his entire life. Fifty-nine years later, while writing his memoirs, Franklin lingered on the merits of his virtue journal longer than on any other topic, reconfirming his commitment to the habit.[1]

Franklin's aims were ambitious, but his virtue journal was a success: the black spots in the notebook, initially numerous, became scarcer over time. Perhaps this is no surprise, since Franklin had a habit of doing whatever he set out to do. He lived one of the most celebrated lives in history. He charted the Gulf Stream; he invented bifocals, the lightning conductor, and the flexible urinary catheter; he was the first U.S. postmaster general, served as America's ambassador to France, and was president of Pennsylvania. And, of course, Benjamin Franklin's signature is on the U.S. Declaration of Independence.

Yet the great man had one weakness—or so he thought.

Ben Franklin's third virtue was: *Order. Let all your things have their places; let each part of your business have its time.* Franklin never mastered this seemingly simple task. "My scheme of ORDER gave me the most trouble," he wrote in frustration in his memoirs, adding, "my faults in it vexed me so much, and I made so little progress in amendment, and had such frequent relapses, that I was almost ready to give up the attempt."

He was not exaggerating. One scholar wrote, "Strangers who came to see him were amazed to behold papers of the greatest importance scattered in the most careless way over the table and floor."[2] Franklin's diary and his home remained chaotic, resisting sixty years of focused effort from one of the most determined men who ever lived. No matter how many disorderly decades passed, Franklin remained convinced that orderliness was an unalloyed virtue: that if only he could fix this deficiency in his character, and become less messy, he would become a more admirable, successful, and productive person.

Franklin was surely deluding himself. It is hard to believe such a rich life could possibly have been made still richer by closer attention to filing papers and tidying up. His error is no surprise. We are tidy-minded people, instinctively admiring order and in denial about the way mess tends to be the inevitable by-product of good things, and is sometimes a good thing in its own right.

What seems more surprising is not Franklin's error, but his failure to keep his ill-advised resolution. This is a man who did almost everything he set out to do; why is it that he failed on this one occasion? Perhaps he realized, on some unconscious level, that disorderliness was no bar to success. Many of us have yet to make the same realization, in areas that define much of our daily lives: organizing our documents, tasks, and time; looking for love; socializing; raising our kids. Benjamin Franklin's mistake is a mistake from which we can all learn, every day of our lives.

There is one bit of everyday wisdom in Franklin's motto "Let all your things have their places." As the psychologist Daniel Levitin explains in *The Organized Mind*, our spatial memory is powerful, so it's easier to remember things when they are anchored to a particular location.[3] Things such as keys and corkscrews have a tendency to wander about in the course of being used. That is why they are easy to lose. And it is no accident that computer filing systems use a spatial metaphor—manila folders nestled inside other manila folders—to help humans keep track of documents that are, in reality, chopped up and scattered across the surface of some hard drive.

Keeping things in their places will help you keep track of your keys and your corkscrew. Yet it will be much less help in dealing with your documents or your e-mail, because the system will buckle under not only the volume of incoming information but its fundamental contradictions and ambiguities.

Merlin Mann, a productivity expert, has skewered the desire to over-organize a list of tasks in a fast-moving world. Imagine you're making sandwiches in a deli, says Mann. The first sandwich order comes in and you start spreading the mayonnaise on a slice of rye bread. But wait—the lunchtime rush is coming. Wouldn't it be a good idea to stop and check whether any more sandwich orders have arrived? Gosh, yes: two more sandwich orders. Now, how best to organize them? In order of arrival, perhaps. Or maybe it's best to segregate the vegetarian orders from those involving meat? Another possibility is to distinguish the toasted orders from the fresh ones. Hm. Let's check to see if any more sandwich orders have arrived. Yes! Three more. Now there are six. So many ways to organize them . . .[4]

Mann's point is not only that we are often too busy to get organized, but that if we focused on practical action, we wouldn't *need* to get organized. Of course, some situations call for a sophisticated reference system (a library, for example), and some for careful checklists (a building site, an operating room). But most of us don't work in a library or an operating room, and our faith in organization is often misplaced. Many of us share Franklin's touching belief that if only we could get ourselves organized with some rational system, our lives would be better, more productive, and more admirable—but the truth is that Franklin was too busy inventing bifocals, catching lightning, publishing newspapers, and signing the Declaration of Independence ever to get around to tidying up his life. If he had been working in a deli, you can bet he wouldn't have been organizing sandwich orders. He would have been making sandwiches.

Organizing things into categories is not as easy as it might at first seem. The philosophically irrepressible writer Jorge Luis Borges once told of the "Celestial Emporium of Benevolent Knowledge," a fabled Chinese encyclopedia. This Oriental tome, according to Borges, organizes animals into categories thus: (a) those that belong to the emperor; (b) embalmed ones; (c) those that are trained; (d) suckling pigs; (e) mermaids; (f) fabulous ones; (g) stray dogs; (h) those that are included in this classification; (i) those that tremble as if they were mad; (j) innumerable ones; (k) those drawn with a very fine camel's-hair brush; (l) etcetera; (m) those that have just broken the flower vase; (n) those that at a distance resemble flies.

This looks like a joke, but like other Borgesian jokes, it is serious. Most of these apparently absurd categories have practical merit. Sometimes we need to classify things according to who owns them; at other times we must describe their physical attributes, and different physical attributes will matter in different contexts. Sometimes we must be terribly specific—a cat is not a good substitute for a suckling pig if you are preparing a feast, and if we are to punish wrongdoing (whether breaking a vase or committing an armed robbery), we must identify the wrongdoer and no one else. But while each category is useful, in combination they are incoherent, and the encyclopedia sounds delectably unusable. Borges shows us why trying to categorize the world is not as straightforward as we like to believe. Our categories can map to practical real-world cases, or they can be neat and logical, but rarely both at once.

A widely used system of classification reduces Borges's fourteen categories to three: filing in triplicate has become a byword for the tidily organized bureaucracy. Making three copies of correspondence and filing once by date, once by topic, and once by correspondent is a logical solution for a world in which we cannot predict whether we might need to look up all the letters sent and received late in October 2015, or all the letters about the faulty rumbleflange, or all the letters from a Mrs. Trellis. But the system still requires three times the space and tremendous time and energy to maintain. And where do we file the letter that's a ransom note? What about a letter that has three topics rather than one? What about the letter that is a glowing endorsement, suitable for use in advertising? Borges was on to something with the category "etcetera."*

For some organizations, filing in triplicate may be unavoidable. For most of us, such a system is a colossal waste of time, space, and energy. If you need to file physical documents, what about the following beautiful alternative, invented by Japanese economist Yukio Noguchi? Forget about categories. Instead, place each incoming document in a large envelope. Write the envelope's contents neatly on its edge, and line them up on a bookshelf, their contents visible like the spines of books. Now the moment of genius: every time you use an envelope, place it back on the left of the shelf. Over time, recently used documents will shuffle themselves toward the left, and never-used documents will accumulate on the right. Archiving is easy: every now and again, you remove the documents on the right. To find any document, simply ask yourself how recently you've seen it. It is a filing system that all but organizes itself, and it has won many fans.

But wait a moment. Isn't there something strangely familiar about the arrangement? Eric Abrahamson and David Freedman, authors of the exuberant book *A Perfect Mess*, offer the following suggestion: "Turn the row of envelopes so that the envelopes are stacked vertically instead of horizontally, place the stack on your desktop, and get rid of the envelopes."[6]

After following those instructions, what have you got? Any old pile of papers on a messy desk. Every time you pull a document out, you replace it on the top of the pile. Unused documents gradually settle at the bottom. Of course this arrangement lacks the neat labeling of the Noguchi system, but it offers intuitive physical clues such as the thickness of a document, the shade of the paper, the appearance of

*For digital documents, we now have a messier alternative to filing: the tag. A single copy of a document can be in only one folder, but it can be tagged in as many different ways as we like.

dog-ears or Post-it notes. These signals are fallible, but they can be powerful.

This is not to argue that a big pile of paper is the best possible filing system. But despite appearances, it's very far from being a random assortment. A messy desk isn't nearly as chaotic as it at first seems. There's a natural tendency toward a very pragmatic system of organization based simply on the fact that the useful stuff keeps on getting picked up and left on the top of the pile.

That's the thing about a messy desk or a messy office: it's full of clues about recent patterns of working, and those clues can help us work effectively. David Kirsh, a cognitive scientist at the University of California, San Diego, studies the working styles of "neats" and "scruffies." For example, how do people orient themselves after arriving at the office or finishing a phone call? Kirsh finds that "neats" orient themselves with to-do lists and calendars, while "scruffies" orient themselves using physical cues—the report that they were working on is lying on the desk, as is a letter that needs a reply, and receipts that must be submitted for expenses. A messy desk is full of such cues.*[7] A tidy desk conveys no information at all, and it must be bolstered with the prompt of a to-do list. Both systems can work, so we should hesitate before judging other people based on their messy desks.[8]

Of course, it is intolerable to have to work in the middle of somebody else's mess. But that is because the subtle cues that the mess contains are all irrelevant. They are signposts for somebody else's journey.

But surely even our own mess, laden with clues about what to do next, must be less efficient than well-organized tidiness? That depends. As Borges taught us, tidying things into categories is not as easy as it

*The French essayist Paul Valéry argued that if you want to always be able to find your treasured possessions, simply be yourself and put them wherever your instinct tells you. It is only once you start trying to organize everything in a conscious way that things get lost. Valéry may have been overstating the case, but he was on to something: nothing is ever quite so totally lost as when it has been tidied away according to an organizational system that is opaque.

might appear. And while the categories will sometimes help, it's worth pondering whether the filing system will consume more time than it saves.

Academics who study workplace behavior sometimes make the distinction between "filers" and "pilers"—people who establish a formal organizational structure for their paper documents, versus people who let piles of paperwork accumulate on and around their desks. A few years ago, two researchers at AT&T Labs, Steve Whittaker and Julia Hirschberg, studied how a group of office workers dealt with their paperwork. Who hoarded the most paper? Who used their archives more actively? When an office relocation forced everyone to reduce the size of their archives, who coped best?

The answers surprised Whittaker and Hirschberg. "We predicted that filers' attempts to evaluate and categorize incoming documents would produce smaller archives that were accessed frequently," they wrote. But that isn't what they found. The filers didn't have lean archives full of useful and oft-accessed documents; they had capacious cabinets full of neatly filed paper that they never used. The filers were filing prematurely. In an effort to keep their desks clear, they would swiftly file documents that turned out to have no long-term value. In their bloated archives it was hard to find anything useful, despite the logical organization, because the good stuff was surrounded with neatly filed dross. The Borges problem made things harder—as one person told Whittaker and Hirschberg:

"I had so much stuff filed. I didn't know where everything was, and I'd found that I had created second files for something in what seemed like a logical place, but not the only logical place . . . In some cases, things could legitimately be filed under the business unit or a technology. And I ended up having the same thing in two places, or I had the same business unit stuff in five different places."

And because they were devoting so much effort to their filing systems, the filers became unduly attached to their archives and found it difficult to let go of things.

The pilers, in contrast, would keep documents on their desks for a while and sooner or later would pick them up, realize they were useless, and dump them in the recycling bin. Any archives were small and practical and frequently used. When the time came for the office move, the pilers had an easy job—they simply kept the top half of every pile and discarded the rarely used lower documents. (It's that informal Noguchi system again.) The biggest disadvantage that the pilers suffered was that because their offices looked so messy, somebody else might sneak in and tidy everything up, a ruinous act of vandalism.[9]

The main filing headache in the modern world comes not from paper documents but from e-mail. How best to organize that? Borges rears his head again. Does this e-mail from the boss mentioning a performance review, the office party, and the Acme account go under Work > Human Resources or under Work > Boss or under Personal > Diary or under Work > Accounts > Acme? Or perhaps follow the file-in-triplicate tradition, and file copies in each folder? That's easy to accomplish by tagging the file, and the triplicate e-mails don't take up physical space. Nevertheless the triplication is a problem: each extra copy takes up space on the screen as you scan through the folder trying to find what you're really looking for; it is more hay on the haystack the next time you're looking for the needle.

And the folders themselves proliferate: one study found that people create a new e-mail folder every five days.[10] For those of us who've been on e-mail since the late twentieth century, that's more than a thousand folders. A thousand folders are manageable if they're organized into folders of folders of folders. But these deep tree structures can create their own problems. And all this e-mail filing takes time—around 10 percent of all e-mail time is spent organizing e-mail, according to researchers at Xerox PARC.[11]

Still, it's worth the effort, right? Wrong. A fine research paper with the title "Am I Wasting My Time Organizing Email?" by Steve Whittaker (again) and researchers at IBM Research concluded that, broadly, yes, you are.[12] Whittaker and his colleagues got permission to install logging software on the computers of several hundred office workers, and tracked around 85,000 attempts to find e-mail by clicking through folders, or by using ad hoc methods—scrolling through the inbox, clicking on a header to sort by (for example) the sender, or using the search function. Whittaker found that clicking through a folder tree took almost a minute, while simply searching took just 17 seconds. People who relied on folders took longer to find what they were looking for, but their hunts for the right e-mail were no more or less successful. In other words, if you just dump all your e-mail into a folder called "archive," you will find your e-mails more quickly than if you hide them in a tidy structure of folders.*

If carefully filing paper documents is counterproductive and carefully organizing e-mails is a waste of time, what should we conclude about the way to manage a calendar? There are two broad approaches to calendar management. One is that a calendar should be used only for noting fixed points—a doctor's appointment, a flight, a business meeting. Most of the calendar should be left blank to allow us to do whatever seems appropriate in the moment. But an alternative view is that a calendar should be used to plan more carefully, blocking out time to work on different tasks.

Fortunately, we don't need to guess at which approach works best:

*Of course there may be folder systems that work well for certain situations; Whittaker's research shows not that folder trees are always a waste of time, just that they are typically a waste of time. I create a folder when I am asked to go to a particular event, such as a book festival. Every e-mail on that event can be saved in the folder and quickly found, and once the festival is over the entire folder can be archived. I use the search function for almost everything else.

three psychologists, Daniel Kirschenbaum, Laura Humphrey, and Sheldon Malett, have already run the experiment. Kirschenbaum and his colleagues recruited a group of undergraduates to participate in a short course designed to improve their study skills. The students were then split randomly into three groups: a control group who were given simple tips on time management (for example: "Take breaks of 5–10 minutes after every ½–1½ hour study session") and two groups who were given the time-management tips plus instructions as to how to plan their time. The "monthly plan" group was instructed to set out goals and study activities spanning a month or so at a time; the "daily plan" group was told to plan activities and goals day by day. The researchers assumed that the planners would be more successful than the control group, and that the daily plans, with their brief, quantifiable goals, would work better than the rather amorphous monthly plans.[13]

The researchers were in for a surprise. The daily plans were catastrophic. Students using them started by working 20 hours a week but by the end of the course they were down to about 8 hours a week. Having no plan at all was just as bad, although arguably it encouraged more consistent work effort: students began by working 15 hours a week and sagged to 10 hours a week later in the course. But the monthly plans were a tremendous success in motivating students to study—they put in 25 hours a week, and even studied slightly harder at the end of the 10-week course than at the beginning. These are huge effects—the monthly plan motivated about twice as much work as the daily plan. When the researchers followed up a year later, these trends had continued and were reflected in the students' grades: the students with monthly plans were doing better than ever, the students with no plans were treading water, and the students with daily plans were sliding ever further down the scale of academic achievement.

Why was this happening? The researchers had two theories. First, that the daily plans took too much time and effort (many students soon gave up on them, although perhaps not soon enough). Second, that the daily plans sapped the motivation of students once they realized that they kept falling short of their own plans. Both of those speculations sound plausible, but they raise the question of why students weren't able to follow their own daily plans.

The answer is that daily plans can't adjust to unexpected events. Things come up: you catch a cold; you need to stay home for a plumber; a friend calls to say he's visiting town unexpectedly. With a broad plan, or no plan, it's easy to accommodate these obstacles and opportunities.

Some people manage to take this to extremes. Marc Andreessen is one of the first Internet wunderkinds: he cofounded Netscape in 1994, sold it for over $4 billion, and founded a Silicon Valley venture capital firm that invested in companies such as Skype, Twitter, and Airbnb. Besieged by invitations and meetings, Andreessen decided that he would simply stop writing anything in his calendar. If something was important, then it could be done immediately. Otherwise it wasn't worth signing away a slice of Andreessen's future. "I've been trying this tactic as an experiment," he wrote in 2007. "And I am so much happier, I can't even tell you."[14]

Another example: Arnold Schwarzenegger insisted on keeping his diary clear when he was a film star, and even tried to do so when he was governor of California. "Appointments are always a no-no. Planning ahead is a no-no," he told *The New York Times*. Politicians, lobbyists, and activists had to treat him like they treated a popular walk-up restaurant: they showed up and hoped to get a slot. This wasn't some strange status play. Well, perhaps it was, a little. But Schwarzenegger had also realized that an overstuffed diary allows no flexibility.

Of course, it is much easier to make the world queue up to meet you if you're a billionaire venture capitalist or a global star of film and politics. But even if we cannot emulate Andreessen or Schwarzenegger in a point-blank refusal to make appointments, we probably could benefit from nudging ourselves a little in that direction—making fewer firm commitments, and leaving more flexibility to adapt to circumstances. A plan that is too specific will soon lie in tatters. Daily plans are tidy, but life is messy.[15]

In the mid-1960s, some young Harvard students found themselves drinking and keeping each other company on a Saturday night, having failed to persuade any women to spend the evening with them. The dating scene was tough, they agreed. There were two ways to meet girls: blind dates or parties. To the students, both seemed unsatisfyingly messy. Blind dates were too random, parties too awkward (especially as the girls tended to focus on the more senior students). The friends agreed that there had to be a better way to get a date, and so they set up an impressive-sounding organization with the name "Compatibility Research Inc."

Compatibility Research was a computerized dating agency, better known by the trading name Operation Match. For three dollars—about $25 in today's terms—hopeful singles could fill out a questionnaire. It would be converted into a punch card and the all-knowing computer—an IBM mainframe the size of a bus—would do the rest. In those days, number crunchers would typically rent processing time on a shared computer, which tended to be expensive. The Operation Match team managed to buy cheap time on the computer by waiting until the early hours of a Sunday morning. Their venture was not solely aimed at making money: according to Dan Slater's book *Love in the Time of Algorithms*, the founders of Operation Match were hoping for the first pick of the ladies themselves.[16] But they had chosen a clever business. It turns out we are suckers for the idea that finding a date can be turned into a tidy, neatly quantified affair.

At the time, computers were mysterious and seemed almost omniscient. It was easy to imagine that they might produce brilliant results, especially armed with a long questionnaire to chew over. Some questions were simple and numerical: age, height, grade point average (this was Harvard, after all). Others sought responses to *Cosmo*-style provocations: "Is romantic love necessary for a successful marriage?" "Do you believe in a God who answers prayer?" "Is extensive sexual activity in preparation for marriage part of 'growing up'?" And there were hypothetical scenarios (What would you do if sent on a blind date with an embarrassingly ugly person?) offering a multiple-choice format for answers. With all this information, how could a supercomputer fail to produce a perfect, quantified match?

"The computer had a legitimacy," recalls Dave Crump, one of the company's founders, and that was an idea they were keen to encourage. One advertisement promised, "Let a computer scientifically find the right date for you . . . during Singles Week."

The truth was more prosaic, as Crump's colleague Jeff Tarr later explained.

"The first thing we did was to make sure they were in the same area. Mostly girls wanted to go out with boys who were the same age or older, their height or taller, the same religion. So after we had these cuts, then we just kind of randomly matched them."[17]

That's it. So much for "compatibility research." The IBM computer did what computers do very easily: found a match for zip code, religion, age, and height. Further sorting was usually unnecessary, and the implication of Jeff Tarr's account is that most of the questions were there purely for effect.

The computer was simply figuring out who else was single and local. This is a perfectly valuable service, as Grindr and Tinder have since demonstrated. But Operation Match's founders weren't in a hurry to call attention to what their computer was really doing. The idea of scientific compatibility matching was just irresistible to everybody, especially the media—such was the curiosity that Jeff Tarr even appeared on a popular TV panel show. And aside from being good publicity, the computer made for a fine conversation starter, allowing people to spend their first date trying to figure out together why the computer, in its digital wisdom, had seen fit to pair them off. This idea that a computer algorithm could find the perfect match was so powerful that actually implementing any such algorithm was superfluous.

Surely algorithmic dating is more sophisticated today? That is certainly what most dating websites would have us think. Starting with the very names of popular sites (Match, eHarmony), the sales pitch is the same as ever it was: Give the computer your data and it will find you love. Online dating is now a massive business, and the promise of tidily quantified compatibility remains a key selling point. We seem convinced that if only the machines were powerful enough, and were fed enough data, they could find us a soul mate. OkCupid, a site with geek appeal and a witty, naughty tone, allows you to answer literally hundreds of thousands of questions: anything from "Do you like the taste of beer?" to "Would you ever read your partner's e-mail?" Users typically answer several hundred such questions, as well as indicating what answer they would hope for from a would-be date—and how important they feel the question is.

But while modern dating websites are incomparably larger, there is little reason to believe that their algorithms work much better. In the summer of 2014, OkCupid published the results of a few experiments it had been running on the site's users.[18] One of these experiments deployed a kind of placebo matching algorithm: users were told that they were 90 percent compatible (what does that even mean?) when in fact the computer believed them to be barely compatible at all.

It soon emerged that being *told* that the algorithm rated you as a good match was just as effective at promoting an extended online chat as actually *being* a good algorithmic match. Just as with Operation Match, compatibility was a placebo: believing that you were compatible was all that was necessary; the algorithm itself was worth very little.

This really should not be a surprise. Hannah Fry, the author of *The Mathematics of Love*, explains why OkCupid is fundamentally limited in what it can do: "Their algorithm is doing exactly what it was designed to do: deliver singles who meet your specifications. The problem here is that you don't really know what you want."[19]

The problem runs deeper than that. If we did know what we wanted, we still wouldn't be able to express that desire to the computer. We can easily specify height, age, religion, location, and income. We can list hobbies and interests, too. But while these things matter, what we really want in a romantic partner cannot be tidily measured: "makes me laugh," "turns me on," "gets along with my friends," or "understands me." If the computer cannot pose the right questions for you, it is hardly likely to produce the right answers.

Searchable attributes such as location can help us find a partner. And they're particularly useful for people with the kind of requirement that you can verify, such as an unusual sexual preference or dietary restriction. A site like "Positive Singles" will help people with a sexually transmitted condition such as HIV or herpes meet others in the same situation. If you have very specific needs of the sort that can be specified in a database, then Internet dating is a godsend. But what is strange is that even people with fairly generic preferences—to find a nice girl/boy with vanilla sexual tastes and a good sense of humor—have faith that, armed only with a list of our hobbies and the answers to a few pop psychology questions, a computer can find us the perfect match.

The experience of Chris McKinlay suggests otherwise.

Touted by *Wired* magazine as "the math genius who hacked OkCupid," McKinlay—a computer science researcher in his mid-thirties—was looking for romance and created some software that slurped up information about twenty thousand women on the dating website OkCupid. This wasn't easy: OkCupid blocks attempts to scrape data from its website, and so McKinlay had to program his own software to imitate human search behavior. He left it running around the clock in a quiet corner of the UCLA math department, and three weeks later he had the answers to six million questions.[20]

McKinlay then identified clusters of "types" of women he found promising. Armed with a deep pool of data, he was able to optimize his own profile, answering truthfully but choosing the perfect answers to emphasize. Finally he unleashed software bots to attract attention to his own profile. The result was a perfect dating storm: Chris was swamped by messages from interested women. The only trouble was that he then needed to date them.

First date number one—lunch—went nowhere. First date two was depressing. First date three produced nothing more than a hangover. McKinlay continued to watch the messages roll in and became ever more ruthless about squeezing in more first dates. Over the course of the summer, he managed fifty-five first dates—of which fifty-two flopped.

Before online dating took off, most people didn't manage fifty-five first dates in their entire lives—and yet somehow people developed serious relationships and enjoyed happy marriages with no less success than they do today. Perhaps McKinlay was being picky, given that he was suddenly faced with more potential dates than anyone could manage. But it's hard to avoid the conclusion that if the algorithms were any good at finding the right kind of woman, McKinlay wouldn't have had so many disastrous dates.

McKinlay eventually had a date with someone whom he really liked, and who liked him back. Her name is Christine Tien Wang, and it wasn't long before Chris and Christine had announced their engagement. McKinlay's marathon dating season had ended, and ended happily. This wasn't thanks to McKinlay's hacking, however. Christine wasn't a particularly good match according to his algorithm; she wasn't in the top ten thousand matches in Los Angeles. And he didn't find her; she found him. She searched for someone who was local, tall, and had blue eyes, and Chris McKinlay popped up.

Christine Tien Wang was Chris McKinlay's eighty-eighth first date.

While few people have tested the limits of online dating as systematically as Chris McKinlay, many of those who continue to place their faith in the computer nonetheless admit to being somewhat disenchanted with the experience. A simple survey conducted by three behavioral scientists, Michael Norton, Jeana Frost, and the author of *Predictably Irrational*, Dan Ariely, revealed that people were unhappy in three obvious ways. The first was that online dating itself was a mechanical drop-down menu experience, like trying to book a cheap hotel. The second was that online dating took too long—the typical survey respondent spent twelve hours a week browsing through profiles and sending and receiving messages, for 106 minutes of offline interaction in the form of a phone call or a meeting. And those 106 minutes, however they were spent, were a let-down: people tended to have high expectations before the dates they had arranged online, but feel disenchanted afterward. To adapt a Woody Allen joke: not only are the dates terrible, but there are so few of them.[21]

The problem with the tidy, checkbox-ticking approach to date finding, then, is not that it is less likely to find us an acceptable life partner than the traditional, messier tactic of initiating conversations at social events. It's probably no better or no worse—but it promises far too much, sucks up time and effort, and then delivers a date no better than you might have found at random. Online dating seems to be just as much a waste of effort as painstakingly sorting all our e-mails into folders: the messier approach is at least as effective, and it's much quicker.

A few years ago, Jeana Frost devoted her PhD research to fixing online dating. Gone was the search for a close match in a database, the algorithm that said that because you liked Johnny Depp movies and long walks on the beach, you'd be a great match for another Deppite beachcomber. Instead, Frost matched people up entirely at random.

Rather than rely on an algorithm to set up the perfect face-to-face date, Frost wanted to use the online environment to stimulate a conversation. She created a virtual image gallery in which people had a virtual date, represented by simple geometric avatars with speech bubbles. The images—from Lisa Simpson and Jessica Simpson to George Bush and John Kerry—were conversation starters. For example, this exchange was prompted by an image of Fred Astaire and Ginger Rogers:[22]

M: do you like to dance?
D: yes, waltz?
M: does that mean you like also disco freestyle?
D: haha . . . i don't know how to disco freestyle
M: the big easy is a fun place to go to dance . . . you been there?
D: yes, i liked it. Would be fine too! What would be important to you, before you would go there with a chatroom acquaintance?

It's not exactly the balcony scene from *Romeo and Juliet*, but it is a friendly and mildly flirtatious chat that nods toward the possibility of a proper date. People enjoyed these virtual dates, and a quarter of them exchanged phone numbers during the virtual dates, which isn't bad for an entirely arbitrary match.

Two days later, the virtual dating experience was followed up with an evening of speed dating in which the experimental participants would have a series of four-minute chats, some with people they'd had virtual dates with, and others whom they'd gotten to know only by reading the regular Internet dating profile. The virtual dates showed promise: people who had enjoyed a virtual date together in the art gallery chat room also tended to like each other in person. The regular online dating profile generated no such affection. In short, it was better if you forgot the algorithm, and just tried to make random online dates more like actual dates.

Unfortunately, while we are starting to question the idea that a clever algorithm searching a tidy database can deliver magical results in our love life, we're also trusting the algorithms well beyond their original role. The founder of eHarmony, Neil Clark Warren, wants to get into matching people with the perfect job or the perfect financial adviser or even the perfect friend. That may be good business, but you have to wonder whether this effort will work any better for recruiters and job seekers than it does for singles.[23]

Consider the tale of the Reverend Paul Flowers. Flowers, a Methodist minister, was chairman of the Co-operative Bank, a British institution that ran into serious problems after trying to snap up other banks in the aftermath of the 2008 financial crisis. In 2013, he was asked to step down, and before long the story was less about the struggles of the Co-op Bank and more about the Reverend Flowers himself. At a Treasury select committee hearing, he seemed to lack the most basic grasp of how banking worked. For example, he guessed that Co-op's assets were £3 billion; in fact they were £47 billion. Things took a further turn for the worse when a newspaper published photographs showing the Reverend Flowers buying drugs. Lurid text messages emerged in a subsequent court case, and he was eventually convicted of possessing cocaine, crystal meth, and ketamine.[24]

More important than the drug offenses is the fact that the "Crystal Methodist" was by all appearances grossly incompetent to be overseeing a bank. He had no meaningful banking experience or qualifications, but had risen to prominence within the unusual governance structure of the Co-operative Group, which is owned and run by members. Still—how did he secure the job of chairman? The answer eventually emerged: Reverend Flowers had aced a psychometric test, the recruiters' equivalent of an online dating profile.[25]

No doubt such tests can play a role in sorting and sifting candidates, who are asked to agree or disagree with questions such as "I often get angry at the way people treat me" or "I really like most people I meet." They can even help to correct some of the biases of face-to-face interview methods, in which unconscious racism and sexism can often play a role. But if we think that a tidy multiple choice test is a decent measure of a candidate's suitability for a job, we're making the online dating error all over again. John Rust, a psychometric expert at the University of Cambridge, sums up the problem: "Openness to experience is one of the big five scales in personality testing, and clearly one that Flowers may have scored highly on. But you would need to follow that with an interview that asked exactly what type of experiences he is open to."[26]

Will we ever realize that there are some parts of life that the algorithms cannot improve? Perhaps not. The more the test sounds scientific and authoritative, the more we are likely to trust it. And we've been suckers for whatever looks like cutting-edge science for a long time—to the extent that the idea of algorithmic dating is actually far older than computers themselves. In 1924 the inventor and writer Hugo Gernsback declared in *Science and Invention* magazine: "We take extreme care in breeding horses . . . but when we come to ourselves we are extremely careless and do not use . . . the means that science puts into our hands."[27] These scientific means included the "electrical sphygmograph" (it takes your pulse) and a "body odor test" (sniffing a hose attached to a large glass capsule that contains your beau or belle).

When it comes to breeding horses, it's reasonable to think we can arrange the qualities we're looking for into a tidy list: temperament, strength, speed. When it comes to finding someone who can make us happy, or manage not to nearly bankrupt one of our venerable financial institutions, the qualities we want are altogether harder to define.

Algorithmic compatibility matching has promised so much for so long, yet it fails—and it fails for reasons that are easy to understand. Why, then, do we continue to ask the computers to lead the way for us? Perhaps it's because we find an actual, unscripted conversation with a stranger to be such a frightening prospect. Even once the interaction does move to a face-to-face environment—which, for most romantic relationships, is part of the point—we often continue to rely on a script whenever we can.

In 1950, the mathematician, codebreaker, and computer pioneer Alan Turing proposed a test of artificial intelligence. In Turing's "imitation game," a judge would communicate through a teleprompter with a human and a computer. The human's job was to prove that she was, indeed, human. The computer's job was to imitate human conversation convincingly enough to confuse the judge.[28] Turing optimistically predicted that by the year 2000, computers would be able to fool 30 percent of human judges after five minutes of conversation. He was almost right: in 2008, at an annual Turing test tournament called the Loebner Prize, the best computer came within a single vote of Turing's benchmark. How?

The science writer Brian Christian had an answer: computers are able to imitate humans not because the computers are such accomplished conversationalists, but because we humans are so robotic.[29]

An extreme example is the "pickup artist" subculture, devoted to seducing women through prescripted interactions. On Internet forums, these men will swap ideas for "openers"—the Jealous Girlfriend opener, the My Little Pony opener, the You Guys Can Settle a Debate opener—which men can use to approach "sets," or what you and I might call "groups of women talking to one another." In this strange game, there seems to be little interest in paying attention to what the other player is doing: the pickup forums suggest a series of scripted follow-ups, regardless of how the woman responds. In one Internet forum, laden with ads for "Love Systems" and "Magic Bullets," one man wrote that he tried the Jealous Girlfriend opener on a group of women and was mocked because they'd heard the same line before. He asked for advice. The response: "Eject. Find another set." That makes sense—if you think all women are interchangeable.[30]

Another technique of the pickup artist is "negging," firing off small insults. The theory behind negging seems to be that if a man undermines a woman's confidence, she will be eager for validation, and that validation will come from sleeping with the pickup artist. But I wonder if the true secret of negging is that insults are very simple and elicit simple responses. It's possible to get through a conversation full of little insults without ever really having to listen, or to improvise a response. If you needle a woman about her weight, you need never engage with the intimidating fact that she is another human being, someone who has her own story to tell, her own talents, friends, history, and hopes. No script could hope to deal with such messy complexity.

The "negging" technique is similar to a surprisingly compelling chatbot, MGonz, which fools humans simply by firing off insults: "cut this cryptic shit speak in full sentences," "ah thats it im not talking to you any more," and "you are obviously an asshole." MGonz would never pass a Turing test with an informed judge, but it has drawn unsuspecting humans into abusive dialogues on the Internet that last for over an hour without its ever being suspected of being a chatbot. The reason? People in the middle of a slanging match share something with computers: they find it hard to listen.[31]

Even for those who aspire to more meaningful connections than the pickup artist, there are temptations to simplify and tidy by using scripts or algorithms. For an illustration of this, take a look at your smartphone. Start typing and see what it suggests. Composing a text message to my wife, I typed "Ju" into my phone and waited for the phone to suggest the rest, word by word. Here's the message my wife received:

"Just wanted to let you know that I think you're awesome."

My contribution to that was two letters at the beginning and a full stop at the end. My wife seems not to have suspected that anything was amiss. After a delay, she wrote back:

"Thank you! Sorry have been busy! XXXX you are totally amazing! Xx"

Or at least I think the message was from her. But much of it may have been from her phone. The reason a smartphone is able to produce a plausible and indeed affectionate sentence is that we repeat ourselves. There is nothing wrong with a little formulaic chat from time to time—why else would we talk of "sweet nothings"? But as Brian Christian observes, our conversations are often surprisingly predictable exchanges of "How are you?" and observations about the weather, ending with "Let's do lunch sometime." Again, there is nothing wrong with this in itself, any more than there is anything wrong with the fact that a letter begins "Dear . . ." and ends "Yours sincerely . . ." But while a real conversation can have an automatic start and end, there should be something more interesting going on in between.

We can look to chess computing for a parallel. Computers have an opening "book"—a large database full of possible openings, responses, responses to responses, responses to responses to responses. They also have a closing book instructing them on perfect play in the endgame. Most chess games do not simply progress from opening book to closing book, because a book that listed the optimal move from any position would be far too large for any computer. But some chess games stay in book throughout, and a game of chess that never gets out of book is not much of a game. Similarly, a conversation that never gets out of book is not much of a conversation.

It is surprising how many of our conversations take this ritualistic format, even when we are desperate to make a human connection. It is easy to mock the pickup artists with their "openers" and their willingness to "eject" from an interaction that isn't going well. But do the rest of us really do any better? Is this line, transcribed from a first date, delivered by a human or a computer?

"Dwight Owens. Private wealth group at Morgan Stanley. Investment management for high-net-worth individuals and a couple pension plans. Like my job, been there five years, divorced, no kids, not religious. I live in New Jersey, speak French and Portuguese. Wharton business school. Any of this appealing to you?"

It's a trick question: these words actually come from the TV comedy *Sex and the City*. Still: it's close to home. Even without the manipulative tactics of the pickup artist, first dates are often highly formal exchanges of useless biographical information because nobody wants to take the risk of saying something interesting. The behavioral scientist Dan Ariely once ran an experiment that combined online dating with something akin to Brian Eno's Oblique Strategies. Participants in the experiment were given access to an instant-messaging system, which they used to chat online while discussing a possible first date. The system, however, forced them to pick from a choice of rather disruptive conversational moves—"How many romantic partners did you have?" "When was your last breakup?" "Do you have any STDs?" "How do you feel about abortion?" People loved the conversations that resulted, because instead of tidily moving through a rather ritualistic exchange, these questions put the conversation somewhere new, dangerous, and exciting.[32] I can't say whether Dwight Owens would have been more likely to get a phone number from his date, Miranda, if he had opened with "Have you ever broken someone's heart?" but I can guarantee that both of them would have had a more interesting conversation.

Crazy as this might seem, there's a long tradition of using courageous questions to get us out of our tidy conversational habits. One list of questions was made famous by the novelist Marcel Proust, including "What is your most treasured possession?" "What is the trait you most deplore in yourself?" "What is your favorite journey?" and "How would you like to die?" All of these questions beat "What do you do for a living?"

Brian Christian and his girlfriend answered Proust's questions as part of an icebreaker at a wedding: "Reading that questionnaire was a stunning experience: the feeling, one of doubling in an instant our understanding of each other. Proust had helped us do in ten minutes what we'd taken ten months to do on our own."

Dan Ariely's provocative questions, and Jeana Frost's PhD research, demonstrate that even a computer chat room can be used to start a very human process of conversation. But perhaps we shouldn't hold our breath waiting for the dating websites to popularize these messy approaches. After all, they want us to come back to the online environment again and again; a happily hitched customer is a customer no longer.

Similarly, social media sites have no incentive to act in ways that encourage deep and meaningful conversations among friends. Consider Facebook's announcement, late in 2015, that it was increasing the range of one-click responses from the traditional "Like" to

"Angry," "Sad," "Wow," "Haha," and "Love." At first glance, it might have seemed that Facebook was expanding our conversational palate. As one newspaper reported, "Mark Zuckerberg hinted . . . that his site was looking to expand the Like button, making a way for people to communicate that they were upset by news."[33] But a moment's thought reveals that this is nonsense. Facebook always offered people the option to communicate that they were upset by news—perhaps by typing, "I am upset by this news," and adding some words of sympathy or advice. The new Facebook "reactions" tempt us not to bother with anything so human; a single click will suffice. The change is not for our benefit, but for the benefit of advertisers, who find it far easier to analyze one-click reaction data than to make sense of natural language. But there is little doubt that we will embrace the simplification, because given a tidy option, we tend to take it.

The sociologist Sherry Turkle recently started interviewing young people about the way they viewed old-fashioned face-to-face conversation, now that it was so easy to communicate through a text message or chat room. They told her that they found traditional discussions difficult, even frightening. "I'll tell you what's wrong with conversation!" one high school senior replied. "It takes place in real time and you can't control what you're going to say."[34] It is hard to think of an expression more opposed to the spirit of improvisation that we saw in Miles Davis ("First-take feelings, if they're anywhere near right, they're generally the best") or Martin Luther King ("It was astonishing, the man spoke with so much force"). This is a young man so obsessed with control that he is intimidated by the prospect of simply talking "in real time."

But much as we might wish otherwise, life takes place in real time. Life cannot be controlled. Life itself is messy. And it isn't just high school seniors who like to fool themselves about that. From Marco "Rubot" Rubio's strange repetitive glitch, to the *schwerfällig* British generals outmaneuvered by Erwin Rommel, to the managers who try to tie performance down to a reductive target, we are always reaching for tidy answers, only to find that they're of little use when the questions get messy.

Each year that the computers fail to pass the Turing test, the Loebner Prize judges award a consolation prize for the best effort: it is the prize for the Most Human Computer. But there is also a prize for the human confederates who participate in the contest: the Most Human Human. Brian Christian entered the 2009 Loebner contest with the aim of winning that honor. He understood that it was not enough simply to chat away as humans often do, because too much human chat is itself formulaic and robotic. His strategy was to make a mess.

First, he got off the script, out of "the book" of tidy, formalized exchanges, lunging for the question that might connect. "How are you?" is too safe. "Tell me about your first kiss" risks ending a conversation, but better that than never starting a conversation at all. Faced with irate customers, O_2's "How much for the bird?" quip was risky, too. We don't have to be a genius like Keith Jarrett or Martin Luther King to make a risk pay off.

Second, he stepped away from the generic, always looking for the details of the world around him. Chatbots, automated phone menus, and pickup artists flourish in a sterile bubble, devoid of context and history. Human conversation works best when it is rooted in the subtleties of a particular moment. At one point in the 2009 Loebner Prize competition, two participants realized that they were both from Toronto and started geeking out about ice hockey. It was instantly clear that neither of them was a computer. When a Zappos customer service rep realizes that the customer is physically just down the street in Las Vegas, she proves she isn't a computer, either.

Third, Brian Christian disrupted the conversation, because that is what real humans do. People don't speak in complete sentences and wait for each other to finish. They um and ah; they interrupt excitedly;

they finish each other's ideas. In a text-message environment, replies will stack up; people often find themselves having two or three parallel conversations with the same person at the same time. The chaos of all this is quintessentially human. Brian Christian typed three times as much as his robot rivals, and talking in and over and through the judge's responses, drawing meaning from hesitations and moments of confusion as much as from complete sentences. Isn't that sort of animated cross-talk exactly what makes a truly human conversation?

Brian Christian's risky, context-rich, and messy conversations earned him the title of the Most Human Human. Real creativity, excitement, and humanity lie in the messy parts of life, not the tidy ones. And an appreciation of the virtues of mess in fulfilling our human potential is something we can encourage in our children from an early age—if we dare.

Carl Theodor Sørensen, a landscape architect, designed playgrounds in Denmark in the 1930s. He had a problem: he noticed that while the adults who commissioned and paid for the playgrounds were perfectly satisfied with them, the local children didn't seem to like them very much. Quickly tiring of swings and slides, they would endlessly be tempted to sneak into local building sites instead.

Sørensen decided that he would build a playground that *was* a building site, all sand and gravel, hammers and nails. It was an enormous hit with the children, who started to build dens and other structures, before tearing them down to build something else.

Sørensen's playground opened in 1943 in Emdrup, a district of Copenhagen, at a time when Denmark was occupied by Nazi Germany. Grown-ups had bigger problems to worry about than whether young Tomas accidentally nailed himself to the ramparts of his own fortified castle. But slowly, tentatively, the idea spread.

A similar playground, The Yard in Minneapolis, set up in 1949, initially seemed doomed, as children stashed the tools away, trying to monopolize them in the race to build the most spectacular structure. For a while it seemed like the adults would have to step in and tidy up both the playground and the rules of engagement; yet eventually that proved unnecessary. There was no *Lord of the Flies* descent into brutality. The children came together to figure out their own rules. What was at first an opportunity for creative expression became a catalyst for learning how to work together as a community.[35]

The same benefits come from playing messy, informal games (a pickup soccer game in the park, with sweaters for goalposts) as formal ones (a timed game on a marked pitch with a referee). In fact, the informal game may be far superior in ways that we tend not to appreciate. Recent research has found a correlation between playing informal games as a child, and being creative as an adult; the opposite was true of the time spent playing formal, organized games.[36]

Peter Gray, a psychologist at Boston College, points out that in an informal game, everyone must be kept happy: if enough players stop wanting to play, the game will end.[37] That implies the need to compromise, to empathize, and to accommodate younger, weaker, and less skillful playmates; no such need arises in formal games, where those who are having a miserable time on the losing team are obliged to keep going until the final whistle blows. As different children arrive and leave, people must switch sides to keep things interesting, evening up the numbers and the skill levels: "them and us" is alien to informal play. No wonder the skills we learn from informal games stand us in better stead for many real-life situations than the skills we learn from formal ones.

The Yard and Emdrup are venerable examples of playground success, but another mess-pit of a playground, The Land, in North Wales, is just a few years old. It embraces similar principles with similar results and has become famous thanks to a documentary produced by Erin Davis[38] and a feature article in *The Atlantic* by Hanna Rosin.

It is hard to exaggerate quite what a mess The Land is. It is a muddy scrap of ground with a few trees, most grass long since trampled into the muck. A waterlogged ditch runs through the middle of it. There's a trash can over there; three tires piled together next to it; beside that, an abandoned bike with stabilizers, lying on its side. There's an overturned chair, a large wooden spindle that looks like it once held industrial cable; another tire filled with indeterminate rubbish. And that's just a random area of flat ground—the ditch is far worse, filled with random junk—a bike wheel, another tire, some kind of stool, bits of plastic and pipework. It quite literally looks as though someone took an undistinguished patch of scrubland, backed a truck into it, emptied a skip loaded with scrap metal and plastic, and then drove off before anyone called the police.

There is no sign that this is a playground: no bright colors, no shiny slide, no rubberized matting. There is a swing, of sorts—a large green segment of plastic pipe slung from a tree. It seems likely that the children made it themselves, as they made the trampoline built from grimy mattresses, the scrappy fortress made from wooden pallets, and the fire in the oil drum. Fire is a commonplace here—as are saws and nails and mad spinning rope swings. Nor are they part of some carefully supervised craft activity. There are adults at The Land, but they rarely intervene. One ten-year-old boy saws with frantic abandon at a heavy-duty piece of cardboard. His fingers are exposed; the saw slips and bends; he has no workbench or firm mounting; he's in too much of a hurry to take care. It's awful to watch, like the ominous opening to some gruesome public safety film. Nevertheless his fingers survive intact, and the cardboard becomes part of an extended polearm that he uses to swat at snowballs.

Writes Rosin:

"These playgrounds are so out of sync with affluent and middle-class parenting that when I showed fellow parents back home a video of kids crouched in the dark lighting fires, the most common sentence I heard from them was 'This is insane.'"[39]

But is it? It is surprisingly hard to prove that places like The Land are any more likely to lead to grievous injuries than the sterile, prefabricated play spaces defined by the abbreviation KFC—Kit, Fence, Carpet—that schools and municipalities nowadays install in the hope of minimizing mishaps, and the lawsuits that might result. Tim Gill, a researcher and writer on childhood, estimates that the rubbery surface that has become standard in most playgrounds constitutes up to 40 percent of the entire cost of the playground.[40] Yet it's unclear that these expensive KFC playgrounds play host to fewer accidents. David Ball, a professor of risk management at Middlesex University, has been unable to find any indication that injury rates are falling in these sanitized playgrounds in either the United States or the United Kingdom.[41]

Recently, a team of fifteen academics tried to systematically review all the data they could find about risky outdoor play.[42] The categories of risk were a catalogue of parental nightmares: great heights; high speeds; dangerous tools such as knives and axes; dangerous elements such as fire and water; rough play such as fighting; and the risk of getting lost. And yet, the researchers concluded, such play offers benefits: more exercise, improved social skills, reduced aggression, and reduced injuries. The researchers were cautious: not many good studies have been conducted, and so it is hard to draw firm conclusions. But it is quite possible that a space where children clumsily wield saws and set fire to things is just as safe as a space carefully designed by experts.

How could it possibly be that allowing children to play on a building site is as safe as—maybe safer than—letting them play on approved equipment with rubber-matted floors and carefully padded climbing apparatus? Hammers and hoists and open fires and trees and all the rest can actually be dangerous, after all. But it turns out that children adjust for risk: if the ground is harder, the play equipment sharp-edged, the spaces and structures uneven, they will be more careful.

Indeed, some play experts argue that standardizing playgrounds encourages children to become careless and may make them more likely to have accidents in other environments. Helle Nebelong, an award-winning playground architect, says:

"When the distance between all the rungs in a climbing net or a ladder is exactly the same, the child has no need to concentrate on where he puts his feet. Standardization is dangerous because play becomes simplified and the child does not have to worry about his movements. This lesson cannot be carried over to all the knobbly and asymmetrical forms with which one is confronted throughout life."[43]

Learning to be alert to risk is a better preparation for self-preservation outside the playground than bouncing around like a pinball in a padded funhouse.

The benefits of messy play don't end there. Grant Schofield, a professor of public health at Auckland University of Technology, has been running a research project in which schools opened up nearby unused land for primary-age children to roam free in during breaks. There were no more serious injuries than when the children played in their conventional playgrounds—indeed, there were fewer. And other results were dramatic: when they returned to the classroom from their feral wanderings, their behavior was better. They paid attention in class. Bullying fell to the extent that the school abolished a "time-out" room and halved the number of teachers on duty at playtime.[44]

Jared Diamond, author of *The World Until Yesterday*, makes much the same point about hunter-gatherer societies he studied in New Guinea, who "consider young children to be autonomous individuals whose desires should not be thwarted, and who are allowed to play with dangerous objects such as sharp knives, hot pots, and fires." Though plenty of these kids grow up with physical scars, argues Diamond, they are the opposite of being emotionally scarred. Their "emotional security, self-confidence, curiosity, and autonomy" set them apart from children brought up by cautious Westerners.[45]

When we overprotect our children, denying them the opportunity to practice their own skills, learn to make wise and foolish choices, experience pain and loss, and generally make an almighty mess, we believe we're treating them with love—but we may also be limiting their scope to become fully human.

James Scott, author of *Two Cheers for Anarchism*, points out that Emdrup's playground was open and accommodating to the "purposes and talents" of the people who use it. Its designer, Carl Theodor Sørensen, was strikingly modest about how much he really understood about what children might choose to do. Whatever that might be, and however messy, the playground was open to the possibility. Jane Jacobs pointed out that only an arrogant man would try to anticipate all the uses to which a building might be put; the same thing is true of a playground.

This openness to mess is the same quality we found in MIT's Building 20, in the provocations of Brian Eno's Oblique Strategies, and in the modular furniture of Robert Propst. Brian Christian's risky, context-rich, and messy conversations earned him the title of the Most Human Human. Jeff Bezos and John Boyd sought to break away from tidy formulas, seeking an advantage through rapid improvisation despite its risks and their mistakes. Keith Jarrett and Miles Davis and Martin Luther King drew magic out of the unique challenges and atmosphere of a particular moment, stepping away from structure and control but gaining an indefinable energy as a result. We've seen, again and again, that real creativity, excitement, and humanity lie in the messy parts of life, not the tidy ones.

Most playgrounds are not open to the talents and purposes of the children who use them. A swing is for swinging; a merry-go-round is for merrily going around. But it is not only children who find themselves nudged and controlled as they wander curiously through life. A good job, a good building, even a good relationship, is open and adaptable. But many jobs, buildings, and relationships are not. They are monotonous and controlling. They sacrifice messy possibility for tidy predictability. And too often, we let that happen, because we feel safer that way. That is a shame.

Openness and adaptability are inherently messy. A playground such as The Land is profoundly disconcerting to adult eyes. It seems a dangerous, anarchic mess. That is why it's fun to play in. And that is why it is a good preparation for a messy life.

ACKNOWLEDGMENTS

I've been working on this book for five years; I hope that anyone whose contribution has been left out will forgive me. I could have kept a list, but that would have been a little too tidy.

David Bodanis, Paul Klemperer, and above all Andrew Wright read the manuscript repeatedly and with great care. Their suggestions have improved it immeasurably. All three of them have shown me many other kindnesses over the years. Thank you all. Other thoughtful comments came from Dom Camus, Jess Chiappella, Oliver Johnson, William Klemperer, Mark Lynas, and Fran Monks.

Many people helped by pointing me toward the right idea or person at the right time. Thanks to Adele Armstrong, Katerina Billouri, Wolfango Chiappella, Sir Andrew Dilnot, Alice Fishburn, Richard Fisher, Bruno Giussani, Cesar Hidalgo, Nigel House, Emma Jacobs, Richard Knight, Martin Lloyd, Patricia Ryan Madson, Sue Matthias, and Scott Page. I am also grateful to my colleagues at the *Financial Times* and the BBC for being such inspirational people to work with.

Thanks to everyone who gave up their time to be interviewed for the book: David Allen, Gwyn Bevan, Stewart Brand, Shelley Carson, Mathijs de Vaan, Brian Eno, Digby Fairweather, Tim Gill, Nicola Green, Andy Haldane, Guy Haworth, Craig Knight, John Kounios, Charles Limb, Michael Norton, Gerald Ratner (interviewed by Emma Jacobs), Ken Regan, Keith Sawyer, Balázs Vedres, and Holly White.

Acknowledgments

As a glance at the references will reveal, I have a considerable debt to the journalists, writers, and thinkers whose reporting or analysis has informed my own ideas, but in particular:

On music: Ashley Kahn, Paul Trynka, and the BBC documentary teams behind *For One Night Only: The Cologne Concert* and *Oblique Strategies*.

On creative prodigies: Paul Hoffman and Ed Yong.

On architecture: Warren Berger, Stewart Brand, Alain de Botton, and Jonah Lehrer.

On Martin Luther King, Jr.: Taylor Branch, David Garrow, and Stephen Oates.

On Bezos, Rommel, and Stirling: Virginia Cowles, David Fraser, and Brad Stone.

On Flight 447: William Langewiesche, Jeff Wise, and the staff of *99% Invisible*.

On Hans Monderman: Tom Vanderbilt.

On being human: Dan Ariely, Brian Christian, Hanna Rosin, and Muzafer Sherif.

On the microbiome: Emily Eakin.

On mess: Eric Abrahamson, David Freedman, Jane Jacobs, and James C. Scott.

Thank you to my excellent agents and editors, Sally Holloway, Iain Hunt, Jake Morrissey, Zoë Pagnamenta, and Tim Whiting, and to everyone at all of my publishers and agents around the world.

Finally, my love and gratitude to Fran Monks. She knows why.

NOTES

INTRODUCTION

1. Corinna da Fonseca-Wollheim, "A Jazz Night to Remember: The Unique Magic of Keith Jarrett's 'The Köln Concert,'" *The Wall Street Journal*, October 11, 2008, http://www.wsj.com/articles/SB122367103134923957.
2. Vera Brandes was speaking to a BBC documentary team. See *For One Night Only: The Cologne Concert*, BBC Radio 4, December 29, 2011, http://www.bbc.co.uk/programmes/b0103z8j.
3. *For One Night Only: The Cologne Concert*. Jarrett himself later described the instrument as "a seven-foot piano which hadn't been adjusted for a very long time and sounded like a very poor imitation of a harpsichord or a piano with tacks in it." Ian Carr, *Keith Jarrett: The Man and His Music* (London: Paladin, 1992), p. 71.
4. Carr, *Keith Jarrett*, pp. 71–73.

1. CREATIVITY

1. David Bowie, interview by *Uncut* magazine, 1999. Available at http://www.bowiegoldenyears.com/low.html.
2. Paul Trynka, "Berlin: Follow in David Bowie's Tracks," *The Independent*, March 4, 2011, http://www.independent.co.uk/travel/europe/berlin-follow-in-david-bowies-tracks-2232296.html.
3. Tobias Rüther, *Heroes: David Bowie and Berlin* (London: Reaktion Books, 2014), p. 45.
4. Sasha Frere-Jones, "Ambient Genius," *The New Yorker*, July 7, 2014.
5. Paul Trynka, *Starman: David Bowie: The Definitive Biography* (London: Sphere, 2011), p. 289.
6. I'm indebted to my friend Dom Camus for this example and a very useful conversation about it on January 12, 2016.
7. Shaun Larcom, Ferdinand Rauch, and Tim Willems, "The Benefits of Forced Experimentation: Striking Evidence from the London Underground Network," Oxford University Department of Economics Working Paper, September 2015, http://www.economics.ox.ac.uk/materials/papers/14046/paper-755.pdf.
8. Author interview with Brian Eno, February 24, 2015.
9. Ludovic Hunter-Tilney, "Sound Visionary," *Financial Times*, July 1, 2011, http://next.ft.com/content/6407cc22-a226-11e0-bb06-00144feabdc0.
10. Author interview with Brian Eno, February 24, 2015.
11. Amit Sood, Mayo Clinic, "Multitasking Isn't Working for Me: How Can I Focus My Attention and Improve My Concentration?" http://www.mayoclinic.org/healthy-lifestyle/adult-health/expert-answers/how-to-focus/faq-20058383; Margarita Tartakovsky, "12 Foolproof Tips for Finding Focus," Psych Central, psychcentral.com/lib/12-foolproof-tips-for-finding-focus/; Caroline Williams, "Concentrate! How to Tame a Wandering Mind," BBC Future, October 16, 2014, http://www.bbc.com/future/story/20141015-concentrate-how-to-focus-better.

12. In addition to the research described in the text, readers may be interested in Shelley Carson, "Cognitive Disinhibition, Creativity, and Psychopathology," in *The Wiley Handbook of Genius*, ed. Dean Keith Simonton (Chichester, England: John Wiley & Sons, 2014), and Örjan de Manzano, Simon Cervenka, Anke Karabanov, Lars Farde, and Fredrik Ullén, "Thinking Outside a Less Intact Box," *PLoS One* 5, no. 5, e10670 (May 17, 2010), DOI: 10.1371/journal.pone.0010670.
13. Shelley Carson, Daniel Higgins, and Jordan Peterson, "Decreased Latent Inhibition Is Associated with Increased Creative Achievement in High-Functioning Individuals," *Journal of Personality and Social Psychology* 85, no. 3 (2003), pp. 499–506, DOI: 10.1037/0022-3514.85.3.499.
14. Holly A. White and Priti Shah, "Creative Style and Achievement in Adults with Attention-Deficit/Hyperactivity Disorder," *Personality and Individual Differences* 50, no. 5 (2011), pp. 673–677, DOI: 10.1016/j.paid.2010.12.015.
15. Charlan Jeanne Nemeth and Julianne L. Kwan, "Originality of Word Associations as a Function of Majority vs. Minority Influence," *Social Psychology Quarterly* 48, no. 3 (1985), pp. 277–282.
16. E. Langer, Y. Steshenko, B. Cummings, N. Eisenkraft, and S. Campbell, "Mistakes as a Mindful Cue," prepublication manuscript, Harvard University, 2004; the work is described in Ellen Langer's *On Becoming an Artist* (New York: Random House, 2006), p. 82.
17. Paul Howard-Jones, Sarah-Jayne Blakemore, Elspeth A. Samuel, Ian R. Summers, and Guy Claxton, "Semantic Divergence and Creative Story Generation: An fMRI Investigation," *Cognitive Brain Research* 25, no. 1 (September 2005), pp. 240–250.
18. Trynka, *Starman: David Bowie*, p. 290.
19. Author interview with Brian Eno, February 24, 2015.
20. Ibid.
21. C. Diemand-Yauman et al., "Fortune Favors the Bold (and the Italicized): Effects of Disfluency on Educational Outcomes," *Cognition* 118, no. 1 (January 2010), DOI: 10.1016/j.cognition.2010.09.012.
22. David Sheppard, *On Some Faraway Beach* (Chicago: Chicago Review Press, 2009), p. 5.
23. "President Obama Honors Outstanding Early-Career Scientists," White House Press Release, July 23, 2012, https://www.whitehouse.gov/the-press-office/2012/07/23/president-obama-honors-outstanding-early-career-scientists; Erez Aiden, "Zoom!" GE & Science Prize for Young Life Scientists, *Science*, December 2, 2011, http://www.sciencemag.org/content/334/6060/1222.full.pdf; "NIH Announces 79 Awards to Encourage Creative Ideas in Science," NIH Press Release, September 20, 2011, http://www.nih.gov/news/health/sep2011/od-20.htm.
24. Ed Yong, "The Renaissance Man: How to Become a Scientist Over and Over Again," *Not Exactly Rocket Science* (blog), June 8, 2011, http://blogs.discovermagazine.com/notrocketscience/2011/06/08/the-renaissance-man-how-to-become-a-scientist-over-and-over-again/.
25. Ibid.; also Amy Barth, "Five Questions for the Man Who Put Three D's in DNA," *Discover*, March 2010, http://discovermagazine.com/2010/mar/05-questions-he-put-three-d-in-dna-explains-how-it-works.
26. Robert S. Root-Bernstein, Maurine Bernstein, and Helen Gamier, "Identification of Scientists Making Long-Term, High-Impact Contributions, with Notes on Their Methods of Working," *Creativity Research Journal* 6, no. 4 (1993), pp. 329–343, DOI: 10.1080/10400419309534491.
27. Oliver Johnson, "Jurassic Park Past: My Time with Michael Crichton," *Hodderscape*, June 16, 2015, http://www.hodderscape.co.uk/jurassic-park-past-my-time-with-michael-crichton/.
28. Mihaly Csikszentmihalyi, *Creativity: Flow and the Psychology of Discovery and Innovation* (New York: HarperCollins, 1996).
29. Jonah Lehrer, *Imagine: How Creativity Works* (Edinburgh: Canongate, 2012), pp. 25–27, 39–41.
30. Ibid., p. 29.
31. Howard E. Gruber and Sara N. Davis, "Inching Our Way Up Mount Olympus: The Evolving-Systems Approach to Creative Thinking," in Robert J. Sternberg, *The Nature of Creativity* (New York: Cambridge University Press, 1995); see also Keith R. Sawyer, *Explaining Creativity: The Science of Human Innovation* (Oxford: Oxford University Press, 2012), p. 376.

32. Howard Gruber, *Darwin on Man: A Psychological Study of Scientific Creativity* (London: Wildwood House, 1974).
33. "David Bowie: Verbatim," *Radio 4 Archive Hour*, January 30, 2016, http://www.bbc.co.uk/programmes/b06z5pts.
34. Kerri Smith, "Neuroscience: Idle Minds," *Nature*, September 19, 2012, http://www.nature.com/news/neuroscience-idle-minds-1.11440.
35. Nick Stockton, "What's Up with That: Your Best Thinking Seems to Happen in the Shower," *Wired*, August 5, 2014, http://www.wired.com/2014/08/shower-thoughts/.
36. John Kao, *Jamming: The Art & Discipline of Business Creativity* (London: HarperCollins, 1997), p. 46.
37. Gia Kourlas, "Twyla Tharp's Fifty Years of Forward Movement," *The New York Times*, April 4, 2015, http://www.nytimes.com/2015/04/05/arts/dance/twyla-tharps-50-years-of-forward-movement.html.
38. Twyla Tharp, *The Creative Habit* (New York: Simon & Schuster, 2007), pp. 80–83.
39. Simon Armitage, *Oblique Strategies*, BBC Radio 4, May 12, 2014, http://www.bbc.co.uk/programmes/b02qncrt.
40. Carlos Alomar, interview by Simon Armitage for his documentary *Oblique Strategies*, BBC Radio 4, May 12, 2014, http://www.bbc.co.uk/programmes/b02qncrt.
41. Carlos Alomar, speaking on the BBC TV documentary *Five Years*, May 25, 2013, available at http://artvod.com/music/david-bowie-five-years-documentary/.
42. Alomar, interview by Armitage, *Oblique Strategies*.

2. COLLABORATION

1. Ben Hunt-Davis and Harriet Beveridge, *Will It Make the Boat Go Faster?* (Kibworth Beauchamp, England: Matador, 2011), pp. 38–39.
2. Ibid., p. 81.
3. Winston A. Reynolds, "The Burning Ships of Hernán Cortés," *Hispania* 42, no. 3 (September 1959), pp. 317–324.
4. Paul Hoffman, *The Man Who Loved Only Numbers* (London: Fourth Estate, 1999), p. 49.
5. Bruce Schechter, *My Brain Is Open: The Mathematical Journeys of Paul Erdős* (Oxford: Oxford University Press, 1998), p. 182. Also see the Erdős Number Project at Oakland University: http://wwwp.oakland.edu/enp/. The Erdős number graph continues to evolve because mathematicians continue to publish research based on their collaborations with Erdős, crediting him as a coauthor.
6. Jukka-Pekka Onnela et al., "Analysis of a Large-Scale Weighted Network of One-to-One Human Communication," February 19, 2007, arxiv.org/pdf/physics/0702158.pdf.
7. Mark Granovetter, "The Strength of Weak Ties," *American Journal of Sociology* 78, no. 6 (May 1973), pp. 1360–1380, and his *Getting a Job: A Study of Contacts and Careers* (Chicago: University of Chicago Press, 1974).
8. Schechter, *My Brain Is Open*, pp. 176–177.
9. Ibid., p. 195.
10. Mathijs de Vaan, David Stark, and Balázs Vedres, "Game Changer: The Topology of Creativity," *American Journal of Sociology* 120, no. 4 (January 2015).
11. Author interview with Balázs Vedres, June 8, 2015.
12. Except where otherwise stated, descriptions of the Robbers Cave experiment are from Muzafer Sherif et al., *The Robbers Cave Experiment: Intergroup Conflict and Cooperation* (Middletown, CT: Wesleyan University Press, 1988).
13. Gary Alan Fine, "Forgotten Classic: The Robbers Cave Experiment," *Sociological Forum* 19, no. 4 (December 2004), DOI: 10.1007/s11206-004-0704-7.
14. The study is described in Cass Sunstein and Reid Hastie, *Wiser: Getting Beyond Groupthink to Make Groups Smarter* (Boston: Harvard Business Review Press, 2015), pp. 81–83.
15. Irving L. Janis, *Victims of Groupthink* (Boston: Houghton Mifflin, 1972).

16. The Asch experiments are often known as the "conformity" experiments, although most subjects did not conform every time. However, given the fact that the group members—actors working for Solomon Asch—were clearly wrong, it is striking that people conformed at all. See S. E. Asch, "Studies of Independence and Conformity: I. A Minority of One Against a Unanimous Majority," *Psychological Monographs* 70, no. 9 (1956), pp. 1–70; and Christian Jarrett, "Textbook Coverage of This Classic Social Psychology Study Has Become Increasingly Biased," *BPS Research Digest*, March 25, 2015, http://digest.bps.org.uk/2015/03/textbook-coverage-of-this-classic.html.
17. Scott Page, *The Difference: How the Power of Diversity Creates Better Groups, Firms, Schools and Societies* (Princeton, NJ: Princeton University Press, 2008).
18. Scott Page, interview by Claudia Dreifus, "In Professor's Model, Diversity = Productivity," *The New York Times*, January 8, 2008, http://www.nytimes.com/2008/01/08/science/08conv.html?_r=1&.
19. Samuel R. Sommers, "On Racial Diversity and Group Decision Making: Identifying Multiple Effects of Racial Composition on Jury Deliberations," *Journal of Personality and Social Psychology* 90, no. 4 (April 2006), pp. 597–612, http://dx.doi.org/10.1037/0022-3514.90.4.597.
20. D. L. Loyd, C. S. Wang, K. W. Phillips, and R. B. Lount, Jr., "Social Category Diversity Promotes Premeeting Elaboration: The Role of Relationship Focus," *Organization Science* 24, no. 3 (2013), pp. 757–772. See also the discussion in Katherine W. Phillips and Evan P. Appelbaum, "Reinterpreting the Effects of Group Diversity," in Margaret A. Neale and Elizabeth A. Mannix, *Looking Back, Moving Forward: A Review of Group and Team-Based Research* (Bingley, England: Emerald, 2012), pp. 185–209.
21. Katherine W. Phillips, Katie A. Liljenquist, and Margaret A. Neale, "Is the Pain Worth the Gain? The Advantages and Liabilities of Agreeing with Socially Distinct Newcomers," *Personality and Social Psychology Bulletin* 35, no. 3 (March 2009), pp. 336–350.
22. Brooke Harrington, *Pop Finance* (Princeton, NJ: Princeton University Press, 2008).
23. Ibid., p. 58.
24. Ibid., p. 133.
25. P. Ingram and M. W. Morris, "Do People Mix at Mixers? Structure, Homophily, and the 'Life of the Party,'" *Administrative Science Quarterly* 52, no. 4 (2007), pp. 558–585. For a discussion, also see Jonah Lehrer, "Opposites Don't Attract (and That's Bad News)," *Wired*, January 6, 2012, http://www.wired.com/2012/01/opposites-dont-attract-and-thats-bad-news/.
26. Howard Aldrich and Martha A. Martinez-Firestone, "Why Aren't Entrepreneurs More Creative? Conditions Affecting Creativity and Innovation in Entrepreneurial Activity," in *The Oxford Handbook of Creativity, Innovation, and Entrepreneurship*, ed. Christina Shalley, Michael A. Hitt, and Jing Zhou, June 2015, DOI: 10.1093/oxfordhb/9780199927678.013.0026. For a useful discussion, see Keith Sawyer, "Why Aren't Entrepreneurs More Creative?" https://keithsawyer.wordpress.com/2015/09/02/why-arent-entrepreneurs-more-creative/.
27. A. J. Bahns, K. M. Pickett, and C. S. Crandall, "Social Ecology of Similarity: Big Schools, Small Schools and Social Relationships," *Group Processes & Intergroup Relations*, DOI: 10.1177/1368430211410751.
28. Jeremy Greenwood, Nezih Guner, Georgi Kocharkov, and Cezar Santos, "Marry Your Like: Assortative Mating and Income Inequality," NBER Working Paper No. 19829, January 2014, www.nber.org/papers/W19829.
29. Bill Bishop with Robert G. Cushing, *The Big Sort: Why the Clustering of Like-Minded America Is Tearing Us Apart* (Boston: Houghton Mifflin, 2008).
30. On this point, see Ethan Zuckerman's excellent *Rewire: Digital Cosmopolitans in the Age of Connection* (New York: W. W. Norton, 2013).
31. Nick Bilton, "Ferguson Reveals a Twitter Loop," *The New York Times*, August 28, 2014, http://www.nytimes.com/2014/08/28/fashion/ferguson-reveals-a-twitter-loop.html?_r=0.
32. Emma Pierson, "See How Red Tweeters and Blue Tweeters Ignore Each Other on Ferguson," *Quartz*, November 25, 2014, http://qz.com/302616/see-how-red-tweeters-and-blue-tweeters

-ignore-each-other-on-ferguson/; and Pierson's FAQ on the study, "Ferguson FAQ," *Obsession with Regression* (blog), November 27, 2014, http://obsessionwithregression.blogspot.co.uk/2014/11/ferguson-faq.html. A larger study of political tweeting also found similar "echo chamber" characteristics: Yosh Halberstam and Brian Knight, "Homophily, Group Size, and the Diffusion of Political Information in Social Networks: Evidence from Twitter," NBER Working Paper No. 20681, November 2014, http://www.nber.org/papers/w20681 DOI 10.3386/w20681.

33. Author interview with Balázs Vedres, June 8, 2015.
34. Author interview with Mathijs de Vaan, June 8, 2015.
35. William Fotheringham, "Dave Brailsford Hails Team Sky Rethink for Chris Froome's Tour de France Win," *The Guardian*, July 27, 2015, http://www.theguardian.com/sport/2015/jul/27/dave-brailsford-team-sky-chris-froome-tour-de-france-2015-win.
36. Remarks made by Dave Brailsford at a conference in November 2015 at which the author was present.

3. WORKPLACES

1. Alain de Botton, *The Architecture of Happiness* (London: Penguin, 2007), pp. 163–166, 178.
2. Ed Catmull with Amy Wallace, *Creativity, Inc.: Overcoming the Unseen Forces That Stand in the Way of True Inspiration* (London: Bantam, 2014), chap. 2.
3. Walter Isaacson, *Steve Jobs* (London: Little, Brown, 2011), p. 486.
4. Ibid., pp. 430–432.
5. The first Ed Catmull quotation is from Isaacson, *Steve Jobs*, p. 430. The second is from Catmull with Wallace, *Creativity, Inc.*, p. ix.
6. Isaacson, *Steve Jobs*, pp. 430–432.
7. Julie Jargon, "Neatness Counts at Kyocera and at Others in the 5S Club: Sort, Straighten, Shine, Standardize, Sustain; Getting Mr. Scovie to Go Through His Boxes," *The Wall Street Journal*, October 27, 2008, http://www.wsj.com/articles/SB122505999892670159.
8. S. Alexander Haslam and Craig Knight, "Cubicle, Sweet Cubicle," *Scientific American Mind*, September/October 2010. Also author interview with Craig Knight, July 29, 2015.
9. Jargon, "Neatness Counts at Kyocera."
10. T George Harris, "Psychology of the New York Work Space," *New York*, October 31, 1977, pp. 51–55.
11. Robert Sommer, *Tight Space: Hard Architecture and How to Humanize It* (Englewood Cliffs, NJ: Prentice-Hall, 1974); Sommer's work is neatly summarized by Harris, "Psychology of the New York Work Space," pp. 51–55.
12. Jargon, "Neatness Counts at Kyocera."
13. Alex Haslam and Craig Knight, "Your Place or Mine?" BBC News, November 17, 2006, http://news.bbc.co.uk/2/hi/uk_news/magazine/6155438.stm.
14. This and the following rules are from a 2012 internal BHP Billiton document, "City Square: Work Environment Guidelines, Frequently Asked Questions," via the *Australian Financial Review* website: http://www.afr.com/rw/2009-2014/AFR/2012/07/08/Photos/09a66320-c8cb-11e1-a18b-e5c71f70dca5_BHP_City_Square.pdf.
15. Frank Duffy, *The New Office* (London: Conran Octopus, 1997), p. 197.
16. For my account of the goings-on at Chiat/Day, I have relied heavily on Warren Berger's magnificent feature article for *Wired*, "Lost in Space," February 1, 1999, http://archive.wired.com/wired/archive/7.02/chiat_pr.html.
17. Scott Adams, *Dilbert*, January 10, 1995.
18. Useful resources on Building 20 include: Alex Beam, "A Building with Soul," *The Boston Globe*, June 29, 1988; Jonah Lehrer, "Groupthink: The Brainstorming Myth," *The New Yorker*, January 30, 2012, http://www.newyorker.com/reporting/2012/01/30/120130fa_fact_lehrer?currentPage=all; "A Last, Loving Look at an MIT Landmark—Building 20," *RLE Undercurrents* 9, no. 2 (Fall 1997), http://www.rle.mit.edu/media/undercurrents/Vol9_2_Spring97.pdf; Philip J. Hilts, "Last Rites for a 'Plywood Palace' That Was a Rock of Science," *The New York Times*, March

31, 1998, http://www.nytimes.com/1998/03/31/science/last-rites-for-a-plywood-palace-that-was-a-rock-of-science.html?pagewanted=all&src=pm; Eve Downing, "Letting Go," *Spectrum* (Spring 1998), http://spectrum.mit.edu/articles/letting-go/; and Steven Levy, *Hackers: Heroes of the Computer Revolution*, 25th Anniversary Edition (Sebastopol, CA: O'Reilly Media, 2010).

19. A lovely half-hour documentary, "Building 20: The Magical Incubator" was made by MIT in 1998. It's tape T1217 in the MIT archives, online at: http://teachingexcellence.mit.edu/from-the-vault/mits-building-20-the-magical-incubator-1998; a definitive account of the merits of Building 20 is in chapter three of Stewart Brand, *How Buildings Learn: What Happens After They're Built* (New York: Viking, 1994).
20. Robert Campbell, "Dizzying Heights in Frank Gehry's Remarkable New Stata Center at MIT, Crazy Angles Have a Serious Purpose," *The Boston Globe*, April 25, 2004.
21. Robin Pogrebin and Katie Zezima, "M.I.T. Sues Frank Gehry, Citing Flaws in Center He Designed," *The New York Times*, November 7, 2007. See also Spencer Reiss, "Frank Gehry's Geek Palace," *Wired* (May 2004), http://www.wired.com/wired/archive/12.05/mit.html.
22. Reiss, "Frank Gehry's Geek Palace."
23. Steven Levy, *In the Plex: How Google Thinks, Works, and Shapes Our Lives* (New York: Simon & Schuster, 2011), p. 32.
24. Ibid., pp. 34, 125.
25. Ibid., p. 126.
26. Ibid., p. 129.
27. Ibid.
28. "Inside the Box: How Workers Ended Up in Cubes—and How They Could Break Free," *The Economist*, January 3, 2015; John Wetzel, "The Action Office: The Secret History of the Cubicle," YouTube, https://www.youtube.com/watch?v=RgDHifV62WI; Nikil Saval, "The Cubicle You Call Hell Was Designed to Set You Free," *Wired*, April 23, 2014, http://www.wired.com/2014/04/how-offices-accidentally-became-hellish-cubicle-farms/.
29. Robert Propst, *The Office: A Facility Based on Change* (Elmhurst, IL: The Business Press, 1968), p. 27.
30. Harris, "Psychology of the New York Work Space," pp. 51–55.
31. *The Business Etiquette Handbook*, 1965, p. 17.
32. Author interview with Craig Knight, July 29, 2015.
33. A. K. Korman, *Organizational Behavior* (Englewood Cliffs, NJ: Prentice Hall, 1977), p. 181.
34. Catmull with Wallace, *Creativity, Inc.*, p. 301.
35. Ibid., p. 303.
36. Ibid., p. 3.
37. Ibid., p. x.

4. IMPROVISATION

1. Stephen B. Oates, *Let the Trumpet Sound: A Life of Martin Luther King, Jr.* (New York: Harper Perennial, 1994), p. 9.
2. David Garrow, *Bearing the Cross: Martin Luther King, Jr., and the Southern Christian Leadership Conference* (Vintage: London, 1993), p. 35; Oates, *Let The Trumpet Sound*, p. 16.
3. Oates, *Let the Trumpet Sound*, p. 20.
4. Garrow, *Bearing the Cross*, p. 49.
5. Oates, *Let the Trumpet Sound*, p. 55.
6. Oates, *Let the Trumpet Sound*, p. 56, has a detailed account of Dr. King's routine for writing a sermon. The recollections of Dr. King's assistant John Thomas Porter are on p. 50.
7. Mark Hemingway, Twitter account @Heminator, September 22, 2011, https://twitter.com/Heminator/status/117063712136904704.
8. Ewen MacAskill, "Rick Perry Forgets Agency He Wants to Scrap in Republican Debate Disaster," *The Guardian*, November 9, 2011, http://www.theguardian.com/world/2011/nov/10/rick-perry-forgets-agency-scrap.

9. "Ed Miliband: I Forgot Parts of My Speech," *The Daily Telegraph*, September 24, 2014, http://www.telegraph.co.uk/news/politics/ed-miliband/11117748/Ed-Miliband-I-forgot-parts-of-my-speech.html.
10. Tim Harford and Emma Jacobs, "Regrets? I've Had a Few," *FT Magazine*, June 4, 2011, http://www.ft.com/cms/s/2/8817953e-8bf1-11e0-854c-00144feab49a.html#axzz1OIHMeKJu.
11. Fred Laico, interview by Ashley Kahn, *Kind of Blue: The Making of the Miles Davis Masterpiece* (London: Granta Books, 2000), p. 75.
12. Quoted in Kahn, *Kind of Blue*, p. 105.
13. See Richard Williams, *The Blue Moment* (London: Faber & Faber, 2009), which charts the influence of *Kind of Blue*.
14. Quotes from Quincy Jones and Chick Corea from Kahn, *Kind of Blue*, pp. 20, 178.
15. Bill Evans's liner notes for *Kind of Blue* compare the album to a Japanese style of painting in which the artist cannot hesitate for a moment without ruining the effect. "Miles conceived these settings only hours before the recording dates," Evans explains, although that is not quite true. Both Bill Evans and arranger Gil Evans seem to have had a hand in composing certain pieces, and band members recalled trying some of the arrangements at live gigs.
16. Miles Davis with Quincy Troupe, *Miles: The Autobiography* (New York: Simon & Schuster, 1990), p. 235.
17. Mark Lewisohn, *The Complete Beatles Chronicle: The Definitive Day-by-Day Guide to the Beatles' Entire Career* (Chicago: Chicago Review Press, 1992), p. 253.
18. Charles Limb, "Your Brain on Improv," TEDxMidAtlantic Talk, November 2010, https://www.ted.com/talks/charles_limb_your_brain_on_improv/.
19. See, for example: A. Pinho, O. Manzano, P. Fransson, H. Eriksson, and F. Ullén, "Connecting to Create: Expertise in Musical Improvisation Is Associated with Increased Functional Connectivity Between Premotor and Prefrontal Areas," *The Journal of Neuroscience* 34 (April 30, 2014), DOI: 10.1523/JNEUROSCI.4769-13.2014; A. Berkowitz and D. Ansari, "Expertise-Related Deactivation of the Right Temporoparietal Junction During Musical Improvisation," *Neuroimage* 49 (2010), DOI: 10.1016/j.neuroimage.2009.08.042.
20. Charles Limb and Allen Braun, "Neural Substrates of Spontaneous Musical Performance: An fMRI Study of Jazz Improvisation," *PLoS ONE* 3, no. 2 (February 27, 2008), DOI: 10.1371/journal.pone.0001679.
21. Author interview with Charles Limb, October 24, 2014.
22. S. Liu, H. M. Chow, Y. Xu, M. Erkinnen, K. Swett, M. Eagle, D. Rizik-Baer, and A. Braun, "Neural Correlates of Lyrical Improvisation: An fMRI Study of Freestyle Rap," *Scientific Reports* 2:835, DOI: 10.1038/srep00834.
23. Author interview with Charles Limb, October 24, 2014. A similar perspective can be found in Aaron Berkowitz, *The Improvising Mind* (Oxford: Oxford University Press, 2010), p. 143, which endorses Limb's view that the brain's systems for monitoring and correction seem to be suppressed during musical improvisation.
24. Author telephone interview with Nicola Green, October 28, 2014. Many articles covered the social media responses at the time, for example: Alex Hern, "When Life Gave O_2 Network Failure It Made Networkfailureade on Twitter," *New Statesman*, July 12, 2012, http://www.newstatesman.com/blogs/alex-hern/2012/07/when-life-gave-o2-network-failure-it-made-networkfailureade-twitter.
25. Kate Krader, interview by Ben Schott for *The Art of the Menu*, BBC Radio 4, September 29, 2014, http://www.bbc.co.uk/programmes/b04jjz3v. The restaurant in question was 11 Madison Park.
26. Max Chafkin, "The Zappos Way of Managing," *Inc.*, May 1, 2009, http://www.inc.com/magazine/20090501/the-zappos-way-of-managing.html; Armando Roggio, "The Zappos Effect," *Practical Ecommerce*, March 21, 2011, http://www.practicalecommerce.com/articles/2662-The-Zappos-Effect-5-Great-Customer-Service-Ideas-for-Smaller-Businesses; Ben Popken, "Zappos

Saves Best Man from Going Barefoot at Wedding," *Consumerist*, May 19, 2011, http://consumerist.com/2011/05/19/zappos-saves-best-man-from-going-barefoot-at-wedding/.

27. Nat Hentoff, "An Afternoon with Miles Davis," *The Jazz Review*, December 1958, pp. 11–12.
28. Quoted in Patricia Ryan Madson, *Don't Prepare, Just Show Up* (New York: Bell Tower, 2005), p. 28.
29. "Magic Words," *This American Life*, episode 532, http://www.thisamericanlife.org/radio-archives/episode/532/transcript.
30. M. Neal and P. Barton Wright, "Validation Therapy for Dementia," *Cochrane Database of Systematic Reviews* 2003 (3): CD001394, http://www.ncbi.nlm.nih.gov/pubmed/12917907.
31. Gilbert Ryle, "Improvisation," *Mind* 85, no. 337 (January 1976), pp. 69–83.
32. Harford and Jacobs, "Regrets? I've Had a Few."
33. Carl Czerny, *Letters to a Young Lady on the Art of Playing the Pianoforte, from the Earliest Rudiments to the Highest Stage of Cultivation* (Vienna, 1839), trans. J. A. Hamilton (New York: Firth, Pond, 1851), pp. 74–77.
34. Jimmy Cobb, interview by Ashley Kahn, *Kind of Blue*, p. 79.
35. Oates, *Let the Trumpet Sound*, pp. 64–68; Garrow, *Bearing the Cross*, pp. 17–23.
36. Garrow, *Bearing the Cross*, p. 23; Oates, *Let the Trumpet Sound*, p. 69; Taylor Branch, *Parting the Waters: America in the King Years, 1954–63* (New York: Simon & Schuster, 1988), p. 138.
37. Branch, *Parting the Waters*, pp. 138–142; James Scott's *Two Cheers for Anarchism: Six Easy Pieces on Autonomy, Dignity, and Meaningful Work and Play* (Princeton, NJ: Princeton University Press, 2012), pp. 22–29, contains insightful commentary on the speech and what it tells us about the nature of leadership.
38. Garrow, *Bearing the Cross*, p. 282; Oates, *Let the Trumpet Sound*, pp. 256–259; Branch, *Parting the Waters*, pp. 878–882.
39. Branch, *Parting the Waters*, p. 882.

5. WINNING

1. David Fraser, *Knight's Cross: A Life of Field Marshal Erwin Rommel* (London: HarperCollins, 1994), p. 39.
2. "A Sinister Advantage," *The Economist*, December 9, 2004, http://www.economist.com/node/3471297.
3. Monte Cox, "Southpaws: Doing It Right the Wrong Way," *Fightbeat/Fightworld*, May 2005, republished at http://coxscorner.tripod.com/southpaws.html.
4. Tyler Cowen, *Average Is Over* (New York: Dutton, 2013), pp. 101–104; Jonathan Rowson, "Carlsen: The Nettlesome World Champion," *The Herald*, December 29, 2013; republished on Chessbase at http://en.chessbase.com/post/carlsen-the-nettlesome-world-champion.
5. Author interview with Guy Haworth, December 9, 2014.
6. Fraser, *Knight's Cross*, pp. 62–67.
7. Brad Stone, *The Everything Store: Jeff Bezos and the Age of Amazon* (London: Corgi, 2014), p. 25.
8. Robert Spector, *Amazon.com: Get Big Fast* (London: Random House, 2000), pp. 82, 87.
9. Stone, *The Everything Store*, pp. 56–58.
10. Ibid., pp. 41–42.
11. Ibid., p. 203.
12. Ibid., p. 114.
13. Ibid., p. 122.
14. Ibid., pp. 131, 143.
15. Ibid., p. 117.
16. Ibid., pp. 213–225.
17. Erwin Rommel, letter to Lucie Rommel, February 26, 1941, in David Irving, *Rommel: The Trail of the Fox* (Ware, England: Wordsworth Military Library, 1999), p. 63. I hesitate to cite David Irving. His later work was discredited in a high-profile libel trial; he was eventually sentenced

to three years in prison in Austria for the crime of denying the Holocaust. However, his biography of Rommel continues to be cited by serious historians.

18. Fraser, *Knight's Cross*, pp. 228–231.
19. Ibid., pp. 232, 235.
20. Ibid., p. 5; Daniel Allen Butler, *Field Marshal: The Life and Death of Erwin Rommel* (Oxford, England: Casemate, 2015), p. 218.
21. "Donald Trump Under Fire for Mocking Disabled Reporter," BBC News, November 26, 2015, http://www.bbc.co.uk/news/world-us-canada-34930042.
22. Robert Coram, *Boyd: The Fighter Pilot Who Changed the Art of War* (Boston: Little, Brown, 2002), pp. 329–330.
23. Ibid., p. 332.
24. Josh Marshall, "The William T. Sherman of Crazy," *Talking Points Memo*, August 27, 2015, http://talkingpointsmemo.com/edblog/the-william-t-sherman-of-crazy; also see his follow-up, "The Way of the Doofus Warrior," August 28, 2015, http://talkingpointsmemo.com/edblog/the-way-of-the-doofus-warrior.
25. Fraser, *Knight's Cross*, p. 271.
26. David Kirkpatrick, "Barnes & Noble's Jekyll and Hyde," *New York*, July 19, 1999, http://nymag.com/nymetro/news/bizfinance/biz/features/47/.
27. Spector, *Amazon.com: Get Big Fast*, p. 133.
28. Stone, *The Everything Store*, p. 87.
29. Ibid.
30. Ibid., p. 80.
31. Stefanie Olsen, "FTC Fines E-tailers $1.5 Million for Shipping Delays," CNET News, July 26, 2000, http://news.cnet.com/FTC-fines-e-tailers-1.5-million-for-shipping-delays/2100-1017-3-243684.html.
32. Stone, *The Everything Store*, p. 315.
33. Ibid., pp. 316–317.
34. Ken Auletta, "Paper Trail," *The New Yorker*, June 25, 2012, http://www.newyorker.com/magazine/2012/06/25/paper-trail-2.
35. Leslie Hook, "Amazon Cloud Service Key to Sustaining Profitability," *Financial Times*, January 26, 2016, https://next.ft.com/content/d837a4f6-c390-11e5-b3b1-7b2481276e45.
36. Result of a search on Amazon.com conducted January 9, 2015.
37. "Amazon Japan 'Co-Operating' with Tokyo Police After Raid," BBC News, January 27, 2015, http://www.bbc.co.uk/news/technology-31000904; "Islamic State Magazine Dabiq Withdrawn from Sale by Amazon," BBC News, June 6, 2015, http://www.bbc.co.uk/news/world-middle-east-33035453.
38. Tim Maly, "Algorithmic Rape Jokes in the Library of Babel," *Quiet Babylon* (blog), http://quietbabylon.com/2013/algorithmic-rape-jokes-in-the-library-of-babel/.
39. Henry Blodget, "I Asked Jeff Bezos the Tough Questions," *Business Insider*, December 13, 2014, http://uk.businessinsider.com/amazons-jeff-bezos-on-profits-failure-succession-big-bets-2014-12.
40. Marcus Wohlsen, "Amazon Could Finally Grow Its Profits—By Selling Other People's Stuff," *Wired*, January 5, 2015, http://www.wired.com/2015/01/secret-amazon-finally-making-profit-selling-peoples-stuff/.
41. "The Best Performing CEOs in the World," *Harvard Business Review*, November 2014, https://hbr.org/2014/11/the-best-performing-ceos-in-the-world.
42. Gavin Mortimer, *The SAS in World War II* (Oxford: Osprey, 2011), p. 10.
43. Virginia Cowles, *The Phantom Major: The Story of David Stirling and the SAS Regiment* (1958; Barnsley, England: Pen and Sword Books, 2010), pp. 12–15; Gavin Mortimer, *Stirling's Men: The Inside History of the SAS in World War II* (London: Cassell, 2005), pp. 10–11.
44. Alan Deutschman, "Inside the Mind of Jeff Bezos," *Fast Company*, August 1, 2004, http://www.fastcompany.com/50541/inside-mind-jeff-bezos.

45. Coram, *Boyd: The Fighter Pilot Who Changed the Art of War*, p. 371.
46. Mortimer, *Stirling's Men*, p. 28; Mortimer, *The SAS in World War II*, pp. 25–31.
47. Cowles, *The Phantom Major*, pp. 60–66.
48. Ibid., pp. 71–72.
49. Quoted ibid., p. 97.
50. Cowles, *The Phantom Major*, pp. 98–103.
51. Mortimer, *Stirling's Men*, pp. 56–57; Cowles, *The Phantom Major*, pp. 178–180.
52. Mortimer, *Stirling's Men*, pp. 59–62; Cowles, *The Phantom Major*, pp. 200, 205–208.
53. Fraser, *Knight's Cross*, pp. 534–552. The detail about the wreath is from Irving, *Rommel: The Trail of the Fox*, pp. 402–405.

6. INCENTIVES

1. Isabel Oakeshott, "Mother Catches Out Blair over GPs," *Evening Standard*, April 29, 2005, http://www.standard.co.uk/news/mother-catches-out-blair-over-gps-7272924.html; Nicholas Timmins, "Blair Bemused over GP Waiting Times," *Financial Times*, April 30, 2005, http://www.ft.com/cms/s/0/483307e2-b915-11d9-bfeb-00000e2511c8.html#axzz3l572UdzP.
2. For details about Beckmann and the scientific forestry project, see Henry E. Lowood, "The Calculating Forester: Quantification, Cameral Science, and the Emergence of Scientific Forestry Management in Germany," chap. 11 in Tore Frangsmyr, J. L. Heilbron, and Robin Rider, eds., *The Quantifying Spirit in the Eighteenth Century* (Berkeley: University of California Press, 1990), http://ark.cdlib.org/ark:/13030/ft6d5nb455/. Chris Maser, in *The Redesigned Forest* (San Pedro, CA: R. & E. Miles, 1988), gives more details of the fate of German forests, including extensive reports of Richard Plochman's conclusions, drawn in 1968. I owe a great debt to James C. Scott's *Seeing Like a State* (New Haven, CT: Yale University Press, 1998) for alerting me to the story of German forestry and to its wider implications.
3. Brian M. Casey, Donald D. McIntire, and Kenneth J. Leveno, "The Continuing Value of the Apgar Score for the Assessment of Newborn Infants," *New England Journal of Medicine* 344 (February 15, 2001), pp. 467–471, DOI: 10.1056/NEJM200102153440701.
4. Atul Gawande, "The Score: How Childbirth Went Industrial," *The New Yorker*, October 9, 2006, http://www.newyorker.com/magazine/2006/10/09/the-score.
5. David Dranove, Daniel Kessler, Mark McClellan, and Mark Satterthwaite, "Is More Information Better? The Effects of 'Report Cards' on Health Care Providers," *Journal of Political Economy* 111, no. 3 (2003), pp. 555–588.
6. Melissa Korn and Rachel Louise Ensign, "Colleges Rise as They Reject: Schools Invite More Applications, Then Use Denials to Boost Coveted Rankings," *The Wall Street Journal*, December 25, 2012, http://www.wsj.com/articles/SB10001424127887324731304578189282282976640; Max Kutner, "How to Game the College Rankings," *Boston Magazine*, September 2014, http://www.bostonmagazine.com/news/article/2014/08/26/how-northeastern-gamed-the-college-rankings/.
7. Stephen Burd and Rachel Fishman, "Ten Ways Colleges Work You Over," *Washington Monthly*, September/October 2014, http://www.washingtonmonthly.com/magazine/septemberoctober_2014/features/ten_ways_colleges_work_you_ove051760.php.
8. Paul Jump, "Twenty per cent Contracts Rise in Run-up to REF," *Times Higher Education*, September 26, 2013, https://www.timeshighereducation.com/news/twenty-per-cent-contracts-rise-in-run-up-to-ref/2007670.article; Chris Bertram, "Research Excellence Framework: The Denouement," *Crooked Timber*, December 18, 2014, http://crookedtimber.org/2014/12/18/research-excellence-framework-the-denouement/.
9. Alan Beattie, "Development: Crumbs of Comfort," *Financial Times*, September 15, 2010, http://www.ft.com/cms/s/0/f575ec76-c0f8-11df-99c4-00144feab49a.html#axzz3AvlCdxTN.
10. Steven Kerr, "On the Folly of Rewarding A, While Hoping for B," *Academy of Management Journal* 18, no. 4 (December 1975), pp. 769–783, http://www.jstor.org/stable/255378.

11. Peter Smith, "On the Unintended Consequences of Publishing Performance Data in the Public Sector," *International Journal of Public Administration* 18, no. 2–3 (1995), pp. 277–310, http://dx.doi.org/10.1080/01900699508525011.
12. Harvey Goldstein and David Spiegelhalter, "League Tables and Their Limitations: Statistical Issues in Comparisons of Institutional Performance," *Journal of the Royal Statistical Society Series A* 159, no. 3 (1996), DOI: 10.2307/2983325.
13. Gwyn Bevan and Richard Hamblin, "Hitting and Missing Targets by Ambulance Services for Emergency Calls: Effects of Different Systems of Performance Measurement Within the UK," *Journal of the Royal Statistical Society Series A* 172, no. 1 (2009), pp. 161–190.
14. "History of the Basel Committee," Bank for International Settlements, last modified October 1, 2015, http://www.bis.org/bcbs/history.htm; Charles Goodhart, *The Basel Committee on Banking Supervision: A History of the Early Years 1974–1997* (New York: Cambridge University Press, 2011).
15. Josef Korte and Sascha Steffen, "A 'Sovereign Subsidy'—Zero Risk Weights and Sovereign Risk Spillovers," VoxEU.org, September 7, 2014, http://www.voxeu.org/article/sovereign-subsidy-zero-risk-weights-and-sovereign-risk-spillovers.
16. Andrew Haldane and Vasileios Madouros, "The Dog and the Frisbee," Bank of England Speech 596, given August 31, 2012, http://www.bankofengland.co.uk/publications/Documents/speeches/2012/speech596.pdf. Also author interview with Andy Haldane, May 16, 2015.
17. I. McCammon and P. Hageli, "An Evaluation of Rule-Based Decision Tools for Travel in Avalanche Terrain," *Cold Regions Science and Technology* 47 (2007), pp. 193–206.
18. Julian N. Marewski and Gerd Gigerenzer, "Heuristic Decision Making in Medicine," *Dialogues in Clinical Neuroscience* 14, no. 1 (March 2012), pp. 77–89; Gerd Gigerenzer, *Gut Feelings: The Intelligence of the Unconscious* (New York: Viking, 2007).
19. Lee A. Green and Mark P. Becker, "Physician Decision Making and Variation in Hospital Admission Rates for Suspected Acute Cardiac Ischemia: A Tale of Two Towns," *Medical Care* 32, no. 11 (November 1994), pp. 1086–1097.
20. Victor DeMiguel, Lorenzo Garlappi, and Raman Uppal, "Optimal Versus Naive Diversification: How Inefficient Is the 1/N Portfolio Strategy?" *The Review of Financial Studies* 22, no. 5 (2009), pp. 1915–1953.
21. Jeremy Bentham, *Constitutional Code* (London: R. Heward, 1830), vol. 1, chap. IX, §16, Art 60.1, cited in Florian Ederer, Richard Holden, and Margaret Meyer, "Gaming and Strategic Ambiguity in Incentive Provision," Oxford University Department of Economics Working Paper Number 640, January 2013.
22. Tom Braithwaite, "Banks Strive to Weather the Fed's Stress Test Storms," *Financial Times*, February 24, 2014, http://www.ft.com/cms/s/0/4db4b096-9d66-11e3-a599-00144feab7de.html#ixzz3mSGcZY25; see also Paul Glasserman and Gowtham Tangirala, "Are the Federal Reserve's Stress Test Results Predictable?" Office of Financial Research Working Paper 15-02, March 3, 2015.
23. Author interview with Andy Haldane, May 16, 2015.
24. Gwyn Bevan and Christopher Hood, "Targets, Inspections, and Transparency: Too Much Predictability in the Name of Transparency Weakens Control," *British Medical Journal* 328, no. 7440 (March 13, 2004), p. 598, DOI: 10.1136/bmj.328.7440.598; Sir Andrew Dilnot and Sir David Spiegelhalter both advocated the use of randomly chosen measures in personal conversations with the author.
25. "The Volkswagen Scandal: A Mucky Business," *The Economist*, September 26, 2015, http://www.economist.com/news/briefing/21667918-systematic-fraud-worlds-biggest-carmaker-threatens-engulf-entire-industry-and; Brad Plumer, "Volkswagen's Appalling Clean Diesel Scandal Explained," *Vox*, September 23, 2015, http://www.vox.com/2015/9/21/9365667/volkswagen-clean-diesel-recall-passenger-cars; "Clean Air Act Diesel Engine Cases," US Department of Justice, May 14, 2015, http://www.justice.gov/enrd/diesel-engines; Jeff Plungis and Dana Hull, "VW's Emissions Cheating Found by Curious Clean-Air Group," Bloomberg, September 20, 2015, http://www.bloomberg.com/news/articles/2015-09-19/volkswagen-emissions-cheating-found-by-curious-clean-air-group.

7. AUTOMATION

1. Jeff Wise, "What Really Happened Aboard Air France 447," *Popular Mechanics*, December 6, 2011, http://www.popularmechanics.com/flight/a3115/what-really-happened-aboard-air-france-447-6611877/; William Langewiesche, "The Human Factor," *Vanity Fair*, October 2014, http://www.vanityfair.com/news/business/2014/10/air-france-flight-447-crash; "Air France Flight 447 and the Safety Paradox of Automated Cockpits," *Slate*, June 25, 2015; "Children of the Magenta," *99% Invisible* (podcast), June 23, 2015, http://99percentinvisible.org/episode/children-of-the-magenta-automation-paradox-pt-1/.
2. William Langewiesche, speaking on "Children of the Magenta," *99% Invisible* (podcast), http://99percentinvisible.org/episode/children-of-the-magenta-automation-paradox-pt-1/.
3. Robert Charette, "Automated to Death," *IEEE Spectrum*, December 15, 2009, http://spectrum.ieee.org/computing/software/automated-to-death; for details about AirAsia 8501, also see Jeff Wise, "AirAsia Flight 8501 Crash Reveals the Dangers of Putting Machines in the Driver's Seat," *New York*, December 2, 2015, http://nymag.com/daily/intelligencer/2015/12/airasia-flight-8501-and-the-risks-of-automation.html.
4. James Reason, *Human Error* (Cambridge, England: Cambridge University Press, 1991), p. 180.
5. Mike M. Ahlers, "Pilots of Wayward Jet Lose Licenses," CNN, October 28, 2009, http://edition.cnn.com/2009/US/10/27/airliner.fly.by/index.html.
6. Cited in Langewiesche, "The Human Factor."
7. Andy Greenberg and Ryan Mac, "How a 'Deviant' Philosopher Built Palantir, a CIA-Funded Data-Mining Juggernaut," *Forbes*, September 2, 2013, http://www.forbes.com/sites/andygreenberg/2013/08/14/agent-of-intelligence-how-a-deviant-philosopher-built-palantir-a-cia-funded-data-mining-juggernaut/.
8. "Man in Bradford Traffic Queue Given Parking Ticket," BBC News, February 6, 2014, http://www.bbc.co.uk/news/uk-england-leeds-26074514; "Motorist Slapped with Parking Ticket While Waiting in Traffic Queue," *Daily Mirror*, February 7, 2014, http://www.mirror.co.uk/news/uk-news/bradford-council-slap-motorist-victor-3120354.
9. Ian J. Goodfellow, Yaroslav Bulatov, Julian Ibarz, Sacha Arnoud, and Vinay Shet, "Multi-digit Number Recognition from Street View Imagery Using Deep Convolutional Neural Networks," December 20, 2013, http://arxiv.org/abs/1312.6082; see also "How Google Cracked House Number Identification in Street View," *Technology Review*, January 6, 2014, http://www.technologyreview.com/view/523326/how-google-cracked-house-number-identification-in-street-view/.
10. Natasha Singer, "When No One Is Just a Face in the Crowd," *The New York Times*, February 1, 2014, http://www.nytimes.com/2014/02/02/technology/when-no-one-is-just-a-face-in-the-crowd.html?_r=3.
11. See David Kravets, "FBI Checks Wrong Box, Places Student on No-Fly List," *Wired*, February 6, 2014, http://www.wired.com/threatlevel/2014/02/no-fly-list-bungle/, and, for much more detail, the judge's ruling, posted at http://www.wired.com/images_blogs/threatlevel/2014/02/ibraruling.pdf.
12. Pam Dixon, "What Information Do Data Brokers Have on Consumers?" Congressional Testimony, December 18, 2013, http://www.worldprivacyforum.org/2013/12/testimony-what-information-do-data-brokers-have-on-consumers/.
13. See Frank Pasquale, *Black Box Society* (Cambridge, MA: Harvard University Press, 2015), and Cathy O'Neil, *Weapons of Math Destruction* (New York: Crown, 2016).
14. Akiko Fujita, "Tracking Disaster: Japanese Tourists Drive Straight into the Pacific," ABC News, March 16, 2012, http://abcnews.go.com/blogs/headlines/2012/03/-tracking-disaster-japanese-tourists-drive-straight-into-the-pacific/. Also see Lauren Hansen, "8 Drivers Who Blindly Followed GPS into Disaster," *The Week*, May 7, 2013, http://theweek.com/articles/464674/8-drivers-who-blindly-followed-gps-into-disaster.
15. Richard Thaler, *Misbehaving* (London: Penguin/Allen Lane, 2015).

16. Gary Klein, *Streetlights and Shadows: Searching for the Keys to Adaptive Decision Making* (London: MIT Press, 2009), pp. 118–119.
17. Sarah O'Connor, "Leave the Robotic Jobs to Robots and Improve Humans' Lives," *Financial Times*, January 5, 2016, https://next.ft.com/content/da557b66-b09c-11e5-993b-c425a3d2b65a.
18. Klein, *Streetlights and Shadows*, pp. 123–124.
19. "Will Self-Driving Cars Spell the End of the American Road Trip?" *99% Invisible* (podcast), available on *The Eye: Slate's Design Blog*, July 3, 2015, http://www.slate.com/blogs/the_eye/2015/07/03/self_driving_cars_and_the_paradox_of_automation_from_99_invisible.html. Raj Rajkumar's comments below are from the same podcast.
20. Jack Stewart, "What May Be Self-Driving Cars' Biggest Problem," BBC Future, August 25, 2015, http://www.bbc.com/future/story/20150824-what-may-be-self-driving-cars-biggest-problem.
21. Cited in Langewiesche, "The Human Factor."
22. M. L. Cummings, C. Mastracchio, K. M. Thornburg, and A. Mkrtchyan, "Boredom and Distraction in Multiple Unmanned Vehicle Supervisory Control," *Interacting with Computers* 25, no. 1 (2013), pp. 34–47, http://hdl.handle.net/1721.1/86942.
23. Tom Vanderbilt, "The Traffic Guru," *The Wilson Quarterly*, Summer 2008.
24. Ibid.
25. Simon Jenkins, "The Removal of Road Markings Is to Be Celebrated. We Are Safer Without Them," *The Guardian*, February 4, 2016, http://www.theguardian.com/commentisfree/2016/feb/04/removal-road-markings-safer-fewer-accidents-drivers.

8. RESILIENCE

1. Michael Specter, "Germs Are Us," *The New Yorker*, October 22, 2012, http://www.newyorker.com/magazine/2012/10/22/germs-are-us.
2. Michael Pollan, "Some of My Best Friends Are Germs," *The New York Times Magazine*, May 15, 2013, http://www.nytimes.com/2013/05/19/magazine/say-hello-to-the-100-trillion-bacteria-that-make-up-your-microbiome.html.
3. The most widely reported estimate is that the microbial cells in our body outnumber our own cells ten to one. This is a guess. We do not know to within two orders of magnitude how many cells there are in the human body. Peter Andrey Smith calls the ten-to-one ratio "a crude estimate from 1972 that established itself as a fact through repetition." Smith reports on more recent work and suggests a range between 1 to 1 and 100 to 1. All that suggests that while enormously uncertain, the crude estimate from 1972 is holding up quite well. "Is Your Body Mostly Microbes? Actually, We Have No Idea," *The Boston Globe*, September 14, 2014, https://www.bostonglobe.com/ideas/2014/09/13/your-body-mostly-microbes-actually-have-idea/qlcoKot4wfUXecjeVaFKFN/story.html.
4. See Martin Blaser, *Missing Microbes* (New York: Henry Holt, 2014), p. 35, for a discussion of the correlation between microbiome diversity and obesity. The UC San Francisco research is described in Specter, "Germs Are Us"; the University of Toronto research—published in Ruth Brown et al., "Secular Differences in the Association Between Caloric Intake, Macronutrient Intake, and Physical Activity with Obesity," *Obesity Research and Clinical Practice*, September 14, 2015, pii: S1871-403X(15)00121-0, DOI: 10.1016/j.orcp.2015.08.007—is described in "Why It Was Easier to Be Skinny in the 1980s," *The Atlantic*, September 30, 2015, http://www.theatlantic.com/health/archive/2015/09/why-it-was-easier-to-be-skinny-in-the-1980s/407974/.
5. "CDC Puts C Difficile Burden at 453,000 Cases, 29,000 Deaths," University of Minnesota Center for Infectious Disease Research and Policy, February 25, 2015, http://www.cidrap.umn.edu/news-perspective/2015/02/cdc-puts-c-difficile-burden-453000-cases-29000-deaths.
6. Emily Eakin, "The Excrement Experiment," *The New Yorker*, December 1, 2014, http://www.newyorker.com/magazine/2014/12/01/excrement-experiment; Freakonomics Radio, "The Power of Poop," March 3, 2011, http://freakonomics.com/2011/03/03/the-power-of-poop-full-transcript/.

7. Emily Eakin, "Bacteria on the Brain," *The New Yorker*, December 7, 2015, http://www.newyorker.com/magazine/2015/12/07/bacteria-on-the-brain.
8. This study was done by researchers at the Biology and the Built Environment Center at the University of Oregon. See Jessica Green, "Are We Filtering the Wrong Microbes?" TED Talks, 2011, http://www.ted.com/talks/jessica_green_are_we_filtering_the_wrong_microbes/transcript?language=en.
9. Alanna Collen, "'Microbial Birthday Suit' for C-Section Babies," *BBC Magazine*, September 11, 2015, http://www.bbc.com/news/health-34064012.
10. Blaser, *Missing Microbes*.
11. Ed Yong, "There Is No 'Healthy' Microbiome," *The New York Times*, November 1, 2014, http://www.nytimes.com/2014/11/02/opinion/sunday/there-is-no-healthy-microbiome.html, and Gabrielle Canon, "Sorry, Your Gut Bacteria Are Not the Answer to All Your Health Problems," *Mother Jones*, October 27, 2014, http://www.motherjones.com/environment/2014/10/microbiome-health-gut-bacteria; Blaser, *Missing Microbes*, pp. 31–32.
12. Jane Jacobs, *The Death and Life of Great American Cities* (New York: Vintage, 1992), p. 50.
13. Ibid., p. 193.
14. Maryann P. Feldman and David B. Audretsch, "Innovation in Cities: Science-Based Diversity, Specialization and Localized Competition," *European Economic Review* 43 (1999).
15. AnnaLee Saxenian, *Regional Advantage: Culture and Competition in Silicon Valley and Route 128* (Cambridge: Harvard University Press, 1994).
16. Cesar Hidalgo, *How Information Grows* (London: Allen Lane, 2015), chap. 9.
17. Thomas Schelling, who won the Nobel Memorial Prize for Economics in 2005, famously demonstrated this effect using a simulation that is simple enough to run with nickels and dimes on a chessboard. In the simulation, the nickels don't want to be surrounded by dimes and the dimes don't want to be surrounded by nickels, but both are happy with a mix of neighbors. Schelling showed that as one or two surrounded coins moved to a new place on the board, a cascade could begin, leading to total segregation. For more about the Schelling model, see my book *The Logic of Life: The Rational Economics of an Irrational World* (New York: Random House, 2008).
18. Bill Bishop and Robert Cushing, *The Big Sort* (New York: Houghton Mifflin, 2008). For the data on the 2012 election, see Alan Greenblatt, "The 'Politics of Self-Expression' Increasingly Divides Americans," *Governing*, December 26, 2014, http://www.governing.com/topics/politics/gov-american-politics-gets-sorted-by-tribe.html.
19. Jonathan Rothwell, "Housing Costs, Zoning, and Access to High-Scoring Schools," Brookings Institution policy paper (2012), http://www.brookings.edu/~/media/research/files/papers/2012/4/19-school-inequality-rothwell/0419_school_inequality_rothwell.pdf.
20. Diederik Stapel, *Faking Science: A True Story of Academic Fraud*, trans. Nicholas J. L. Brown, available for download, http://nick.brown.free.Fr./stapel/FakingScience-20141214.pdf, p. 112.
21. Diederik A. Stapel and Siegwart Lindenberg, "Coping with Chaos: How Disordered Contexts Promote Stereotyping and Discrimination," *Science* 332, no. 6026 (April 8, 2011), pp. 251–253, DOI: 10.1126/science.1201068.
22. Stapel, *Faking Science*, p. 113.
23. Ibid., p. 103.
24. Yudhijit Bhattacharjee, "The Mind of a Con Man," *The New York Times Magazine*, April 28, 2013, http://www.nytimes.com/2013/04/28/magazine/diederik-stapels-audacious-academic-fraud.html?pagewanted=all&_r=0.
25. George L. Kelling and James Q. Wilson, "Broken Windows," *The Atlantic Monthly*, March 1982, http://www.theatlantic.com/magazine/archive/1982/03/broken-windows/304465/.
26. "What Broken Windows Policing Is," *The Economist*, January 27, 2015, http://www.economist.com/blogs/economist-explains/2015/01/economist-explains-18.
27. Kelling and Wilson, "Broken Windows."
28. Steven D. Levitt, "Understanding Why Crime Fell in the 1990s: Four Factors That Explain the Decline and Six That Do Not," *Journal of Economic Perspectives* 18, no. 1 (Winter 2004),

pp. 163–190. For the fifth explanation, focusing on removal of lead from gasoline, see Jessica Wolpaw Reyes, "Environmental Policy as Social Policy? The Impact of Childhood Lead Exposure on Crime," *The B.E. Journal of Economic Analysis & Policy* 7, no. 1 (2007), Article 51, http://www.bepress.com/bejeap/vol7/iss1/art51.

29. Bernard E. Harcourt and David E. Thacher, "Is Broken Windows Policing Broken?" *Legal Affairs*, October 17, 2005, http://legalaffairs.org/webexclusive/debateclub_broken windows1005.msp.
30. Robert J. Sampson and Stephen W. Raudenbush, "Seeing Disorder: Neighborhood Stigma and the Social Construction of 'Broken Windows,'" *Social Psychology Quarterly* 67, no. 4 (December 2004), pp. 319–342.
31. For a description of the situation of Jewish scientists and mathematicians in Germany, and the discrimination they suffered even before the Nazi ascendancy, see Fritz Stern, *Einstein's German World* (London: Penguin, 1999), especially chap. 3.
32. Constance Reid, *Hilbert* (New York: Springer, 1996), p. 205.
33. Fabian Waldinger, "Bombs, Brains and Science: The Role of Human and Physical Capital for the Creation of Scientific Knowledge," working paper, University of Warwick, March 7, 2015; *The Review of Economics and Statistics*, November 16, 2015, http://www.mitpressjournals.org/doi/abs/10.1162/REST_a_00565#.VwbCa7dIir8; an earlier-dated version is available at http://www.dal.ca/content/dam/dalhousie/pdf/faculty/science/economics/seminars/Waldinger-Bombs-Brains.pdf.
34. "Donald J. Trump Statement on Preventing Muslim Immigration," December 7, 2015, https://www.donaldjtrump.com/press-releases/donald-j.-trump-statement-on-preventing-muslim-immigration.
35. Gianmarco Ottaviano and Giovanni Peri, "The Economic Value of Cultural Diversity: Evidence from US Cities," NBER Working Paper No. 10904, November 2004, http://www.nber.org/papers/w10904.

9. LIFE

1. Franklin's discussion of his virtue journal is in Part Two of his autobiography (New York: Henry Holt, 1916 ed.), available online at http://www.gutenberg.org/ebooks/20203.
2. John Bach McMaster, as quoted ibid., n. 70.
3. Daniel Levitin, *The Organized Mind* (London: Penguin, 2015).
4. Merlin Mann, "Inbox Zero," talk delivered at Google Tech Talks, July 23, 2007, https://www.youtube.com/watch?v=z9UjeTMb3Yk.
5. Jorge Luis Borges, "John Wilkins' Analytical Language" (1942), *Selected Non-Fictions*, ed. and trans. Eliot Weinberger (New York: Viking, 1999), p. 231.
6. Eric Abrahamson and David Freedman, *A Perfect Mess* (London: Orion, 2007), pp. 156–157.
7. Maria Popova, "Order, Disorder, and Oneself: French Polymath Paul Valéry on How to Never Misplace Anything," *Brain Pickings*, October 30, 2015, https://www.brainpickings.org/2015/10/30/paul-valery-analects-order-disorder/.
8. Abrahamson and Freedman, *A Perfect Mess*, p. 159.
9. Steve Whittaker and Julia Hirschberg, "The Character, Value and Management of Personal Paper Archives," *ACM Transactions on Computer Human Interaction* 8 (2001), pp. 150–170.
10. R. Boardman and M. A. Sasse, "'Stuff Goes into the Computer and Doesn't Come Out': A Cross-Tool Study of Personal Information Management," *Proceedings of the SIGCHI Conference on Human Factors in Computing Systems*, 2004, pp. 583–590.
11. V. Bellotti, N. Ducheneaut, M. Howard, I. Smith, and R. Grinter, "Quality vs. Quantity: E-mail-Centric Task Management and Its Relationship with Overload," *Human-Computer Interaction* 20, no. 1–2 (2005), pp. 89–138.
12. Steve Whittaker, Tara Matthews, Julian Cerutti, Hernan Badenes, and John Tang, "Am I Wasting My Time Organizing Email? A Study of Email Refinding," *Proceedings of the SIGCHI Conference on Human Factors in Computing Systems*, 2011.

13. Daniel S. Kirschenbaum, Laura L. Humphrey, Sheldon D. Malett, "Specificity of Planning in Adult Self-Control: An Applied Investigation," *Journal of Personality and Social Psychology* 40, no. 5 (1981), pp. 941–950. For the one-year follow-up, see Daniel S. Kirschenbaum, Laura L. Humphrey, Sheldon D. Malett, and Andrew Tomarken, "Specificity of Planning and the Maintenance of Self-Control: 1 Year Follow-Up of a Study Improvement Program," *Behavior Therapy* 13 (1982), pp. 232–240.
14. Marc Andreessen, "Pmarca Guide to Personal Productivity," June 4, 2007, http://pmarchive.com/guide_to_personal_productivity.html.
15. Charlie LeDuff and John Broder, "Schwarzenegger, Confident and Ready for Prime Time," *The New York Times*, June 24, 2004, http://www.nytimes.com/2004/06/24/us/schwarzenegger-confident-and-ready-for-prime-time.html?pagewanted=all; also see Eric Abrahamson and David Freedman, *A Perfect Mess* (London: Orion, 2007), pp. 75–77, for discussion.
16. Dan Slater, *Love in the Time of Algorithms* (London: Current, 2013), p. 17.
17. The FiveThirtyEight website made a short documentary interviewing founders and customers of Operation Match: http://fivethirtyeight.com/features/what-online-dating-was-like-in-the-1960s/.
18. Christian Rudder, "We Experiment on Human Beings!" *OK Trends*, July 28, 2014, http://blog.okcupid.com/index.php/we-experiment-on-human-beings/.
19. Hannah Fry, *The Mathematics of Love* (London: TED Books, 2015), p. 44.
20. Kevin Poulsen, "How a Math Genius Hacked OkCupid to Find True Love," *Wired*, January 21, 2014, http://www.wired.com/2014/01/how-to-hack-okcupid/.
21. Author interview with Michael Norton, February 1, 2016.
22. Jeana Frost, Zoe Chance, Michael Norton, and Dan Ariely, "People Are Experience Goods: Improving Online Dating with Virtual Dates," *Journal of Interactive Marketing* 22, no. 1 (2008).
23. Emma Jacobs, "A Heartfelt Mission to End Career Hookups," *Financial Times*, September 4, 2014, http://www.ft.com/cms/s/0/8c5d408a-2f63-11e4-a79c-00144feabdc0.html#axzz3pxipi4Dk.
24. "Paul Flowers at Treasury Select Committee," BBC News, November 19, 2013, http://www.bbc.co.uk/news/business-24999781; Helen Warrell and Miles Johnson, "Ex-Co-op Bank Chairman Paul Flowers Charged with Drug Offenses," *Financial Times*, April 16, 2014; Helen Pidd, "Former Co-op Bank Boss Paul Flowers Pleads Guilty to Drug Charges," *The Guardian*, May 7, 2014.
25. Sharlene Goff and Emma Jacobs, "Psychometric Tests Led Co-op Bank to Make Paul Flowers Chairman," *Financial Times*, January 28, 2014.
26. Gill Plimmer, "How to Cheat a Psychometric Test," *Financial Times*, April 3, 2014, http://www.ft.com/cms/s/2/eeda84e4-b4f6-11e3-9166-00144feabdc0.html#axzz3pxipi4Dk.
27. Matt Novak, "Mechanical Matchmaking: The Science of Love in the 1920s," *Smithsonian*, May 23, 2013, http://www.smithsonianmag.com/history/mechanical-matchmaking-the-science-of-love-in-the-1920s-103877403/#Dl8eC83OzkKhyp75.99.
28. A. M. Turing, "Computing Machinery and Intelligence," *Mind*, 59 (1950), pp. 433–460.
29. Brian Christian, *The Most Human Human* (London: Viking, 2011).
30. "This Really Happened, No Joke (I Got Caught Using Jealous Girlfriend Opener)," The Attraction Forums, http://www.theattractionforums.com/general-discussion/46830-really-happened-no-joke-i-got-caught-using-jealous-girlfriend-opener.html.
31. A full transcript of MGonz's first interaction is on Mark Humphrys's website: http://computing.dcu.ie/~humphrys/Eliza/eliza.anon.html, accessed November 3, 2011. See also Christian, *The Most Human Human*, pp. 36–37.
32. Dan Ariely, "Online Dating: Avoiding a Bad Equilibrium," http://danariely.com/2010/09/20/online-dating-avoiding-a-bad-equilibrium/, accessed November 3, 2011.
33. Andrew Griffin, "Facebook Dislike Button Arrives—in the Form of Reaction Emoji," *The Independent*, October 8, 2015, http://www.independent.co.uk/life-style/gadgets-and-tech/news/facebook-dislike-button-arrives-in-the-form-of-reaction-emoji-a6686331.html.

34. Sherry Turkle, *Reclaiming Conversation: The Power of Talk in a Digital Age* (New York: Penguin, 2015), p. 22.
35. James Scott, *Two Cheers for Anarchism: Six Easy Pieces on Autonomy, Dignity, and Meaningful Work and Play* (Princeton, NJ: Princeton University Press, 2012), chap. 3.
36. Matthew T. Bowers, B. Christine Green, Florian Hemme, and Laurence Chalip, "Assessing the Relationship Between Youth Sport Participation Settings and Creativity in Adulthood," *Creativity Research Journal* 26, no. 3 (2014), DOI: 10.1080/10400419.2014.929420.
37. Peter Gray, *Free to Learn* (New York: Basic Books, 2013), chap. 8.
38. Erin Davis (director), *The Land* (2015), http://playfreemovie.com/.
39. Hanna Rosin, "The Overprotected Kid," *The Atlantic*, April 2014, http://www.theatlantic.com/magazine/archive/2014/04/hey-parents-leave-those-kids-alone/358631/.
40. Author interview with Tim Gill, November 5, 2015.
41. Cited in Tim Gill, *No Fear: Growing Up in a Risk Averse Society* (London: Calouste Gulbenkian Foundation, 2007), p. 29.
42. Mariana Brussoni et al., "What Is the Relationship Between Risky Outdoor Play and Health in Children? A Systematic Review," *International Journal of Environmental Research and Public Health* 12, no. 6 (June 8, 2015), pp. 6423–6454.
43. Helle Nebelong, speech at Designs on Play Conference, 2002, cited in Gill, *No Fear*, p. 35.
44. "Breaking Breaktime's Rules," *The Economist: Babbage Blog*, January 29, 2014, http://www.economist.com/blogs/babbage/2014/01/child-development.
45. Jared Diamond, "Best Practices for Raising Kids? Look to Hunter-Gatherers," *Newsweek*, December 12, 2012, excerpted from *The World Until Yesterday: What Can We Learn from Traditional Societies* (New York: Viking, 2012), http://www.newsweek.com/best-practices-raising-kids-look-hunter-gatherers-63611.

INDEX

Index

Index

Index

Tim Harford has a knack.

For making ideas clear.

Problems easy to understand.

Solutions simple to grasp.

In his books, Harford tackles the big ideas that lie at the hearts of economics, politics, government, and human behavior by sharpening the lens that we see all of them through.

As a result, he makes the murkiest concepts clear and gives readers new ways to understand our fast-changing world better than we ever thought possible.

© Fran Monks

Understanding the global economy (finally).

"Tim Harford is perhaps our very best popular economics writer."
—Tyler Cowen, author of *Create Your Own Economy* and *The Great Stagnation*

THE UNDERCOVER ECONOMIST STRIKES BACK

HOW TO RUN – OR RUIN – AN ECONOMY

TIM HARFORD

bestselling author of *THE UNDERCOVER ECONOMIST*

What would you do if you ran the world's economy?

That's the question Tim Harford poses in *The Undercover Economist Strikes Back: How to Run—or Ruin—an Economy.* His answer is unexpected and insightful, surprising and enlightening.

Stripping away the spin, hype, and jargon that surround economics, Harford offers a provocative assessment of how the world's economy actually works and helps us to truly understand—perhaps for the first time—the global economy.

"Tim Harford is a brave man to write a book about macroeconomics for the layperson; luckily, he is also a funny man. . . . His perky style and chatty asides keep us grinning." ***—The Wall Street Journal***

"With fascinating examples and vivid explanations, Tim Harford succeeds in turning macroeconomics into a gripping read."

—Simon Singh, author of *Fermat's Last Theorem*

A guide to how we got here, one invention at a time.

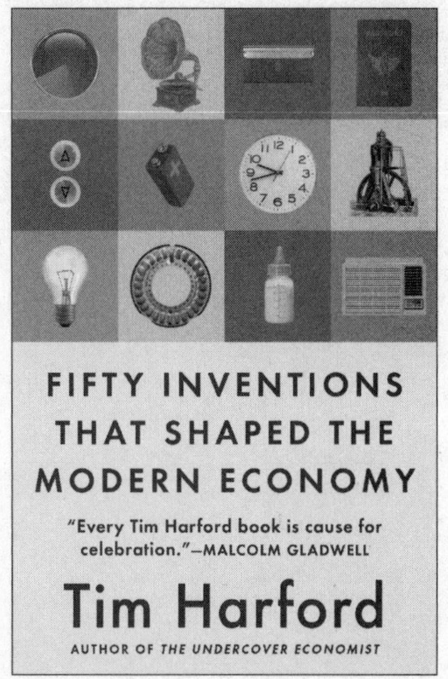

What are civilization's most important inventions? What impact do they have on our lives?

In *Fifty Inventions That Shaped the Modern Economy,* Tim Harford paints an epic yet intimate picture of economic success by recounting the stories behind the ideas and people who created these inventions, and the far-reaching consequences they had for all of us.

It's a readable and imaginative exploration of the world around us, one invention at a time.

"Harford has a knack for writing about economic issues in a clear and gripping way." ***—Worth***

"Tim Harford is perhaps our very best popular economics writer." **—Tyler Cowen, author of *Create Your Own Economy***